SO-AXI-802

FaithWalk

A Daily Journey Through the Bible

Woodrow Kroll & Tony Beckett

BACK TO THE BIBLE
Publishing

FAITHWALK: A DAILY JOURNEY THROUGH THE BIBLE

Copyright © 2000 by The Good News Broadcasting Assoc., Inc.
All rights reserved. International copyright secured.

No part of this book may be reproduced in any form without permission in writing from the publisher, except in the case of brief quotations embodied in critical articles or reviews.

All Scripture quotations, unless otherwise indicated, are taken from the HOLY BIBLE: NEW INTERNATIONAL VERSION (North American Edition), copyright © 1973, 1978, 1984 by The International Bible Society. Used by permission of Zondervan Publishing House. All rights reserved.

All italicizing of words and phrases in Scripture quotations are added by the authors for emphasis.

BACK TO THE BIBLE PUBLISHING
P.O. Box 82808
Lincoln, Nebraska 68501

Editor: Rachel Derowitsch
Cover and interior design: Laura Poe
Cover photo: © Robert Everts/TonyStone
Art and editorial direction: Kim Johnson

Additional copies of this book are available from Back to the Bible Publishing. You may order by calling 1-800-759-2425 or through our Web site at www.resources.backtothebible.org.

1 2 3 4 5 6 7 8 9 10 – 05 04 03 02 01 00

ISBN 0-8474-0702-0

Printed in USA

INTRODUCTION

How much does the Bible mean to you? Does it shape your life? Do you look to it for answers? The Bible can influence every aspect of your being—your thinking, your values, your spiritual destiny. But there's a catch—you have to read it!

We'd like to help you read through the Bible this year through *FaithWalk: A Daily Journey Through the Bible.* Each day directs you to an Old and New Testament reading. The Scripture passage noted in bold type is followed by an inspirational devotional from Back to the Bible's Senior Bible Teacher, Woodrow Kroll, or Associate Bible Teacher, Tony Beckett, that will help you understand the passage you've read and apply it to your life.

Our prayer for you is that this will be a year of commitment to reading God's Word faithfully. We know you'll be the winner as you experience the rich dividends of biblical knowledge and spiritual growth!

FaithWalk is based on the *Old and New Testament* schedule from Woodrow Kroll's *Read Me Bible Guides.* For information on this or the other *Read Me* schedules, please contact Back to the Bible at 1-800-759-2425.

GOOD START GONE BAD

Genesis 1–3, Matthew 1 • *Key Verse: Genesis 3:15*

At God's initiative the world came into existence. Things got off to a great start! Moses records throughout chapter 1 that God's assessment of creation was that "it was good." That phrase is repeatedly used to describe His work.

It was "not good," however, for man to be alone. But chapter 2 does not indicate that God realized that He had made a mistake. His work of creating "a suitable helper" for Adam was not a correcting but a continuing of His creative work. God's work of creation was good—perfect, in fact.

Chapter 3 tells how things went from good to bad. Satan entered the picture with the intent of ruining it. This time he was like a serpent intending to deceive. At other times he is like an angel of light who looks so right but is so wrong.

The wrong in this world is the effect of sin. The right in this world is the work of God. Genesis 3:15 is a prophecy of what Jesus would one day accomplish. By His death, burial and resurrection, He would break the power of sin. In Jesus there is salvation for all who believe.

As you begin this journey of reading the Bible, thank God for His Son, Jesus, who breaks the power of sin, and for His Word, the Bible. Also make it a prayer of commitment that you will finish what you begin today, that you will read the entire Bible this year.

OUT OF EDEN

Genesis 4–6, Matthew 2 • Key Verses: Genesis 6:6–8

After the first sin, more sins followed. That's the way it is with sin, a pattern seen right from the beginning.

God told Cain that sin was like a beast ready to destroy him (4:7). Cain, however, ignored this warning and murdered his brother. But that was only the beginning. As the race of men increased in number, some did seek the Lord, but man's wickedness increased all the more (6:5).

Sin brings not only the pain of its effects now but also the judgment of God. Noah lived a righteous life; "he walked with God" (6:9). By God's favor, not by his own merit, Noah was given the promise that he would be delivered from the flood that God would use to punish the sinful world.

Sin is nothing with which to trifle. It is like a beast that wants to destroy. It is not something done once but is a pattern, a lifestyle, that grows and spreads. The sin of an individual affects others who sometimes are the victims and at other times co-participants.

Escape from the consequences is possible, but it is found only in God's favor and in His way. Noah lived by accepting God's way for his deliverance. We live eternally by receiving God's way for deliverance from our sins—Jesus.

How do you view sin—as something of no consequence, a thing you can do without penalty, or as a dangerous beast? Get God's view! Right now ask God to help you see what sins may be in your life today.

THE RAIN OF DEATH

Genesis 7–9, Matthew 3 • *Key Verse: Genesis 7:1*

Sometimes the account of Noah and the ark is told as a wonderful story for children. Imaginations dance with images of animals on parade, going up a long ramp two by two into the ark.

But we need to keep in mind that this is a scene of judgment. Why the ark? Why the gathering of the animals? Both questions are answered with the word *judgment*.

The sin of mankind had reached such depths that God could not allow it to continue unpunished. But by His grace He provided the ark as a place for those inside to escape. The rain brought death and the ark was the way of salvation.

The reality is the same today. Sin brings judgment. God's grace provides salvation. There was one place of safety in Noah's day: the ark. There is only one place of salvation today: the cross.

Sin must be punished. God warns and provides a way of escape. It is our decision to receive or reject what is offered to us in Jesus. If you have not done so before, acknowledge your need and receive Jesus as Savior today. He died, was buried and rose again so that you can live forever.

Have you received God's offer of salvation? Remember, if Noah had stayed outside the ark, he would have died. Just knowing there is salvation is not enough. You need to receive it.

ONE NATION, SCATTERED UNDER GOD

Genesis 10–12, Matthew 4 • Key Verse: Genesis 11:4

The world was given a fresh start. Noah and his family survived because God chose to spare them and they had obeyed Him. In chapter 8 God gave His word not to destroy the world again by a flood. The changing of the seasons is a reminder of God's unchanging faithfulness to His word (v. 22).

However, a pattern already seen in Genesis repeated itself again. Man continued to do those things that brought judgment. Noah's drunkenness and Ham's disrespect affected succeeding generations. The names of the nations that came into existence later would be identified with wrong and idolatry—names like Magog and Canaan, with cities named Sodom and Gomorrah.

By chapter 11 men were saying that they were ready to "make a name for [themselves]" (v. 4). In pride man is exalted and God is forgotten. Again a judgment came from God. This time He confused the language of the people and scattered them over the face of the earth.

Whenever we hear or read another language, it should remind us that pride is a sin that God hates. The seasons remind us of His faithfulness. The languages should remind us of the serious consequences of sin.

Pride is a dangerous sin, one that causes a person to exalt himself over others—sometimes over God. Examine your heart today. Remember that "when pride comes, then comes disgrace, but with humility comes wisdom" (Prov. 11:2).

TRUST AND OBEY

Genesis 13–15, Matthew 5:1–26 • *Key Verse: Genesis 15:6*

In Romans 4:3, Paul cites Genesis 15:6, which says, "Abram believed the LORD, and he credited it to him as righteousness." Abram's life of belief is evident. When God told him to move, he moved. That was an act of obedience coupled with remarkable trust. God did not tell him where but that He would later show him the place. Without the course clearly marked, Abram believed and did what God wanted.

Abram's belief was commemorated in altars. He built altars in Shechem, Bethel and Hebron. The first was at the place where God promised that the land would be given to Abram's descendants. That altar served as a reminder of that promise. At the other locations Abram "called on the name of the LORD." Those altars were places of prayer.

When returning from the rescue of Lot, Abram met Melchizedek, the priest of God Most High. To him Abram gave a tenth of everything, an act of worship recounted in Hebrews.

Abram believed, and it showed. He remembered God's promise, prayed and worshiped. His belief was not a one-time decision but a lifetime dedication.

Believe! And then live what you believe.

"God, help me not to forget the blessings that come from You. May my worship of You be constant because You are the God of every day and every place."

LETTING GO, LETTING GOD

Genesis 16–17, Matthew 5:27–48 • *Key Verse: Genesis 17:17*

God's ways certainly are not man's ways. We need to remember that or we may be like Abraham, Sarah and Hagar, who at times struggled with what God was doing and tried to do what they thought should be done.

Sometimes the problem is *a lack of patience*. God promised Abraham descendants. When children did not come soon enough, Sarah conceived—not an heir but an error. Mankind still suffers the long-term effects of that decision. God's way was not as fast as what man wanted.

Sometimes the problem is *a lack of imagination*. Hagar could not imagine staying when Sarah mistreated her. Sarah could not imagine that at her age she would have a child. God's way was not imaginable to either of them.

Sometimes the problem is *a lack of perspective*. Abraham was told that Sodom was to be destroyed (Gen. 18). God saw the sin of the city; Abraham saw a city worth sparing. Perhaps there were ten righteous people in it, but evidently not. God's way was not the same perspective.

We can be impatient, think things to be impossible and not see things as God sees them. Or we can study the Bible and learn God's ways. He works things according to His timing and watches over us through even the hardest situations. Our determination must be that God's ways will be our ways.

Do not try to force God into your mold, but allow yourself to be shaped by His ways. Surrendering control to Him can be difficult but is best.

TWO QUESTIONS

Genesis 18–19, Matthew 6:1–18 • *Key Verses: Genesis 18:13–14*

Rhetorical questions are ones asked for effect. No answer is expected. In these chapters there are two such questions. No answer is expected because the answers are obvious. The questions are intended to remind us of two truths about God.

"Is anything too hard for the LORD?" (18:14). Of course not. But sometimes that is easier to affirm than to live. Abraham would have answered "yes" immediately, though his situation might have caused him to balk internally. He and Sarah had just been told that they would have a baby.

Sarah laughed to herself at the thought. "After I am worn out and my master is old?" she asked. The first rhetorical question answered her question.

Sometimes people struggle with the truth that God is a God of love, grace and judgment. We might ask, "How can God do that?" Abraham himself tried to avert judgment on Sodom and Gomorrah by bartering with God. His struggle with judgment was answered with the second rhetorical question: "Will not the Judge of all the earth do right?" (v. 25). Of course He will. He will do right even in exercising His judgment on those cities.

God can do anything, and whatever He does is right. A birth announcement and a judgment pronouncement remind us of these truths.

Is there something you think is too hard, even for God? You just read how God taught Abraham and Sarah that He can do anything and whatever He does is right. Learn both parts of this lesson.

STAY WITH GOD'S PLANS

Genesis 20–22, Matthew 6:19–34 • *Key Verse: Genesis 22:5*

God had promised Abraham and Sarah that they would have children. When Abraham moved to Gerar, however, his trust in this promise was tested. He was afraid that the king would kill him and take Sarah as his wife. Instead of trusting, Abraham planned to survive by telling the king that Sarah was his sister. In Gerar, Abraham trusted in his own plans.

Abraham was 100 years old when Isaac was born. Instead of trusting that God would give them a son, Abraham and Sarah had tried to accomplish God's promise their way, and thus Ishmael was born. The result was great tension after Isaac, the child of promise, was born. In the birth of Ishmael, Abraham trusted in his own plans.

On Moriah, however, Abraham trusted God and experienced His blessing. He obeyed when God told him to sacrifice Isaac. His faith was so strong that he believed God would bring Isaac back to life after being sacrificed. Abraham demonstrated that faith when he told his servants, "We will worship and then *we* will come back to you" (22:5, emphasis mine). He knew Isaac would return with him.

Like Abraham, we do best when we stay with God's plans.

Our plans may seem best but are not unless they are God's plans. We are called to trust and obey. Decide today to make those three words the characteristic of your life—that you trust and obey.

WHEN THE TIMES ARE CHANGING

Genesis 23–24, Matthew 7 • *Key Verses: Genesis 24:26–27*

With growing older comes change. In today's reading, Abraham experienced the loss of his wife and the addition of a daughter-in-law. In these two events he trusted and obeyed God.

When Sarah died, Abraham demonstrated his faith in a remarkable way. He buried her in the land God promised to him. Later, when Abraham died, all that he possessed of the Promised Land was that grave site—and he paid for it. God stayed faithful and kept His promise. The land was given to Abraham's descendents.

Choosing a bride for Isaac was also an act of trust and obedience. Abraham sent his servant to find a wife for his son. He did this believing that God would "send his angel before" the servant and provide a wife for Isaac (24:7). At a well outside of Nahor, the servant met Rebekah, Isaac's future wife.

Abraham had learned his lesson well. He did not take God's plans into his own hands.

The temptation is great to carry out our plans, to do God's will our way. But the hymn says it well: "Trust and obey, for there's no other way to be happy in Jesus."

Did you notice how God was praised and thanked by Abraham's servant? List three things that you praise and thank God for today.

FAITH OF OUR FATHERS

Genesis 25–26, Matthew 8:1–17 • ***Key Verse: Genesis 26:24***

Woven in these two chapters are both belief and disbelief. Isaac believed enough to pray and to stay. He prayed when he and Rebekah were having difficulty conceiving. God answered that prayer with twins. He also stayed in Gerar when God told him not to go to Egypt during a famine. But like his father, there came a point where he disbelieved enough to lie (26:7).

This section concludes with a reciting of God's blessing on Isaac. Even Abimelech, the king to whom he lied, wanted an alliance with Isaac. He wanted to be at peace with the one whom God was blessing. Isaac recognized God's blessing in his life and thus learned a vital lesson.

His sons needed to learn that lesson too. In a moment of fatigue and hunger, Esau gave up his birthright in exchange for some food. Like his father and grandfather, concern for the physical caused him to lose sight of the spiritual.

A good family background and even God's guidance are not enough. In every one of us is the potential to do wrong. We need to realize this, refuse to do what is wrong, determine to do what is right—and then do it.

We can be thankful for the godly heritage we receive, and we can leave one to our children as well. But pleasing God is more than heritage—it involves belief and obedience. Make the choice today to trust and obey.

THE END AND THE MEANS

Genesis 27–28, Matthew 8:18–34 • *Key Verses: Genesis 28:15–16*

Jacob knew what he wanted: his father's blessing. After all, it was God's promise for his life. It was not a question of what he wanted but of how he got it.

Already Esau had surrendered his birthright (25:33). Then Jacob added his own deceit to the situation. Coached by his mother, he pretended to be Esau so his father would bless him. It worked. By deceit he got what God had already promised him. The fact that it was already his by God's promise did not justify his wrong behavior.

The deceiver then had to leave. Under the guise of looking for a wife, he was sent to his uncle Laban. There, the deceiver himself would be deceived.

God always keeps His word. Even as Jacob traveled away from home, God met him at Bethel and blessed him.

Sometimes people think that getting what they want is the most important thing. But how it is obtained is important as well. The end never justifies the means. God's word should be enough. There is no need to scheme or deceive because God is faithful to His promises.

As you follow through the story of Jacob, these scenes of deceit keep reoccurring. If someone were reading a summary of your life, what pattern would be evident? If it's a pattern of wrong, then pray now for God to help you change.

WHAT GOES AROUND COMES AROUND

Genesis 29–30, Matthew 9:1–17 • *Key Verse: Genesis 29:25*

Two men got what they wanted, but both got it the wrong way. Jacob wanted his father's blessing. In yesterday's reading we saw how he deceived Isaac to get the blessing. Laban wanted his older daughter wed. By deception he got what he wanted too.

Jacob wanted to marry Rachel. He served Laban for seven years to get her. It is touching to read that those years "seemed like only a few days to him because of his love for her" (29:20).

Then Laban substituted Leah. What was a touching scene becomes a torturous one. It is hard to imagine the emotions of Jacob when he realized that he had been deceived.

These verses do not teach that if we deceive we will be deceived. But they do show us the pain of sin and the problems sin causes. Ultimately Jacob married Rachel. He worked another seven years for her, and his home became one of division and unhappiness.

When a person is intent on getting what he wants in whatever way possible, he faces a future filled with the problems sin brings. Jacob got what he wanted—and what he did not want.

Think about the family situation of Jacob and his wives. It involved an unloved wife and competition for a husband's affections. Later there is even strife among the children. Getting what we want instead of waiting for what God gives can be very unpleasant.

A TURN FOR THE BETTER

Genesis 31–32, Matthew 9:18–38 • *Key Verses: Genesis 32:9–10*

A veteran missionary once wrote that he would rather be like Jacob than Solomon. In his assessment, Solomon started so promisingly but ended disastrously, while Jacob started disastrously but ended well. In these chapters Jacob's turn begins to be evident.

A dozen sons were born in a setting of dysfunctionality. Wives were competing and using their servants to aid their cause. It may seem surprising that God would continue to work with such a clan of schemers, but He did—not to condone their actions but to accomplish His ultimate purpose.

In some respects things were going well. Jacob's flocks were increasing, and his ability at husbandry brought about great prosperity. But with that came jealousy and discord between him and Laban.

God intervened and put Jacob on the road again. He told him to go back home. Home for Jacob was not just where the hearth was but where Esau waited. This time he did not flee but obeyed. Even when pursued by Laban, he did the right thing. Jacob was willing to face up to what he had done.

No matter how disastrously we may have begun, the example of Jacob encourages us to finish well.

No matter what your past or present, you can aim to finish well. Strengthen your resolve and determine to be more like Jacob than Solomon. Finish well.

MEETING THE PAST IN THE FUTURE

Genesis 33–35, Matthew 10:1–20 • *Key Verse: Genesis 35:3*

There are times when we see the past in the future. We may sing, "The sun'll come out tomorrow," but tomorrow may have clouds of our own making.

God wrestled with Jacob to make him the man He wanted him to be. He left Peniel a changed man, whose limp reminded him with every step of when he "saw God face to face, and yet [his] life was spared" (32:30).

But some effects of past actions are not removed by a decision. Both the reunion with Esau and the rape of Dinah are strong evidence of that. Jacob's deception of his father and the stealing of the birthright destroyed his relationship with his brother. In chapter 33 he faced the ongoing effects of past actions.

When his daughter was raped, his sons followed the family pattern of deception to get their revenge on the people of Shechem. Jacob's weak leadership in the situation allowed them to carry out their wicked plan to restore the family honor. He had a fresh start at Peniel, but the effects of past actions remained.

A right decision does not remove all the remains of our past. We must still determine daily to do what is right.

It's easy to be a person of habit. Patterns get ingrained in our lives and those of our family, but we are not condemned to always live that way. By God's grace we can change.

OBVIOUSLY MORE RIGHTEOUS

Genesis 36–38, Matthew 10:21–42 • *Key Verse: Genesis 38:26a*

The character of Judah was such that he could say about his daughter-in-law, "She is more righteous than I." How painful it must have felt to acknowledge that fact, especially considering Judah said that when he realized she was the "prostitute" he was trying to pay!

Consider his character as recorded in these chapters. First, it was his idea to sell Joseph. He proposed the "profitable alternative to fratricide," as John MacArthur puts it.

Second, it was his shameful neglect that prompted Tamar to disguise herself as a prostitute. Two of Judah's sons had died while married to Tamar. He postponed the marriage to the third, a marriage expected under the practice of Leverite marriage.

Third, while going to where they were shearing sheep, he slept with who he thought was a prostitute. Later he learned that she was his daughter-in-law.

Besides a lack of integrity, he was a hypocrite, as seen in Genesis 38:24–26. He said that Tamar should be burned to death for her prostitution—until she confronted him with proof that he was the man who had slept with her.

Sin and hypocrisy bring shame. Better to live a righteous life of integrity like Joseph than one of sin and hypocrisy like Judah.

Check your integrity today. Ask God to help you have a pure heart before Him, one that shows in clean hands before others.

INTEGRITY INCARCERATED

Genesis 39–40, Matthew 11 • *Key Verse: Genesis 39:23*

After a sequence of individuals with character flaws, the narrative now turns to a man about whom nothing negative is recorded. Joseph truly lived a life of righteousness and integrity. He did it with his mind focused on God and not his circumstances.

It is recorded that "the LORD was with Joseph and he prospered" (39:2). Potiphar promoted him to the highest position of responsibility in his house. It was there that Potiphar's wife propositioned him, repeatedly. Opportunity for immorality presented itself to Joseph day after day.

But Joseph's focus on God kept him from sin. His refusal included these words: "How . . . could I do such a wicked thing and sin against God?" (v. 9). He was not asking how he could sin and get away with it. He was not wondering how it would affect Potiphar or his place in the house if found out. Instead, his concern was that his sin would offend God.

In one sense, Joseph's refusal cost him. He was falsely accused and imprisoned. In another sense, though, his refusal brought God's continual blessing.

Our desire always must be to please God. That involves living a life of righteousness and integrity.

"God, help me to always do what is right, whatever the consequences may be. May I desire Your blessing over anything else, even if I am misunderstood or falsely accused."

GETTING PAST THE PAST

Genesis 41–42, Matthew 12:1–23 • *Key Verses: Genesis 41:51–52*

"Deal with it!" is a phrase often heard today. Sometimes it is accompanied with the encouragement to "get over it." These phrases can be like a form of shock counseling. Hit over the head with a blunt piece of advice, a person realizes, hopefully, that it is time to "move on."

When Manasseh was born to Joseph and his wife, Joseph chose a name that meant "forget" because God had made Joseph to forget all his trouble (41:51). His brother's name, Ephraim, meant "twice fruitful" to remind Joseph that God had made him fruitful in the land of his suffering (v. 52).

Joseph definitely grew up in a dysfunctional family. There was enough wrong done to him to last several generations. He was sold into slavery, falsely accused of attempted seduction, imprisoned and even forgotten by those he helped—more than enough to warrant a lifetime crippled by the past.

Yet the past did not dominate and control Joseph. Instead, he kept his focus on God. By God's grace and with God's help, he put the past behind him and rejoiced in the blessings of the present.

By God's grace and with His help, so can you.

Perhaps there is pain in your past. Leave it there. Don't let the past control your present. By God's grace you can be the person He wants you to be, not one in bondage to previous experiences.

OH, BROTHER!

Genesis 43–45, Matthew 12:24–50 • *Key Verse: Genesis 45:5*

Joseph's life had its shares of downs. His brothers were jealous of him, almost killed him, sold him into slavery and lied to his father about what happened to him. As a result, Joseph lived as a slave, was falsely accused and then imprisoned. He could have become filled with resentment, feeding on thoughts of malicious intent and looking for an opportunity to get back at his brothers.

Opportunity came knocking—not just once but twice! His brothers literally came knocking, needing food. Joseph put them to the test and then finally revealed himself to them. Their reaction of fear was natural. It was Joseph who acted in a supernatural way. He did not use the opportunity to extract his revenge.

His heart had not fed on thoughts of getting even but on the sovereignty of God. His conclusion was that God had sent him to Egypt in order to preserve his family. Joseph knew that to get past the past he had to trust God.

We, too, must rest in the sovereignty of God. We may not understand all that is happening, but we must determine to rest in the truth that He is God.

Is there someone you would like to get back at? When hurt, we are tempted to hurt back—and harder. Instead of bringing that other person to mind, think of Joseph. A heart of revenge hurts first itself, and then others.

SOUNDS GOOD TO ME!

Genesis 46–48, Matthew 13:1–30 • *Key Verses: Genesis 48:15–16*

God providentially paved the way for Joseph's family to sojourn in Egypt. At a time of famine, Jacob's extended family was welcomed there, where food and land was made available to him.

As they prepared to meet the Pharaoh, Joseph gave his family a bit of advice. He knew that Egyptians did not like shepherds, so he scripted an answer for them to use when asked about their occupation. He told them to say, "Your servants have tended livestock from our boyhood on" (46:34).

Imagine his chagrin when his brothers said to Pharaoh, "Your servants are shepherds, just as our fathers were" (47:3). What were they thinking?

Perhaps they were thinking that the Egyptians might not like shepherds, but that was exactly what they were. Instead of being an embarrassment to them, it was an encouragement.

When he blessed Joseph, Jacob spoke of "the God who has been my shepherd all my life to this day" (48:15). The shepherd God is an encouragement to those who are a part of His flock. David would later write, "The LORD is my shepherd" (Ps. 23:1). And Jesus said, "I am the good shepherd" (John 10:14).

It may not sound good to others, but "shepherd" sounds good to God's own.

The New Testament Greek word for "shepherds" is used to describe pastors. Your pastor is an undershepherd of Jesus. It is a blessing of God that He has not left us as sheep without a shepherd.

FROM A GARDEN TO A GRAVE

Genesis 49–50, Matthew 13:31–58 • *Key Verse: Genesis 50:24–25*

Warren Wiersbe comments in his notes on Genesis 50 that "Genesis begins with a garden and ends with a coffin: what a commentary on the results of sin!" The progression is from life to death. Sin brought death. Immediately things changed from the idyllic to sin-cursed.

Yet it is a hope-filled coffin that catches our attention here at the end. It contains the bones of Joseph, who made the sons of Israel swear an oath that when God came to their aid, they must carry his bones up from Egypt (50:25).

Joseph believed God. Until his dying day he never wavered in his belief. The strength of his belief was so strong that he made plans to be twice buried: temporarily in Egypt but ultimately in the Promised Land.

What a strange sight it must have been—the people of Israel trekking through the wilderness, carrying what was probably an elaborate Egyptian mummy case. That coffin carried the hope-filled bones of Joseph.

We suffer the effects of living in this sin-cursed world. Yet if we know Jesus as Savior, we are assured of an eternal home where there is no sin. Don't dwell on the world. Instead, read the Word. Fill your bones with hope!

If we walk by sight our faith will waver. But if we walk by faith, our sight will see things differently. Determine, like Joseph, to interpret what you see by your faith.

ONE IN FOUR

*Exodus 1–3, **Matthew 14:1–21*** • *Key Verses: Matthew 14:16–18*

An indication of the importance of the feeding of the 5,000 is the fact that it is the only miracle of Jesus recorded in all four Gospels. The account in John 6 gives so much emphasis to the meaning of the miracle, presenting it as a sermon in action.

The timing of this event is significant. It is the beginning of a phase in Jesus' ministry in which His primary focus was on His disciples. Jesus used this occasion to stretch their understanding of what He expected of them. They were to undertake responsibilities that looked beyond their ability, things they could accomplish when their inability was coupled with Jesus' ability.

The crowd needed to eat. The disciples' suggestion was to send them to the villages nearby to buy food for themselves. But Jesus said that was not necessary. Instead, He instructed His men to give them something to eat—an overwhelming task for a group with limited resources. The disciples then saw that what they had, when placed in the hands of Jesus, could be used to accomplish what looked impossible.

One of the lessons of the loaves is that we must look past our inability and see His ability. When Jesus works through us, we can accomplish the tasks He gives us.

"God, help me rely on Your ability. The tasks You set before me can appear overwhelming until I see them through Your eyes."

WET ENOUGH TO WORSHIP

Exodus 4–6, Matthew 14:22–36 • *Key Verse: Matthew 14:33*

In our mind we have the basic idea of what happened in this account. The disciples were in a boat, at night, in rough water. Then Jesus appeared out of nowhere. At first the disciples thought they were seeing a ghost. But Jesus calmed them by saying, "Take courage! It is I. Don't be afraid" (v. 27).

Peter then seized the moment. "Lord, if it's you, tell me to come to you on the water." "Come," Jesus said (vv. 28–29). And Peter did— to a point. When he looked at the wind, he was afraid and began to sink.

But one fact is never mentioned. How wet did Peter get? Did he sink ankle deep or go all the way under before Jesus caught him? The text does not say. It does say, however, that after Jesus and Peter got into the boat, those there worshiped Jesus, saying, "Truly you are the Son of God" (v. 33).

Worship is a response. Peter got wet enough to respond to Jesus with worship. The other disciples also responded to Jesus with worship. We may not walk on water like Peter, but our hearts must respond to Him as did the hearts of the disciples. He is Lord. Let us worship Him.

Remember, worship is a response. Do you just read the Bible, or do you respond to what it teaches you? Praise God for sending Jesus, our Lord and Savior.

ROTE OR REAL?

Exodus 7–8, Matthew 15:1–20 • *Key Verses: Matthew 15:8–9*

The previous chapter concluded with an interesting worship service. It took place in a boat and was a spontaneous response to Jesus. Worship is, as Warren Wiersbe defines it, "The believer's response of all that he is—mind, emotions, will and body—to all that God is and says and does."

There were people in Jesus' day who confused going through the motions of worship with the real thing. They said the right things and did the right things, but their words and actions were not from their heart.

It was not a new problem. Isaiah had confronted the people years before on this issue. Then in Matthew 15 Jesus quoted Isaiah, confronting the people yet again.

Today the words of Isaiah confront us too. Perhaps daily devotions have become a ritual or routine. Church attendance can be maintained for the wrong reasons. Even our words may sound right but be wrong.

Worship is not to be treated as a thing but lived out as an action. It is not a matter of art but of heart.

So look at your heart today. Is your worship only of the lips or of the life?

Take a moment to list three things for which you can praise God. Then tell God your praise—and then tell someone else!

SLOW LEARNERS

Exodus 9–11, Matthew 15:21–39 • *Key Verses: Genesis 15:32–33*

In these verses we read of another crowd at mealtime. This time, however, it's Jesus who points out the need for food. The previous time the need was brought up by the disciples. Just as before, however, they appeal to their apparent inadequacy.

Their question, "Where could we get enough bread in this remote place to feed such a crowd?" is responded to with a question: "How many loaves do you have?" (vv. 33–34). Five loaves and two fish were more than enough before. Their collective lunch this time is seven loaves, a few small fish—and Jesus.

It is amazing to see how slow the disciples were to understand His power. They had not yet learned the lesson from the previous miracle when the 5,000 were fed. No wonder Jesus at times called them men of little faith.

Once again the disciples were confronted with their inability. Once again He had them state how much food they had. This provided the evidence that what followed was truly a miracle. Once again they saw Jesus' ability.

Like the disciples, sometimes we are slow learners. We need to keep our faith growing. Our faith grows as we feed on the Word, learning what it says and living it daily. Keep reading, learning and living the Bible.

Is God setting before you a task you think is too great? This passage challenges you to place what you have in His hands and let Him work through you.

NOW I GET IT

Exodus 12–13, Matthew 16 • *Key Verse: Matthew 16:12*

Those of us who enjoy telling a good story usually agonize inwardly when we have to explain it. Hopefully, at some point in the retelling of the story, a light will come on and the person will say, "Oh, now I get it!"

Imagine how Jesus might have felt when His disciples still were not getting it. He said, "Be on your guard against the yeast of the Pharisees and Sadducees" (v. 6). They thought, *Did He say that because we didn't bring any bread?*

So, to those Jesus addressed as "You of little faith," He asked, "Do you still not understand?" (v. 9).

Their focus was on the physical; His was on the spiritual. They thought of bread for the body; He thought of food for the soul. In the miracles of feeding the multitudes, Jesus had demonstrated His ability to meet their needs. They could trust Him to provide for them. Now, though, He wanted their attention to be on spiritual matters, not just physical.

When you pray, "Give us this day our daily bread," are you looking for just that which is physical, or are you asking for that which is food for the soul?

Are you a careful listener? Not all teaching is correct. Listen carefully and then compare all teaching you hear with the Bible.

STAND STILL

Exodus 14–15, Matthew 17 • *Key Verse: Exodus 14:13*

In Exodus 14 Moses told the people, "Don't just do something. Stand there!" Those were not his exact words, but they might make us stop to look more closely at the account of the parting of the Red Sea.

It is easy to miss what it meant for the Israelites when Moses said, "Stand firm and you will see the deliverance the LORD will bring you today" (v. 13). It meant that they had to stand still and do nothing, even though Pharoah's army was pursuing, they were fleeing, and the Red Sea was in the way!

Notice how long they had to stand still—all night. What a long night that must have been. Pursued and pinned in, they had no escape.

God could have delivered them immediately, but He chose not to. Instead, He taught them to trust Him. They were not given anything to do but to wait.

Can you stand still and wait? It is hard sometimes not to do something. Salvation comes to us because Jesus did it all. God's work in our life sometimes is the same way. We stand still, and He works while we wait.

"God, give me patience. Help me to know how to stand still, to wait on You."

ALL TOGETHER NOW

Exodus 16–18, Matthew 18:1–20 • *Key Verse: Matthew 18:15*

One of the toughest things a Christian is called upon to do is confront a believer about sin in his life. Part of what makes this hard is the reaction we anticipate. Yet because we love Christ and the other Christian, we do what is right.

Another thing that makes it difficult is the rejection we anticipate. "That's just your opinion," might be the response.

Here, then, is the beauty of verses 15–17. First we go as an individual. If our efforts are rejected, we return with one or two others. No longer is it just the opinion of one but the shared concern of a small group. If the efforts of the group are rejected, then the church as a whole is brought into the situation—not as a matter of reporting but of enlisting.

As a church, we together lovingly confront. The brother or sister is then met with the fact that the church family sees the wrong. All together now we express our concern in hope that there will be change.

We do not live in isolation but as part of the Body of Christ. At times this body works together for the good of the individual.

Is there someone you need to confront? If sometime you are on the receiving end of confrontation, how will you respond?

FROM SLOW BURN TO NO BURN

Exodus 19–20, Matthew 18:21–35 • *Key Verses: Matthew 18:32–33*

We live in an angry world. Too often there is not even time for the proverbial "slow burn." For example, road rage is typically an immediate response. Another driver's actions cause not an equal but usually greater reaction. Obviously, forgiveness has no place in road rage. Revenge is the preferred route.

Jesus, however, told His followers that forgiveness is the only route to take. In this parable, He pointed out how much we want to be forgiven and not held accountable. The servant fell on his knees and begged, "Be patient with me and I will pay back everything" (v. 26). The remarkable aspect of the story is that the debt was forgiven.

If you have received Jesus as your Savior, your debt of sin has been forgiven. You are like the servant in the parable.

There is more, though. That same servant was not willing to forgive another. When the master heard about it, he confronted the servant, saying, "I canceled all that debt of yours .... Shouldn't you have had mercy on your fellow servant just as I had on you?" (v. 32–33).

To be forgiven like the servant is good. To be unforgiving in return is wrong.

Ask God if you are failing to forgive someone. If in your heart you know that is true, then forgive that person now.

WHAT'S IN IT FOR ME?

*Exodus 21–22, **Matthew 19** • **Key Verse: Matthew 19:27***

The struggle to keep oneself in check can rear its head at the most inappropriate times. A young man came to Jesus asking what he needed to do to get eternal life. He was wealthy and probably thought that, like success, eternal life was something he could achieve or buy.

This man's soul hung in the balance. His seeking had forced him to look at his own values. At that point in his life, however, things meant more than the life Christ offered.

Then the discussion turned to the question of who can be saved. Seemingly out of nowhere came Peter's inquiry, "We have left everything to follow you! What then will there be for us?" (v. 27).

Christ's response was most gentle considering the conversation had turned away from salvation to a question of rewards. There are rewards coming. But Jesus cautioned, "Many who are first will be last, and many who are last will be first" (v. 30).

Those who try to be at the head of the line ultimately will find themselves at the end. Our service is not to be done with a "what's in it for me" attitude but out of love for Christ.

Next time you have the opportunity, go to the end of the line. Ask Jesus to help you let others go first because you love them.

IN IT FOR THE SHORT HAUL

Exodus 23–24, Matthew 20:1–16 • *Key Verse: Exodus 24:3*

The children of Israel had a phenomenal opportunity in the desert. True, they ultimately would be in the wilderness for 40 years, but at this point consider what was happening to them.

God had delivered them from Egypt and was leading them in an unmistakable way. Moses had received the Ten Commandments (Exodus 20), and Israel saw the glory of the Lord on top of the mountain. It looked like a consuming fire.

In chapter 24 the people responded to Moses' instruction by saying, "Everything the LORD has said we will do" (v. 3). The next day, after offering sacrifices and reading the Book of the Covenant, the people again responded, "We will do everything the LORD has said; we will obey" (v. 7).

Unfortunately, they were in it only for the short haul. Before 40 days had passed, they were worshiping a golden calf that was described as the gods who had brought Israel up out of Egypt (32:4).

Commitments are easier made than kept. One month of daily readings is almost concluded. Perhaps you are starting to waver on your commitment to read the Bible through this year. Don't quit; stay in it for the long haul.

Help me, God, to be a person who keeps commitments, especially the ones made before You.

POOR TIMING

Exodus 25–26, Matthew 20:17–34 • *Key Verse: Matthew 20:23*

Sometimes you have to wonder what in the world is going on in the heads of some people. This chapter includes one of those times.

Jesus was again predicting His death, noting that it would involve betrayal, condemnation, mocking, flogging and a crucifixion—but it would end in resurrection.

Then the mother of James and John came to Jesus with a request: "Grant that one of these two sons of mine may sit at your right and the other at your left in your kingdom" (v. 21).

When word got out about her request, the other disciples were indignant with the brothers.

This was an amazing misdirection of focus. Jesus was talking about a humiliating death and they were positioning themselves for prestige!

Jesus corrected their focus when He said that He Himself "did not come to be served, but to serve, and to give his life as a ransom for many" (v. 28).

Jesus did not live for Himself but for others. We are not to live for ourselves either. Pride often tempts us to be self-serving. But Jesus points us to the cross, not to a throne.

Pride affects our focus. Remember the suggestion to be at the end of the line? Pride will keep you toward the front.

ESSENTIAL FOR WORSHIP

Exodus 27–28, Matthew 21:1–22 • *Key Verses: Exodus 28:36–37*

The tendency is to think the details of these chapters hold little significance for today. But God put the details in for a reason. One reason is to vividly remind us of the necessity of holiness in our worship of Him.

The garments for the high priest were sacred, or holy, garments. *Holy* simply means "separated." Specifically, it speaks of something set aside for divine use.

A plate of pure gold was attached to the turban. On it was engraved the words, "Holy to the Lord." This was the most conspicuous feature of the turban. It was a reminder of the importance of holiness in worship and service.

Holiness is a recurring theme in the Bible. God is holy. We are to be holy. Our lives in their entirety are to be set aside for divine use. Holiness is not a negative concept as some would have us think. It is not just a list of "don'ts."

If we are to live lives of holiness there will be "don'ts," things that we must not do. At the same time we must remember that holiness is a positive concept—it is what we do. We live separated to God.

Are there any "don'ts" that you do? If you are to be a holy person, those "don'ts" must stop.

WHO DO YOU THINK YOU ARE?

Exodus 29–30, Matthew 21:23–46 • *Key Verse: Matthew 21:23*

Do you ever question authority? Think about it before you answer "no." Are you sure that there is never a time when you say, "Who do you think you are?" Perhaps you do not say those exact words, but do you ever ignore a sign, like a speed limit sign or one that says "No U Turns" right where you want to turn? We may have a habit of questioning authority and not even notice it.

When Jesus' authority was questioned in the temple courts, it was obvious. The chief priests and elders asked Him in a straightforward way, "By what authority are you doing these things? And who gave you this authority?" (v. 23).

Do you ever question Jesus' authority? Perhaps you don't in a manner as blatant as these religious leaders did, but in other ways.

Like ignoring a traffic sign, a person can ignore the instructions in God's Word. It really is a questioning of Jesus' authority when we know what He says and choose not to obey. It is as if we are saying to Him, "Who do you think you are?"

He knows who He is and He has the authority. The real question is, "Do you obey?"

To know what is right and not do it is sin. To know what is wrong and do it is sin. The issue of authority is significant. Do you do right and not wrong, or are you in charge?

RIGHT GOD, WRONG WAY

Exodus 31–33, Matthew 22:1–22 • *Key Verses: Exodus 32:7–8*

When we talk about worship, one phrase that is not true is, "Anything goes." It is possible to worship the right God in the wrong way, as today's reading indicates.

The incident of the golden calf typically is remembered as a time when the Israelites worshiped the wrong God. Aaron did say, "These are your gods, O Israel, who brought you up out of Egypt" (32:4). But what he said could be translated, "This is a god, O Israel." This verse at times is translated, "This is thy God, O Israel, who brought thee out of Egypt."

Notice the next verse carefully. It says, "Tomorrow there will be a festival to the LORD." When the word *lord* is in capital letters, that indicates the Hebrew word for "Jehovah."

Put it together. The golden calf represented Jehovah. The people were worshiping the right God but in the wrong way. God had said, "You shall not make for yourself an idol" (20:4), but the people did.

Give careful attention to your worship. At times people worship the right God in the wrong way.

It is tempting to worship in a self-pleasing way. Ask God if your worship is acceptable to Him.

LAW AND LOVE

Exodus 34–35, Matthew 22:23–46 • *Key Verse: Exodus 34:6–7*

Critics of the Bible sometimes speak negatively about the God of the Old Testament, stating that the God of the New Testament is preferred. One of the most obvious problems with that viewpoint is that the God of the Old Testament and the God of the New Testament are the same.

In the Old Testament God describes Himself as "'the compassionate and gracious God, slow to anger, abounding in love and faithfulness, maintaining love to thousands and forgiving wickedness, rebellion and sin'" (34:6–7). Those who reject the God of the Old Testament must not have read these verses. When Moses heard these words, however, he worshiped.

The context of this statement adds to its poignancy. Moses had brought a new set of stone tablets upon which God would write the commandments. This was the second set of tablets; Moses had broken the first when he saw how the people had so quickly forgotten their commitment to God's law. After the golden calf incident, God proclaimed Himself compassionate and forgiving.

God is the unchanging God of grace, in both testaments. Be thankful that He does not change.

Think for a moment about how God has forgiven you. Then thank Him for His abundant mercy.

ENOUGH ALREADY!

Exodus 36–38, Matthew 23:1–22 • *Key Verses: Exodus 36:4–5*

Today's reading includes one of the few times in history that a fund-raising effort was too successful.

Exodus gives great detail to the construction and furnishing of the Tabernacle. In almost an incidental way, the funding of the project is mentioned (36:3). The Israelites brought so many freewill offerings that Moses finally had to say, "Enough already!" The people had to be restrained from giving more.

While we marvel at the generosity of the people, we are embarrassed by the lack of generosity in God's people today. Far too often, a work of God struggles with being underfunded.

It is said that God's work, done God's way, will never lack God's supply. A key element in that is the obedience of God's people in their giving. The prevailing attitude is to work hard to get in order to have. But the biblical perspective on finances is that we get in order to give. Paul's specific instruction to us is, "Each one of you should set aside a sum of money in keeping with his income" (1 Cor. 16:2).

Giving is for all of God's people to do, that His work might move forward unhindered by financial needs.

Do you give to support God's work? Generously or begrudgingly? When we think about all He has given us, our hearts should want to give.

THEY DID IT HIS WAY

Exodus 39–40, Matthew 23:23–39 • *Key Verses: Exodus 39:42–43*

Everyone knows that repetition aids learning. With that in mind, read these two chapters again, looking for what is repeated. When you do, the phrase "as the LORD commanded" will keep coming to your attention. Midway through the chapters, Moses records that "the Israelites had done all the work just as the LORD had command- ed Moses" (39:42).

They paid attention to the details and to the procedures they were to follow. They paid attention to what God wanted. Exodus concludes with verses describing the glory of the Lord filling the tabernacle, the one built and furnished exactly as He had commanded.

As one reads the history of the people of Israel, it is readily apparent that they did not always do everything as the Lord commanded. God records both the successes and the failures so that we might learn from their lives. He can teach a good lesson from even a bad exam- ple. Here, then, is a positive lesson from a good example: The people "did everything just as the LORD commanded Moses."

A popular song years ago proclaimed, "I did it my way." Our song should be, "I did it His way!"

"It is so easy for me to get in the way. God, help me to do it Your way."

STAY TRUE

Leviticus 1–3, Matthew 24:1–28 • Key Verses: Matthew 24:4-5

Every generation has had the sense that it could be the last one before Jesus comes. That is the reality of the imminent return of Jesus. As Jesus spoke of the end times in this passage, what He described sounds like the day in which we live.

False prophets will appear and deceive many people (v. 11). The false can be recognized by comparing what they say with the truth of the Bible. The better we know the Bible, the better we will be able to recognize what is true and what is false.

There will be an increase in wickedness (v. 12). Not a hard point to prove today! Among other things, consider how technology has made wickedness more accessible than ever. No need to go to a bookstore to buy pornography or to a seedy movie theater. Today those things are just a few clicks of the mouse away.

The love of most will grow cold (v. 12). Family breakups and the increase of violent crimes indicate a lessening of love for others.

So Jesus tells us to stay true to His Word. Those who do will be saved.

Stay true. It's as simple and as challenging as that!

THE END

Leviticus 4–5, Matthew 24:29–51 • *Key Verse: Matthew 24:42*

If you are reading this, then you survived Y2K. Once again those who forecast the end of the world were wrong.

Throughout history there have been those who have announced that the end was near. Sometimes they even gave the exact date. There is such a curiosity about the end of the world that recently a series of novels about end-time events written from a Christian viewpoint made the best-seller lists, a fact that even *TIME* magazine took note of.

The bottom line is that no one knows when the end will come but God. Jesus said, "You do not know on what day your Lord will come" (v. 42). In light of that fact, the believer needs to live out the admonition at the beginning of verse 42 to keep watch. Live expecting that Jesus will return today.

We often live with deadlines. It helps knowing the schedule for when something is to be completed. Likewise, our lives should be lived anticipating that the deadline for Jesus' return may be today. So live expectantly!

Jesus could come today! That truth should motivate us to live ready for His return.

OPPORTUNITIES KNOCK

Leviticus 6–7, Matthew 25:1–30 • *Key Verse: Matthew 25:19*

The parable of the talents is one of opportunities seized and lost. If talent is understood as it is used today, one thinks of skills or abilities. This train of thought can lead to identifying talents as spiritual gifts. However, the amount given was "according to his ability" (v. 15). That establishes that spiritual gifts are something different than a person's capabilities.

Some look to a literal rendering of the word and think in monetary terms. In Jesus' day, a talent was a significant sum.

Another view is that they represent opportunities. As the master leaves, he gives a portion of his goods to these servants. They now have the opportunity to increase his holdings. Two of the servants do well with what is entrusted to their care. Their rewards, given for their faithfulness, are the same. One servant does not do well and is not rewarded.

The challenge of the parable is very plain. Jesus, the Master, is gone and will one day return. It is our responsibility to advance the kingdom.

The challenge of the parable is also very personal. Each servant is judged individually. Are you a good steward of the opportunities you have to serve Jesus?

What opportunities is God giving You to serve Him today? What will you do? Decide now that you will be a good steward.

BY THE BOOK

Leviticus 8–10, Matthew 25:31–46 • *Key Verse: Leviticus 10:3*

Once again we find that people "did everything the LORD command-ed" (8:36). The sad thing to note in this situation, however, is that the commitment did not last one week.

Two of Aaron's sons, Nadab and Abihu, decided to make some changes. The changes may have been minor, at least in our eyes. What harm could there be in adjusting what they put in the censers? There was a problem. It was not what God had commanded.

The judgment was swift and fatal. They died.

It is tempting to try to improve on God's way. A little fire and incense mix sounded appealing, but it was wrong. This temptation continues to plague God's people.

Another temptation is to do it our way instead of God's way. He had commanded how things were to be done and the people had fol-lowed. But there came a point where Nadab and Abihu decided to make a change.

Do *everything* God's way. Determine to live according to His Word. These chapters show His displeasure when His people fail to live by the Book.

Commit to put God's way in front of your way today.

GOT THE POINT

Leviticus 11–12, Matthew 26:1–25 • *Key Verses: Matthew 26:12–13*

Mary's act of worship is a scene of beauty in many ways. First is the extravagance of it—the perfume is described as being "very expensive" (v. 6). From John's account we learn that she then wiped Jesus' feet with her hair, a touching picture of both love and humility. The fragrance that hung in the air was an unmistakable testimony to her devotion to Jesus.

Her act of worship also was a point of controversy. Judas not only thought of other uses for the perfume but voiced his opinion. In what may have been a ruse to cover his real intent, he suggested that the profit could be used to benefit the poor (John 12:5–6).

Sometimes overshadowed by the giving and the contrasting greed is the fact that Mary was the one who got the point. Jesus said that He was going to be crucified; she understood and prepared Him for burial. But the disciples missed the point. They did not understand what was taking place in the anointing and the rush of events that were leading to Calvary.

Watch your heart, its values and receptiveness to God's truth. The sweet scent of worship lingering in your soul will be the blessing. Do not miss the point.

We may sing, "Open our eyes, Lord, we want to see Jesus," but do we mean it? Ask God to help you have a receptive heart.

WORDS' WORTH

Leviticus 13, **Matthew 26:26–50** • *Key Verses: Matthew 26:34–35*

In the space of just a few verses are recorded words spoken by two disciples. The first was a lie and the second was a boast. Judas lied and did what he denied. Peter boasted and did not do what he declared.

"One of you will betray Me," Jesus said. "Not I," was Judas's reply (vv. 21–25).

"You will deny Me," Jesus said. "Never," was Peter's reply (vv. 34–35).

Sometimes we know ourselves too well, as did Judas. We know our plans for wrong, and our denials are hollow sounds. Sometimes we do not know ourselves well enough, like Peter. We make our boasts, which fall short of reality. Our boasts can be hollow sounds as well.

How it must have grieved the heart of Jesus. In the emotion of that night He heard from His disciples words of deceit and denial.

What words does Jesus hear from you? He knows your plans and your heart, your words of denial or boasting notwithstanding. Think about your words and the heart from which they come. Eliminate deceit and denial and give true worth to your words.

Tell the truth always, to God and to man. Think before you speak, making sure you say what is true.

FROM COURAGE TO COWARDICE

Leviticus 14, Matthew 26:51–75 • Key Verse: Matthew 26:75

In Peter's life there was a slow, downward spiral, a regression from courage to cowardice. It began with a denial, moved to a defense and concluded with a denial of a different kind.

Just prior to these verses is the boast of Peter, the one in which he denied that he would ever deny Jesus.

Then came the scene in the garden. Judas arrived with a group of armed men. With characteristic courage and impetuousness, Peter drew his sword and struck a man.

Peter then moved away from Jesus' side to somewhere in the distance. He hung back, staying just out of sight yet keeping everything in sight. His courage was waning. A servant girl and another girl prompted the first two denials. The third denial in the crowd was inevitable.

In Peter's actions there is a lesson: A step back from Jesus may lead to yet another. He did not go immediately from courage to cowardice. It was a sequence of events.

Watch your every step. Stay close to Christ. When your step is away, make sure the next one is back toward Jesus.

"Help me stay close to You, God, in private and in public. May I always be willing to say, 'You are my God.'"

REPENTANCE AND REMORSE

Leviticus 15–16, Matthew 27:1–26 • *Key Verses: Matthew 27:3–4*

Peter's actions are tragic enough, but ultimately he served Jesus courageously and faithfully. Yes, he denied and deserted Jesus, but he found forgiveness and restoration.

The actions of Judas are tragic but in a far more intense way. Ultimately he faced remorse and took his life. He did not take the path that would lead to forgiveness and restoration.

Did Judas repent? Some versions translate verse three with the word *repented*. The Greek word in that verse, however, does not indicate change. Instead, it carries the meaning of remorse. Judas demonstrated his remorse in his interaction with the priests, by throwing the money into the temple and by his suicide. He did not repent unto salvation.

Judas could not escape responsibility or undo results, and neither can we. Without forgiveness, remorse remains.

Remorse must be replaced with repentance. The proper action is to look to God and receive His forgiveness. First John 1:9 promises that His response to our confession will be forgiveness.

Do not live in remorse. Go to God for forgiveness. Make the necessary changes in how you live, and, like Peter, return to a life of obedience.

Is there a need for repentance in your life right now? Do not let sin drive you away from God. Instead, draw near, asking for His forgiveness.

OVERCOMER

Leviticus 17–18, Matthew 27:27–50
Key Verses: Matthew 27:28–29

The imagery of the crown that was set on Jesus' head is much fuller than the English translation conveys. It was a crudely and cruelly fashioned crown, the branches of a thorn bush hastily twisted together. The blows to Jesus' head undoubtedly added to the torment as the thorns pushed painfully into His scalp. That much of the picture is evident, but there is more.

The crown specifically was a *stephanos*. This is the word for the victor's crown, the type given as the symbol of triumph. The person awarding the victor's crown might be wearing a crown as well—in this case a *diadem*, the ruler's crown. These two Greek words are both translated "crown," the one belonging to the ruler and the other to the overcomer.

The crude and cruel crown of thorns upon Jesus' brow was more than just a crown. It was the symbol of the overcomer.

The next time Jesus is described as wearing a crown is in Revelation 19:12, when He appears as the Rider on the White Horse. On His head are many crowns. This time the word used is *diadem*. The Overcomer has returned to reign.

Worship King Jesus. He overcame death and hell. He is King of kings and Lord of lords.

Jesus is King! Take a moment to pray, to worship, praising Him as King.

RULES FOR RIGHTEOUSNESS

Leviticus 19–20, Matthew 27:51–66 • *Key Verse: Leviticus 19:2*

Is there a child who has not at some point looked at his parent and asked, "Why?" And is there a parent who has not replied, "Because"?

Sometimes when one reads the Old Testament, particularly the sections with various laws, the why question comes to mind. The Book of Leviticus can do that to a person! It includes very specific instructions regarding even mildew. Why?

Our passage today gives two direct reasons. "'Be holy because I, the LORD your God, am holy'" (19:2). One reason is holiness. God's intent is not to give rules just for the sake of giving rules. Carefully considered, the various laws and regulations have as their focus the holiness of God's people.

The other reason is relationship. "'I am the LORD your God'" (v. 3). This theme is repeated throughout these chapters and others. The word translated "LORD" points specifically to the relationship between God and His redeemed people. He is our God, and we are His people. In that relationship we are to serve and honor Him.

Rules for the sake of rules? No. Rules for the sake of righteousness and as a part of our relationship. Does your life reflect the holiness that God requires of His people?

To be holy is to be set apart. Are you set apart from sin and set apart to God? Does your life show holiness?

WHEN THE ROCK ROLLED

Leviticus 21–22, Matthew 28 • *Key Verse: Matthew 28:9*

Pilate had ordered the tomb in which Jesus was buried to be made secure (Matt. 27:65). Three things were used to accomplish this. One, a big stone was already in place that covered the entrance securely. Two, a seal of Rome was placed on the tomb. Such a seal was not to be broken and carried severe penalties if it were. Three, a guard was posted.

It was good that the authorities did these things. By taking these measures, they removed the possibility of anybody stealing the body of Jesus. But their efforts were ultimately useless. The rock rolled, the seal broke, and the soldiers fainted. Rock, wax and a few armed men could not thwart heaven's plan. Christ arose!

The reactions of Jesus' followers are interesting. The women who heard the angel's announcement were "afraid yet filled with joy" (v. 8). When they saw Jesus, they worshiped Him. When the disciples saw Jesus in Galilee, their response was likewise one of worship.

The Resurrection is a demonstration of God's power that should evoke worship. Our response to this truth today should be the same as that of the followers of Jesus that day.

"Christ the Lord is risen today. Alleluia!"

At the heart of worship is response. You know Jesus rose from the dead. How do you respond to that truth? Worship should be an immediate response. Say a prayer of praise to our living Savior.

GOOD NEWS

Leviticus 23–24, Mark 1:1–22 • *Key Verses: Mark 1:14–15*

The preaching of Jesus is described as "proclaiming the good news of God" (v. 14). The Gospel is the Good News of God. Specifically, it is what Jesus preached about God. What He had to say is indeed good news.

David Garland observes that "preaching the gospel today is not simply giving testimony to timeless truths, providing tips on successful living from pop psychology, or regaling congregations with entertaining stories designed to make them feel good about themselves and the preacher" (*The NIV Application Commentary: Mark,* p. 62). To learn what the Gospel is, one needs look no further than the next verse.

"The time has come." No more delay in the working out of God's plan.

"The kingdom of God is near." No more distance. The kingdom is not far off but at hand.

"Repent and believe." No more doubt. Repentance is a change of mind that brings about a change of life. Jesus included the need to believe. A disciple is not just a morally good person but also believes in Jesus.

This is the good news about believing in Jesus. Through His death, burial and resurrection, He paid completely the penalty for our sin. There is no better news than this!

Do you ever share good news with others? Of course you do. Today tell someone the good news about Jesus.

GOOD FEAR

Leviticus 25, Mark 1:23–45 • *Key Verse: Leviticus 25:17*

As God instructed His people in how they were to live, He gave them reasons. At times the reason was one of relationship. "I am the LORD your God." Other times the reason was one of righteousness. "Be holy because I am holy."

There is yet another reason behind His instructions. It's one that doesn't get much attention but is a theme of Scripture. In this chapter the reason given is reverence. "Fear your God" (vv. 17, 36, 43).

Sometimes we emphasize God's love exclusively. The fact that He is a God of grace overshadows that He also is a God to be feared.

The inadequacy of understanding the fear of God also keeps its emphasis diminished. There is a fear that debilitates and destroys. This is the most common way of understanding fear. Then there is the fear that is beneficial. The fear of God is not baneful but a blessing.

The fear God commands is a reverence for Him and a restraining force for us. In reverence one realizes that God truly is the awesome God.

God warns us to fear Him, and we should. Do not take lightly the consequences of disobeying God.

Ask God to help you fear Him—not in the frightened sense, but in a life of reverential awe.

LEAVE NO DOUBT

Leviticus 26–27, Mark 2 • *Key Verse: Mark 2:5*

In the account of the healing of the paralytic, attention is immediately drawn to the actions of his friends. They are determined enough to dig through the roof in order to get the man to Jesus. Mark writes that "Jesus saw their faith" (v. 5).

Faith is an intangible. It cannot be weighed on a scale or measured with a ruler. There is no way to biopsy it or to attach it to a monitoring device. Yet Jesus saw their faith.

Specifically, Jesus saw the demonstration of their faith. He recognized that their bold action was evidence of their belief. They really believed Jesus could heal.

Suppose they had done nothing but believe. The man would have stayed a paralytic. To believe is one thing; to live out that belief is another thing—a necessary thing.

James commands us, "Do not merely listen to the word . . . . Do what it says" (James 1:22). Jesus could see their faith by what they did.

Do others see your faith? To believe is one thing; to live out your belief is another. Let there be no doubt in the minds of those who know you. Let them see your faith.

"Help me today, God, to make my faith seen. Give me an opportunity to do something that unmistakably is an act of faith."

KEEP IT QUIET

Numbers 1–2, Mark 3:1–19 • *Key Verses: Mark 3:11–12*

One of the confusing situations in the Gospels is when Jesus instructed someone to keep what He did quiet. In this chapter the evil spirits are given strict orders not to tell that Jesus was the Son of God. Why would Jesus want that fact kept a secret?

Note that in this situation, as in chapter 1, Jesus is muzzling evil spirits. The problem was not with incorrect information. What they said was true; He was the Son of God. The problem was the wrong messenger. As Warren Wiersbe says, "The Savior did not want, nor did He need, the assistance of Satan and his army to tell people who He was."

The right message told by the wrong messenger can bring about the wrong results. People could have confused the ministry of Jesus with their understanding of evil spirits. The two are not aligned in any way. In reality, they are dramatically opposed to each other.

The truthfulness of the message is vitally important. There also needs to be an emphasis on the truthfulness of the messenger. Sometimes the message of Christ is hurt by the one carrying the message.

Are you a fit messenger?

Be the kind of messenger Jesus wants to use to tell others about Him. Your life affects your message!

INTENTIONALLY CONFUSING

Numbers 3–4, Mark 3:20–35 • Key Verse: Mark 3:30

In the first part of this chapter, Jesus gave the evil spirits strict orders not to tell people who He was. While their message was true, those messengers could cause confusion. Some would think that Jesus was associated with demons.

Some people even tried to make others think that. In an intentional effort to make Jesus look demonic, teachers of the Law said, "He is possessed by Beelzebub! By the prince of demons he is driving out demons" (v. 22).

What Jesus sought to keep the evil spirits from doing, the teachers did. What they said not only was wrong but also did not make sense. "How can Satan drive out Satan?" Jesus pointed out (v. 23).

The reality of the ministry of Jesus is that He was destroying the work of Satan and that He is more powerful than Satan.

The conflict with the evil one is real, continues today and will continue until the final judgment. Remember, though, that ultimately Jesus will destroy all the work of Satan.

The battle is raging, but Jesus will win. Do not let anyone confuse you about that.

Jesus has power over the kingdom of darkness. Don't ever admit defeat. Assume that victory will come through Jesus.

THE FACE OF BLESSING

Numbers 5–6, Mark 4:1–20 • *Key Verses: Numbers 6:24–26*

Today when I read these verses, I think of pastors in my youth who concluded the Sunday service with these words or those of other benedictions found in the Bible. As a child, I usually perceived the benediction as the beginning of the end. I would be ready to bolt from the pew as soon as the moment of silence—just long enough to let the pastor get a head start to the door—lasted.

Now I realize that there is more to these verses than the format for a formal conclusion. They are words of blessing, a prayer as such, imploring God to bless the hearer.

What joy there is when we realize that God's face is shining upon us, His graciousness is in our lives, He is watching over us, and He is giving us peace!

In the same way, what joy there should be when we ask God to do that for others. In a self-centered life, we want. In a Christ-centered life, we give. Blessing is ours both to receive and to give. Find someone today for whom you can pray God's blessing.

Fill in the blank: "God, bless _____ today." Then tell that person you prayed for him or her to be blessed.

FROM FEAR TO FEAR

Numbers 7–8, Mark 4:21–41 • *Key Verse: Mark 4:40*

The account of the calming of the sea is so familiar that it can be read almost without thinking. The disciples are in the boat when a threatening storm hits. They wake Jesus, whose sleeping makes them wonder if He cares. He muzzles the wind and all is calm—except the hearts of the disciples.

Jesus asked, "Why are you so afraid?" (v. 40). Their fear makes sense to us! The fear of drowning was real.

What does not make sense is the next verse. After what they had just experienced, the Bible says the disciples were terrified. Instead of going from fear to faith, they went from fear to fear.

There are two parts to explaining this. First, the disciples went from fear to awe. The Greek words used here are different. They went from fright to reverential awe.

Second, they were so accustomed to seeing Jesus in His humanity that the display of His deity astounded them. Typically believers today think first of the deity of Jesus. Divine displays do not astound us as they did His disciples. They should, though.

Do not by familiarity lose sight of the awesomeness of Jesus. Then in times of fear, He will help you move from fear to faith.

Take a few moments to meditate about this passage. As you do, answer this question: "What manner of man is this?"

GRIPERS IN THE GRIP OF GRACE

Numbers 9–11, Mark 5:1–20 • *Key Verse: Numbers 11:23*

Numbers 11 begins with a gripe. When the going gets tough, those with a gripe get going. The Exodus was not a nature walk but a tough trek through the wilderness.

There were hardships, for sure. The first complaint, though, was about the food. In their minds, the Israelites had eaten better when they were slaves. The power of the stomach was so strong that it sounds like they preferred the food of slavery over the menu of the delivered.

Think about all the blessings God was giving them. They were freed from slavery, delivered from the Egyptian army and given a promised land. On a daily basis they experienced God's provision of food and guidance.

Yet in the midst of deliverance, protection, provision and guidance, the people complained. Their discontent was really a rejection of the Lord. Verse 20 makes this plain.

Rejection of God's plan for our lives is a rejection of God. Discontent with our circumstances is a rejection of God. Believers may not think of it in that way, but God does.

The blessing of contentment comes with acceptance of God's work in our lives—no matter what is on the menu.

"God, help me to know contentment, the kind that comes from accepting Your plan for my life."

TEN TO TWO

Numbers 12–14, Mark 5:21–43 • Key Verse: Numbers 13:30–31

A children's chorus begins with the words, "Twelve men went to spy on Canaan, ten were bad, two were good." Can you name the two who were good? The answer, of course, is Caleb and Joshua. But can you name any of the others?

A speaker I knew would at times get out his wallet and offer to pay a dollar for each of those names a person could recall. He never gave away a single bill. As he put away his wallet with all its dollar bills intact, he would say, "We remember the people who stand for God, but not the ones who don't."

Joshua and Caleb stood for God. Shammua, Shaphat, Igal and the others did not. Their collective voices drowned out the faith of the other two. It was not just a matter of a majority vote but of rebellion. When the people decided not to do what God wanted, it was a rebellion that resulted in 40 years of wandering plus the death of all but the younger generation.

But Joshua and Caleb were spared. They ultimately entered the Promised Land.

The lesson is clear: stand for God—whatever the numbers.

There are probably times you do not stand boldly. Perhaps today something will happen and you will have to make a choice either to speak up or be silent. Stand up for Jesus.

WHO'S IN CHARGE?

Numbers 15–16, Mark 6:1–29 • *Key Verse: Numbers 16:11*

Follow this sequence. In Numbers 11:1, the people complained. In 12:1, Miriam and Aaron began to talk against Moses. In 14:2, all the Israelites grumbled against Moses and Aaron. In 16:3, they came as a group to oppose Moses and Aaron.

See a pattern? Leadership is not all privileges and perks. It is also a position of problems. People at times deal with their difficulties by attacking a person rather than by solving the problem.

Now follow this sequence. In Numbers 11:1, the Lord's anger was aroused. In 12:9, the anger of the Lord burned against them. In 14:12, the Lord said He would strike them down. In 16:11, Moses told the complainers that they had banded together against the Lord.

See another pattern? Attacking God's appointed leadership is a serious offense. When His appointed leader is opposed, God takes notice.

Submission to God's appointed leadership is clearly commanded. If there is a time of discontent with leadership in a church or with the direction of a ministry, consider your actions carefully. Do not follow the crowd. Follow the Word and determine to approach the problem in a way that pleases God.

Sadly, God's leaders can be easy targets. Consider what you say about your pastor and other leaders in the church. Is God pleased with what you say?

PRAY TO CHOOSE

Numbers 17–19 • Key Verse: Numbers 17:8

Numbers gives interesting insight into the relationship between God's people and His appointed leaders. On numerous occasions Israel failed. They grumbled and rebelled against Moses. In fact, their actions were against God.

In Numbers 17 God made it very clear for the nation that Aaron was His choice. His staff sprouted, giving the people a sign. It was to be kept as a sign to the rebellious, to put an end to their grumbling.

This passage does not give God's people today a practice to follow. Churches do not choose their leaders by bundling sticks to see which one buds. But we are given some very important principles.

Do not miss the seriousness with which God views rebellion. He made clear His choice of Aaron to keep the people from judgment. In addition, the choosing of leaders must be taken seriously.

The practice of choosing leaders in the New Testament emphasized prayer. Jesus prayed before choosing the Twelve. The disciples prayed in Acts 1 before choosing Matthias. The choosing of the seven in Acts 6 included prayer.

Receiving an objective sign made it easy for Israel to know God's choice. Today, the process of choosing leaders must include prayer.

Pray for the leaders in your church by name. Ask that God will bless and guide so that you may see His name glorified in your church.

THE LESSON OF THE LOAVES
Mark 6:30–56 • Key Verses: Mark 6:51–52

It is easy to get so focused on an event that the significance is lost. Take Christmas, for example. Every December the challenge is to keep the significance in front of the event. Valuable lessons are lost if we don't.

That is what happened to the disciples at the feeding of the 5,000. They participated in the miracle and knew the event, but not its significance.

Immediately afterwards Jesus sent His disciples to Bethsaida by boat. Later, when the wind was against them and they were straining at the oars, they saw the remarkable sight of Jesus walking by them on the water. At first they thought it was a ghost. Jesus calmed them and climbed into the boat, and the wind died down.

Notice verses 51 and 52: "They were completely amazed, for they had not understood about the loaves." The lesson of the event was lost on them.

The lesson of the loaves is that Jesus has the power to meet our needs. His adequacy eliminates our inadequacy and His ability replaces our inability. The voice we should hear in our times of fear is His as He says, "Take courage! It is I. Don't be afraid" (v. 50).

"God, help me look to You when I need help. Teach me that the power is not in me but comes from You."

IT'S ABOUT TIME!

Numbers 20–22, Mark 7:1–13 • Key Verse: Numbers 21:7

Do you ever get frustrated to the point of saying, "It's about time"? Maybe you have tried to get something across to another person but were unsuccessful. Then, finally, he got it and you uttered those words in exasperated relief. Actually, those would be words of hopeful relief. If the person got it now, hopefully he will get it later too.

In Numbers 21 there is such a scenario. It starts with a déjà vu of sorts. "The people grew impatient on the way; they spoke against God and against Moses" (vv. 4–5)—again, we might note. They spoke against God and Moses again.

And God dealt with them for their rebellion—again. This time venomous snakes bit people and many died. Their grumbling rebellion again had resulted in judgment.

This time, though, something different happened after the judgment. The people came to Moses and confessed, "We sinned" (v. 7). They acknowledged their wrong and also asked Moses to pray for them. It was not the first time he had intervened on their behalf. This time, though, he was asked to do so. It was about time!

Too often the people of God fail to come to grips with the reality of their wrong actions. In such times we need to confess, seek God's forgiveness and quit doing what is wrong.

Is there a sin you need to confess? If so, confess it now.

HOW LOW CAN ONE GO?

Numbers 23–25, Mark 7:14–37 • **Key Verse: Numbers 25:3**

The opening verses of Numbers 25 describe a scene of immorality, idolatry and judgment. When the entire story is known, the scene is even sadder than it appears.

Earlier, Balak had sought to hire Balaam to curse Israel. When initially rebuffed, Balak upped the ante and made the offer too good to refuse. He tried, but Balaam could not curse those whom God had determined to bless.

But Balaam still wanted the gold. If he could not get it by cursing, he would try to get it by counseling. He counseled Balak to entice Israel to immorality and idolatry (Num. 31:16). Then they would bring God's judgment on themselves. By so doing, Balaam accomplished the task for which he was hired.

Balaam's "epitaph" in the New Testament is that he "loved the wages of wickedness" (2 Pet. 2:15). He went for the gold and is remembered for it. In Jude 11 there is another New Testament reference to Balaam. Jude writes of those who "have rushed for profit into Balaam's error."

The error of Balaam continues today. A person may not be hired to curse another, but the willingness to put personal gain over others remains. The world places its emphasis on getting. The Christian's worldview should emphasize giving. Do not follow the way of Balaam.

How important are material things to you? Don't let possessions distort your values. Some things are not worth the cost—a lesson Balaam did not learn.

WHOSE SIDE ARE YOU ON, ANYWAY?

Numbers 26–28, Mark 8 • *Key Verse: Mark 8:29*

Never forget that the Christian life is lived on the battlefield. We are in a war. The line is clearly drawn and the sides are diametrically opposed. It is the people of God versus Satan and his emissaries.

Never forget which side you are on, either! Sometimes we can inadvertently aid the enemy, especially when we are not thinking biblically.

What Peter said in Mark 8 is one of the greatest confessions of faith of all times. While some said Jesus was John, Elijah or one of the prophets, Peter said, "You are the Christ" (v. 29).

Then when Jesus began to teach the disciples about His anticipated death, Peter rebuked Him. With that rebuke, he was aiding the enemy. In turn, Jesus rebuked Peter, "Get behind me, Satan!" (v. 33). His words must have startled Peter.

The crux of the matter was that when Peter no longer had in mind the things of God, he was aiding the enemy.

Our views are not to be those of man or of our own reasoning. Our views, attitudes, reasonings and beliefs must be molded by the Word of God. When our thinking turns to minding the things of men instead of the mind of God, we aid the cause of Satan.

Learn to see things God's way. This will come as you learn His Word, pray and allow His Spirit to guide you.

AS GOOD AS YOUR WORD

Numbers 29–31, Mark 9:1–29 • *Key Verse: Numbers 30:2*

Although today a Christian is not under responsibility to fulfill the ceremonial law, the New Testament emphasis on the moral law is strong. We may not make vows as is referenced in Numbers 30:2, but we are to be truthful people. Moses commanded the Israelites that a man "must not break his word but must do everything he said."

In the course of a year, a person makes many more "vows" than is probably realized. For example, each credit card slip we sign is a vow. Don't sign unless you intend to pay. A tax form will ask if the answers given were truthful. Don't sign unless they were. A code of conduct may be included in the regulations for a student or an employer. Don't sign unless you plan to live by it.

Then there are the other slips—not of paper, but of tongue. "I'll get back to you about that." "The check is in the mail." "We'll get together for a meal while you're in town."

Jesus said, "Simply let your 'Yes' be 'Yes,' and your 'No,' 'No'; anything beyond this comes from the evil one" (Matt. 5:37).

How good is your word? And are you as good as your word?

Think before you speak today. Ask yourself, "Will I do what I am about to say?" Keep your word.

DISCOURAGING BY DEFAULT

Numbers 32–34, Mark 9:30–50 • *Key Verses: Numbers 32:6–7*

"Looking out for number one" is an old saying, but its sentiment is as popular as ever. We have been taught that we can have it our way and that we deserve a break today.

Too often a Christian can be subtly sucked into thinking about self with little regard for others. The follower of Christ, however, must remember that every believer is part of the Body and must consider how individual actions affect others.

This is not a new problem. The Reubenites, Gadites and half the tribe of Manasseh liked the look of the land east of the Jordan. It was suitable for livestock. Their request to stay there seemed reasonable.

But Moses saw the effect it would have on Israel: "Shall your countrymen go to war while you sit here? Why do you discourage the [nation]?" (31:6–7).

To their credit, when reminded of similar past situations and when made aware of how their action would affect others, these tribes did not choose to be discouragers. Yes, their families and livestock remained, but the men went to war with the rest of Israel.

Too often people in the church think of themselves and not how their choices might discourage others. Determine to encourage others by your actions as well as your words.

You can be an encourager or a discourager. Putting your interests first can discourage others. Choose to be an encourager.

HARD-HEARTED

Numbers 35–36, Mark 10:1–31 • *Key Verse: Mark 10:5*

More than ever, the prefix "step-" is a part of our vocabulary. Sometimes due to death but more often due to divorce and remarriage, one may speak of a stepparent, stepbrother, stepsister or stepchild. The prefix "ex-" has become a word that can stand alone in a sentence. A former spouse is often referred to as one's "ex."

At first glance, the prevalent use of these terms is probably because of the high divorce rate. That is one cause, but it is not really the heart of the matter.

The heart of the matter is, in fact, the heart. Skip the debate over whether the Bible allows for divorce. Instead, cut to the chase with the words of Jesus: Moses permitted divorce "because your hearts were hard" (v. 5). Without the law of Moses, a husband could impulsively divorce his wife, discarding her, as Warren Wiersbe writes, "like an unwanted piece of furniture."

In reality, divorce does not solve the problem. It just removes the people a step or two from the situation. But the hard heart—the heart of the problem, according to Jesus—stays with the person.

The bottom line for Christians is that our hearts are not to be hard. Keep yours teachable, open and responsive to God's Word and work. Too often the problems we face remain and worsen because our hearts are hard.

"Help me to have a teachable spirit, a heart that is open and responsive to You, O God."

WE HAVE MET THE ENEMY . . .

Deuteronomy 1–3, Mark 10:32–52 • *Key Verse: Mark 10:38*

The old cartoon character Pogo rephrased the words of Admiral Perry: "We have met the enemy and he is us." The struggles and failures so many people experience have as their root nothing other than self. In today's reading, self-focus clashes with the kingdom agenda.

Jesus gave the agenda. "We are going up to Jerusalem," He announced (v. 33). He spoke of His upcoming betrayal, condemnation, mocking, death and resurrection.

Having heard this agenda, James and John made a request—to sit on either side of Jesus in His glory. The clashing of agendas occurred as they shifted focus from Christ's passion to their desired positions of honor.

Just as the request in the Numbers 32 reading (March 5) affected the nation as a whole, so this request affected the disciples as a group. The others became "indignant with James and John" (v. 41). Jesus had to call them together to calm them down.

Consider James 4:1. "What causes fights and quarrels among you? Don't they come from your desires that battle within you?"

Choose to focus on the kingdom agenda. Take the focus off yourself.

Try to see others before yourself. Perhaps today you will be able to put someone in front of you. Learn to live for others.

THE PERIL OF PROSPERITY

Deuteronomy 4–6, Mark 11:1–18 • Key Verse: Deuteronomy 6:12

When things are going well, it is very easy to forget God. He knew that this temptation lay in the path before the people of Israel.

The way had been rough. For 40 years the people had endured the difficulties of being desert nomads, literally burying a generation (see Deut. 1:35). Only the young, along with Caleb and Joshua, were spared from the judgment of God. Now Moses was preparing them to move into the Promised Land.

God was giving them cities that they did not build, houses filled with good things, wells that were in place, and vineyards and olive groves that they did not plant.

With blessing, however, comes a peril. The peril of prosperity is that we sometimes forget God and His blessings. Instead, we rely on self, enjoying the ease.

The words of Moses ring true for us today. He said, "When you eat and are satisfied, be careful that you do not forget the LORD" (6:11–12).

Solomon's prayer also is vital in this regard: "Give me neither poverty nor riches, but give me only my daily bread. Otherwise, I may have too much and disown you and say, 'Who is the LORD?'" (Prov. 30:8–9).

Write out a list of God's blessings, and then add to it each day for a week. It will keep you from forgetting the goodness of God.

FORGET HIM!

Deuteronomy 7–9, Mark 11:19–33 • *Key Verse: Mark 11:25*

It's easy to dismiss the person with whom you disagree or have had a disagreement. A simple, "Forget him!" and you can get on with your life.

Not really. In fact, not at all! Be careful not to get infected with an attitude condoned by this world but condemned by the Word.

Consider what that attitude can do to your praying. Failing to forgive another is one of the things that the Bible says will hinder your prayers. The reason for this is that forgiving others is evidence that we are right with God.

God commands us to forgive. Failure to obey is sin, and sin hinders our prayers. God's will is not followed when we hold a grudge or dismiss another with a "Forget him!" The unforgiving person is then placed in the position of being an unforgiven person. He does not lose his salvation but his fellowship with God is affected.

Commenting on the beginning of the Lord's Prayer, one person noted that the words "Our Father" are significant. They remind us that we may pray in private but never alone. We are part of a family, and together we come before God.

Want your prayers to be effective? Check both your relationship with God and with others.

Yesterday you made a list of blessings. Today list those people whom you should forgive, then cross off each name as you forgive them.

BACKHANDED COMPLIMENT

Deuteronomy 10–12, Mark 12:1–27 • *Key Verse: Mark 12:14*

Not everyone liked Jesus. Some were very open in their opposition. They schemed for opportunities to turn people away from Him. One tactic was to use His own teaching against Him. To accomplish that, they would at times ask trick questions.

In today's reading, a representative group from the Pharisees and Herodians tried to catch Jesus in His words. Part of their strategy was to compliment Jesus first and then hit Him with the question. The compliment speaks volumes. Delivered perhaps with tongue in cheek, these men gave a picture of the One whom the believer is to emulate. We are to be like Jesus, who was a man of integrity and not swayed by men, particularly those of "position." He was a true teacher of the way of God.

Even tongue in cheek, these men spoke the truth. To have said anything else would have precluded the possibility of asking their question. If they had made a misstatement about Jesus, it would have been challenged. They did not want to get sidetracked from their purpose.

Take this description of Jesus. Acknowledge that it is true. Then remember that you are to be like Him. How do you measure up in your integrity, respect of persons and teaching? Are you like Jesus?

Do an integrity check, not of others, but of yourself. Would others say of you what these people said of Jesus?

THIS IS A TEST

Deuteronomy 13–15, Mark 12:28–44
Key Verses: Deuteronomy 13:1–3

It is not uncommon to read of a police department, working on a baffling case or disappearance, to consult a psychic. The "just the facts" approach to crime moves to an "I have a feeling" process of investigation. Sometimes it works! The psychic leads the police to a key piece of evidence.

How should a Christian respond to those times when the paranormal is portrayed as normal?

First, realize that sometimes they will get it right. God's Word tells us that and gives examples of prophets and magicians whose advice was taken and signs believed. Deuteronomy 13:2 says, "And if the sign or wonder of which he has spoken takes place . . . ."

Second, refuse to follow that path. God's specific instruction is "you must not listen to the words of that prophet or dreamer" (v. 3). In other words, do not add Tarot cards to your daily reading. Skip the horoscope.

Third, recognize that it is a test. Our hearts are tested through these seemingly inexplicable happenings. But God explains them. He says they are a test to see if you love Him with all your heart.

Stay true to God. Do not let appearances deceive you.

The better we know the Word, the better we can discern truth and error. Review your commitment to read and learn the Bible.

IN PROPORTION

Deuteronomy 16–18, Mark 13:1–20
Key Verse: Deuteronomy 16:17

Bring up the subject of giving and some reactions are standard. The negative person says, "The church is always asking for money." The self-justifying person says, "I tithe." The evading person says, "I gave at the office."

In the midst of instructions for the "Pilgrim Festivals," annual events that all male Israelites were supposed to attend, is a statement on giving.

First, notice the context is one that emphasizes rejoicing in the Lord (16:11, 14–15). These were times of celebration. Our hearts should be filled with the joy of the Lord.

Second, notice that they were not to come empty-handed (v. 16). Words are cheap, but giving costs. The gifts brought reflected the reality of the heart. To give with joy demonstrates the genuineness of our worship.

Third, notice the gift was to be in proportion to the way they had been blessed (v. 17). Yes, this was a tithe. This, however, was not a percentage gift but a proportionate one. In the same way, our giving is to be as "God has blessed" or "in keeping with [our] income" (1 Cor. 16:2).

Some people find joy as they gain and keep. But followers of God have joy, and from their gain, they give.

Does your giving to the Lord's work follow this pattern? Today you can begin to give as God teaches you to give.

PLAN OR PANIC?

Deuteronomy 19–21, **Mark 13:21–37** • *Key Verse: Mark 13:37*

Deadlines are good. They can help us plan—or they can make us panic. At the beginning of a semester, for example, students are given a variety of deadlines. Some students plan well, budget their time and meet the deadlines.

On the other hand, there are those who say, "I work better under pressure." They ignore the deadlines until panic sets in. Then they do work under pressure—but not necessarily better.

How would a student handle it if an assignment were given without a due date? The only due date announced would be when the professor decided to call for the assignment. One would have to be constantly prepared.

Professors do not typically give assignments without clear due dates, but Jesus did. He gave us His work to do until He comes. Instead of a specific time, He said that it could be "in the evening, or at midnight, or when the rooster crows, or at dawn" (v. 35). His one-word summary instruction was, "Watch!" (v. 37).

If you knew His deadline were today, would you be prepared or would you panic? It could be today. Do you believe that? And are you prepared?

"God, help me to watch today and every day so I will be ready and watching when Jesus comes."

A TEMPTATION TO RESIST

Deuteronomy 22–24, Mark 14:1–26 • **Key Verse: Deuteronomy 22:1**

Among the instructions God gave His people were ones regarding the possessions of others. Straying animals were not to be ignored but returned. At times wandering livestock was to be kept until the owner came to claim it. Even fallen animals were to be assisted. "Do not ignore it" is a twice-repeated instruction in the opening verses of Deuteronomy 22.

It is easier to ignore than get involved. These instructions, though, remind us that God is not concerned just with issues of wrongdoing but with relationships. His people are not to just look out for self, the proverbial "number one" of our lives, but also for the needs and well-being of others. That extends to helping with their livestock. In essence, this instruction aims to involve us in the plights other people face.

Perhaps your neighbor will not have cows loose in your pasture, unless you live in a rural area. If that does happen, you should help. But some other adversity may come into your neighbor's life. When it does, you should help.

Resist the temptation not to be involved with someone else's needs. Read James 2:15–17 and 1 John 3:17–18. Remind yourself that God is concerned that His people help others.

Is there someone you should help today? If no one comes to mind then start looking. Always be ready to help.

WANTS OR WILL?

Deuteronomy 25–27, Mark 14:27–53 • *Key Verse: Mark 14:36*

Life is often lived in pursuit of the "wants." People who live like this frequent the places that provide the food they want, shop the stores that have the products they want, go to the places that feature the entertainment they want, and spend time with those who share similar wants.

The "want-driven" life can become so ingrained that we can adopt "want-driven" praying. The prayer list becomes a wish list, filled with wishes based on wants.

Jesus demonstrated the reality that everyone has wants, but we must seek first God's will. "Take this cup from me," He prayed (v. 36). That was something He wanted and knew was possible because, as He affirmed, with God everything is possible.

His wants, though, were second to God's will. The next words strike at the heart of the want-driven life: "Yet not what I will, but what you will."

James, the brother of Jesus, learned the importance of putting wants second when praying. He wrote, "You do not receive, because you ask with wrong motives, that you may spend what you get on your pleasures" (James 4:3).

When you pray, is it based on your wants or His will?

Look over your prayer list. Ask God to help you sort through the things listed and decide which are merely your "wants" and should be removed.

ON THE BRINK

Deuteronomy 28–29, Mark 14:54–72
Key Verse: Deuteronomy 29:29

The Book of Deuteronomy is a covenant-treaty with stipulations, blessings and curses for the Israelites as they stood on the brink of entering the Promised Land. It describes the way God's people were to live in their new land. They had the promises of God's help, but the future still was unknown to them.

In Deuteronomy 29:29, Moses told them that the future was unknown to them but known to God. What they knew is what He had revealed. They had His Word. God had told them what they needed to know. Now they needed to follow His instructions.

We are so much like Israel. The future is as unknown to us as it was to them. We have God's Word and it tells us how we are to live. Our responsibility is to follow His instructions. This requires us to trust and obey. Demanding to know is not an option because "the secret things belong to the LORD our God" (v. 29).

Life is always lived on the brink of the future. Our knowledge is severely limited, but we do have the revelation of God in His Word. So give obedient attention to it as you, like Israel, live on the brink.

As the saying goes, we may not know what the future holds but we know who holds the future. Ask God for peace in your heart as you look ahead.

LISTEN, LEARN, LIVE

Deuteronomy 30–31, Mark 15:1–25
Key Verse: Deuteronomy 31:11

The attempts of children to answer questions about the Bible can be cute. Names and events get switched around and blended. In their innocence and youthfulness, their statements often bring a smile to one's face.

The expectation is that with growth, their childish mistakes will be replaced with Christian maturity and understanding. But that does not happen automatically. Growing older physically is no guarantee of maturing spiritually.

The emphasis in Deuteronomy 31:11 on reading aloud the Word of God is set in a time in which oral teaching was critical. Today there is easy access to the printed Word. While times have changed in that regard, the truth of verses 11–13 remains.

People need to listen to, learn and live the Word of God. We must live in accordance with the lessons learned from the Bible.

Moses also emphasized the need to pass God's Word to the next generation. Verse 13 says that "their children, who do not know this law, must hear it and learn to fear the LORD your God."

None of this is automatic. Each of us must listen to and learn the Word of God so we may live it. Then, we must pass His truth on to the next generation.

What are you doing to pass along God's truth to the next generation? Think hard about this and pray about what else you should be doing.

THEY SPOKE BETTER THAN THEY KNEW

Deuteronomy 32–34, Mark 15:26–47 • *Key Verses: Mark 15:31–32*

It's an odd thing that we can say one thing and mean another. Sometimes people speak better than they know.

In their mockery, the religious leaders spoke better than they knew when they challenged Jesus to save Himself from the cross (vv. 31–32). They said the right thing. If Jesus were to fulfill His messianic mission, He could not save Himself. His death was necessary for man's redemption.

But their words carried the wrong meaning. In their minds, Jesus was powerless to save. They knew He had healed others, but now since He was staying on the cross, they said that He could not save Himself.

These were the right words, but with the wrong meaning. Jesus is not powerless to save, nor is He unwilling. The nails did not hold Him fast to the cross. It was love—a love as hard as nails. Had He saved Himself from death, He could not have saved others from something more deadly than storms or illnesses. By His suffering, death and resurrection, Jesus taught us to "take up" the cross, not to come down from one.

Many people say the right words about Jesus but do not grasp the real meaning. Do you? Do you truly understand that Jesus had to stay on the cross?

If you have never received Jesus as your Savior, pray to do so now. If you have, thank Him for staying on that cross until His work on our behalf was finished.

STEP INTO THE RIVER

Joshua 1–3, Mark 16 • *Key Verse: Joshua 1:9*

Knowing and doing are two different things. One can know what to do and fail to do it because of fear. At times, obedience is incomplete due to fear.

The Israelites were concluding 40 years in the wilderness due to fear. What they saw as impossible kept them from doing what God had wanted. Now the nation was once again on the brink of entering the land.

A new leader stood before them. His frequent challenge was, "Be strong and courageous." That phrase is repeated four times in chapter 1 (vv. 6, 7, 9 and 18) and expressed in slightly different terms in other verses.

It was time to move out. They knew what they were to do and now they were to do it!

Notice what happened next. The spies brought back an encouraging report and the people prepared to move out. Their first steps, though, were into a flooded river—where their sandals were to meet the mud, so to speak.

"Be strong and courageous" was put to the test when they stepped into that dangerous river. But they obeyed and God blessed (3:15–16).

There will be times in our life of obedience that our courage will be tested. Be ready to step into the river. God is faithful even when the river is wide.

"Today and every day, Lord, give me the courage to obey. I need the strength You give."

THINK SO?

Joshua 4–6, Luke 1:1–20 • *Key Verses: Luke 1:3–4*

E-mail is both used and misused. Hardly a week goes by without some startling story, prayer request or warning of a vicious virus that is circulating. The novice believes whatever has been sent and forwards it on to others. Then come the replies: "It's a hoax." So many of these fabricated stories exist that there are Web sites where one can check to see if the story is true or not.

It's good to question what you read, especially if it is forwarded e-mail! A simple "Think so?" can spare you the embarrassment of passing along incorrect information.

In contrast, Luke begins his Gospel with the comforting statement that "it seemed good . . . to write an orderly account . . . , that you may know the certainty of the things you have been taught" (vv. 3–4). "Think so?" is replaced with a confident "Know so!" because God has given us His certain Word.

The Bible is true, and all teaching must be measured by it. Any teaching that does not match up with the Word is wrong. So, read your Bible with confidence. God gave it to you so you will know the certainty of your faith.

Thank God for the certainty of His Word. Our hope is not an uncertain hope but a confident one.

DIFFICULT BY DESIGN

Joshua 7–9, Luke 1:21–38 • *Key Verse: Luke 1:38*

Smooth sailing is preferred over rough seas; paved roads over potholes. But sometimes the rough seas and potholes are by God's design to accomplish His purpose. At that point, the follower of Christ must decide whether to follow God in the tough times or not.

Mary experienced a time that was difficult by design. These verses record part of her predicament: an unexpected pregnancy. Imagine as best you can the full emotion of the situation. She, an unmarried virgin, was asked to have a baby. Undoubtedly she would become the object of much doubt and ridicule. The truth would be too unimaginable for people to believe. She would bear the shame. In Matthew's account, it is noted that Joseph even considered divorcing her (1:19).

Yet Mary's attitude was remarkable. She said to the angel, "May it be to me as you have said" (v. 38). Her statement revealed her character. She was ready to endure the doubt and ridicule. God's work was more important to her than her reputation.

Following God will take you down rough roads at times. Sometimes you'll be tempted to find the easier path. The best road to travel, however, is always the one of God's choosing.

Are you on the right path, doing God's will? When the way is rough, pray like Mary did, surrendering to God's work in your life.

A HEART OF HUMILITY

Joshua 10–12, Luke 1:39–56 • **Key Verse: Luke 1:43**

Two remarkable women, one older and one younger, teach by example a lesson too easily lost. They teach in what they say and do the amazement every believer should have in sharing the blessings of God. But it is an amazement that can be felt only in a heart of humility.

Elizabeth was amazed to find herself in the presence of Mary, the mother of her Lord. Out of a heart of humility she said that she did not deserve to be there.

Mary, on the other hand, was amazed at the fact that God had chosen her to serve Him in this special way. Her feelings were clear—God owed her nothing. Yet she had received everything from Him. Out of a heart of humility she acknowledged His work in her life.

Humility is a natural result when one truly recognizes the awesomeness of God. These two saints felt honored by God and expressed a deep sense of respect for Him. Their relationship with God was not a casual one, as if He were a friendly neighbor. To them, knowing God was an honor.

Are you too casual about the things of God? Awe is easily lost when familiarity with the Almighty is taken for granted. Keep a heart of humility and be amazed like Mary and Elizabeth.

Humility can be hard to obtain and even more difficult to keep—especially when we think we are humble. Aim low! Stay humble.

INCOMPLETE OBEDIENCE

Joshua 13–15, Luke 1:57–80 • *Key Verse: Joshua 13:13*

Great promises and great victories fill the pages of the Book of Joshua. Israel moved into the Promised Land and conquered it with God's help. Jericho fell, literally. Ai was ultimately defeated. The sun even stood still—all striking evidence that God was fighting for Israel (10:14).

Yet when the details of the conquest are examined beginning in Joshua 13:13, a sad fact needs to be noted. The Israelites did not drive out the people of Geshur and Maacah. The significance is not the names of the people but the fact that they were allowed to remain in the land. As you continue to read Joshua, you will find this phrase repeated: "did not drive them out completely."

The account of Joshua tells us about God's promises and Israel's victories. But it does not hide the fact that sometimes the fulfillment of the promises was limited by Israel's incomplete obedience. Lack of faith and incomplete obedience allowed some of the people to remain in the land.

God's instructions were clear. His promises were certain. The failure was not God's but the people's. They failed and ultimately bore the consequences.

Always strive for complete obedience; never stop short of it.

Whatever God gives you to do, do it completely. Unfinished tasks can be more troublesome than the effort of doing them the first time.

FIRST, MIDDLE AND LAST

Joshua 16–18, **Luke 2:1–24** • *Key Verse: Luke 2:11*

Sometimes when people say, "Lord Jesus Christ," it sounds like that is His full name. First, middle and last names all add up to "Lord Jesus Christ." But do not allow our typical three-part names to inadvertently cause you to miss the significance of those words.

In Luke 2:11, Jesus is described as "Christ the Lord." Jesus is His name. Christ and Lord are titles. Together they give a wonderfully complete picture of Him.

Lord. The word speaks of authority. To say that Jesus is Lord is to acknowledge His right to rule and the power He has to accomplish it. He is Lord over all.

Jesus. This is His name. It is the Greek form of Joshua, which means "Yahweh saves." This name says that He is the one who brings the salvation promised by God.

Christ. In the Old Testament, the word used for this title is *Messiah*, which means "Anointed One." Jesus is the promised Messiah.

The Lord Jesus Christ is the sovereign of the universe, the One who saves us from our sins, the Christ who was promised by God.

Those three words, *Lord Jesus Christ*, resonate with meaning. When you say them, remember they are not just a name but a powerful statement of who He is.

"Jesus, help me understand who and what You are. I want to grow in my understanding of You, my Lord, Savior and Christ."

READY TO WAIT

Joshua 19–21, Luke 2:25–52 • *Key Verses: Luke 2:29–30*

Patience is not a widely practiced virtue anymore. Today is the time for fast food, microwaves and high-speed computers. Just drive through, download and move on to the next thing.

Yet sometimes God says, "Wait." To faithfully follow God, one must be willing to surrender to not only the will of God but also to the "wait" of God.

The Bible tells us that Simeon was a man whom God had instructed to wait, though we don't know for how long. He would not die until he had seen the Lord's Christ (v. 26). Simeon accepted the fact that the timing of his life and death were in God's hands. Once he saw Jesus, he then said, "Sovereign Lord, as you have promised, you now dismiss your servant in peace" (v. 29).

In a similar way, Anna, an 84-year-old widow, was a faithful follower who never left the temple. Hers was a life of worship (v. 37).

Simeon and Anna demonstrated remarkable patience. He waited. She remained faithful. Their days, perhaps months and even years, were in God's hands.

Patient faithfulness is a virtue that needs to be demonstrated in the lives of God's followers today. Have you surrendered to the "wait" of God?

When do you want God to answer your prayers? Probably right now. So, pray this prayer for Him to answer now: "Lord, teach me to wait on You."

THE CURE IS CONTENTMENT

Joshua 22–24, Luke 3 • *Key Verse: Luke 3:14*

Years ago the only clothes people owned were probably handmade. The same was true of their furniture and most everything they had. Then came the rise of manufacturing. More things were available, if you had the money to buy them. With the increase in goods came the increased desire to have.

The finishing touch, of sorts, was the catalog. It made more people aware of how much more there was to have. The catalog stoked the fires of materialism, a fire that rages in epic proportions today.

Manufacturing and marketing, however, are not the source of materialism. The source is the sinful human heart.

Ever notice what John the Baptist said to the soldiers who asked him, "And what should we do?" He replied, "Don't extort money . . . be content with your pay" (v. 14). John knew that soldiers used their position for personal gain. He also knew that the problem was one of the heart. The cure is contentment.

Watch carefully what you feed your heart. Feed it the trappings of materialism, and discontentment will grow. In contrast, Paul said, "Godliness with contentment is great gain" (1 Tim. 6:6). Find true gain by feeding your heart godliness and contentment.

Ask yourself if you have these two qualities: godliness and contentment. Sometimes it is hard to admit they are missing in one's life, but that is the first step in developing them.

FEEL THE POWER

Judges 1–3, Luke 4:1–30 • Key Verse: Luke 4:14

There is nothing wrong with the desire to have the Holy Spirit's power in your life. Sadly, however, teaching on the subject too often strays from biblical truth. In the quest for Holy Spirit power, many people follow paths paved with emotion rather than doctrine.

There is an interesting sequence surrounding the temptation of Jesus. He was full of the Holy Spirit and led by the Spirit (v. 1). Filling comes with surrender. Surrender allows the Spirit to lead. The Spirit-filled believer will be an obedient believer.

In a setting of temptation, He withstood the direct attempts of Satan to get Him to sin. The Spirit-filled believer also will resist temptation and live a righteous life.

After the temptation Jesus is described as returning to Galilee "in the power of the Spirit" (v. 14). It is not incidental that "power" is noted after surrender, obedience and resisting temptation.

There is no short circuit to Holy Spirit power. One must start with surrender and proceed with obedience. Righteousness also is required. A lack of spiritual power is not due to a shortage of emotion. More often it is a shortage of the Christlike life.

If you want Holy Spirit power, follow the example of Jesus. Do not start with emotion but with truth.

To know the power of the Spirit, begin where these verses begin. Ask God to help you follow these steps.

MIGHTY MAN?

Judges 4–6, Luke 4:31–44 • *Key Verse: Judges 6:12*

The name Gideon strikes a few notes in our brain, such as "mighty man of valor" and "hero of the faith." Then the notes sound sour as we can then think, "Not like me." Gideon is seen as a great man, while we often feel like much less.

Yes, he is included in the list of heroes in Hebrews 11. Yes, he was a mighty man of valor. It was not always that way, though. He started out quite fearful.

When we first meet Gideon, he is threshing wheat in a winepress to keep it from the Midianites (6:11). He's hiding out. Then when the angel tells him that he is being sent to save Israel, his reply is not a mighty one. "How can I?" he asks (v. 15).

After a great deal of "coaxing" and encouragement from God, Gideon did finally lead the fight to drive out the Midianites. God patiently worked with His reluctant warrior.

God can meet us where we are and lead us to where He wants us to be. Our lack of self-confidence may seem insurmountable. Remember, though, that our God is the same as Gideon's. The One who saw a mighty man of valor in Gideon sees a choice servant in you. He has equipped you and challenges you to serve Him.

Don't think God works only through "super saints." He uses ordinary believers made extraordinary by being available, teachable and useable.

A QUIET PLACE

Judges 7–8, Luke 5:1–16 • *Key Verse: Luke 5:16*

To read about the life of Jesus is to read of a life filled with activity. His public ministry began with His baptism. Then 40 days of solitude in the wilderness immediately followed. After that, His was a full schedule.

Two interesting observations can be made about the pace of Jesus' ministry. One is that He never hurried anywhere. Jesus was never in a rush. His purpose was so clear that other things were not allowed to put Him in a rush.

The other is that He consistently found the time and the quiet to pray. A healthy prayer life needs those two things: time and quiet.

How can you have a healthy prayer life without taking time to pray? You can't. Some praying we do "on the run." It may be that we pray while driving or while working around the house. Still, we need quality prayer time, undistracted by any other activities.

The other need is for quiet. Finding a time and place where you are undistracted is vital to a healthy prayer life. For some, those times and places are easy to find. For others, it is a challenge.

Jesus set the example. He took time and found a quiet place to pray. Will you?

Do you take time to pray? Why not right now? Jesus did. You should also.

HANGING WITH THE CROWD

Judges 9–10, Luke 5:17–39 • *Key Verses: Luke 5:31–32*

Jesus had a knack for running with the wrong crowd—at least in the eyes of the self-righteous.

Those who were religious believed that the righteous should associate only with those who are righteous. Most of the religious leaders with whom Jesus had contact were hypocritical and legalistic. It was easy for them to criticize Him for His involvement with "sinners."

Matthew was a new follower of Jesus. He did not follow Jesus quietly but publicly. The meal he provided for his friends gave them opportunity to meet Jesus. For the righteous, this was wrong because eating with someone was a sign of friendship. By doing this, Jesus demonstrated that He was a friend of sinners.

To answer His critics, Jesus used the analogy of a doctor. The sick people are the ones who need a physician, not the healthy. He knew their need and wanted to bring healing into the lives of those regarded as sinners.

Jesus did not go along with the crowd, but He was with them. It was there that they heard His message.

Are you ever with the wrong crowd? God does not want us to go along but He does want us to reach out. If you are never with them, how can you ever reach them?

Who are the people you know who need Jesus? Are you trying to find ways to tell them about the salvation He offers? You can't minister to people you avoid.

FRIENDLY FIRE

Judges 11–12, Luke 6:1–26 • *Key Verse: Judges 12:1*

A chaplain friend of mine told me that in the military they say, "There is no such thing as friendly fire." If it's fire, it's not friendly.

Far too often there is "friendly fire" in the church. Typically it is directed at those who are trying to get things done. Those doing the firing seem to remain the same. It's as if once a person or group becomes critical, they stay that way.

For example, look at the Ephraimites. Jephthah was leading the fight against the Ammonites. When called upon, the men of Ephraim did not come. Then when they did show up it was not to help but to hurt. They threatened to burn down Jephthah's house. Friendly fire? No such thing.

This was familiar behavior for the Ephraimites. Look at Judges 8:1. They were offended that Gideon did not call them. While he was pursuing the enemies, they wanted their grievance addressed. They were difficult to please, to say the least!

Whom are you like? Are you like Jephthah and Gideon, men who were actively serving God, or are you like the Ephraimites, always ready with the friendly fire?

Remember, there really is no such thing as friendly fire.

Passages such as these help us see the difference between helping and hurting. Ask God to help you be a helper, joining in wholeheartedly with others who are serving Him.

THE MOST-QUOTED VERSE

Judges 13–15, Luke 6:27–49 • Key Verse: Luke 6:37

Do you know what is the most-quoted Bible verse? I have heard that it is Luke 6:37: "Judge not lest ye be judged." Those are probably not the exact words of the Bible version you use, but accuracy is not always high on the list of people who quote verses, especially when they quote them to prove a point of their own making. Typically, people use this verse to tell others what they should not do.

Jesus did not give us these words to control others but to challenge us. People tend to be hard on others and lax on themselves. This verse is speaking to that issue. Sadly, it is used on others in that hard way. But that is not the way Jesus intended.

Aim this verse at your own heart. You are not to be a censorious person, constantly evaluating everyone and everything around you. God says in Romans 12:17–21 that we are to leave judgment in His hands.

There are judgments to be made, and there is to be accountability in the community of believers. Aim for the balance here, not the extremes. The one extreme takes us to letting anything go on without confrontation, which is wrong. The other extreme is the judgmental spirit. It is this second extreme that Jesus was addressing here.

Don't judge others with this verse. Use it on yourself and reap the benefit Jesus promised.

"God, help me to challenge myself so that I will be neither a censorious person nor undiscerning, but have the balance You desire."

ON OUR OWN

Judges 16–18, Luke 7:1–30 • *Key Verse: Judges 16:20*

One of the easiest temptations to which people succumb is self-sufficiency. We take on tasks in our strength with our own abilities and ingenuity. The more we are self-sufficient, however, the less we are God-dependent.

Samson demonstrated this. His strength was from God, but after a while he forgot that. Then came the day when the Lord left him, "but he did not know that" (16:20). When Delilah called, "Samson, the Philistines are upon you!" he thought nothing had changed. Yet everything had changed.

Whatever physical ability Samson had was insufficient. His resourcefulness could not undo the cords that bound him. The Philistines were able to overcome him and, after blinding Samson, humiliated him.

His final act against the Philistines came when he prayed, "O Sovereign LORD, remember me. O God, please strengthen me just once more" (v. 28). Samson was no longer self-sufficient but was once again God-dependent.

Someone has said that "the Holy Spirit could be removed from the world and most Christians would not even notice." The point is that we tend to live, work and even serve God in self-sufficiency.

Are you dependent on God or independent of Him? The easiest tests to measure this are your prayers and your thoughts. Do you pray for God's help regularly, or only when up against a wall like Samson was? Do you think about needing and receiving God's help, or do you just get things done in your own strength?

Don't be foolish. Why be self-sufficient when you can be God-dependent?

Think about what you will be doing today or tomorrow. Now ask God to help you with those tasks. Do this every day and remember that you need His help.

I SAID I LOVED YOU—ONCE

Judges 19–21, Luke 7:31–50 • *Key Verse: Luke 7:47*

There is an old joke about a wife asking her husband if he loves her. He assures her that he does. When she points out to him that he never tells her that he loves her, he replies, "I told you I loved you at our wedding. If anything had changed, I would have told you."

It would be the exceptional marriage that would thrive in the midst of such a drought of affirmation. For any relationship to continue to strengthen, there needs to be constant reaffirmations of love in both word and deed.

One day a woman expressed her love to Jesus. She did it by taking care of some basic needs, the sort of things a host would provide for a guest. It was a customary act of hospitality for a person's feet to be washed. That is what this woman did, even though Jesus was not a guest in her home. She not only washed His feet but demonstrated her thankfulness and love for Him by bringing perfume, drying with her hair her own tears that had fallen on His feet, and kissing His feet.

Jesus was criticized for her actions by His host, a Pharisee. But Jesus would hear none of it. This woman, who was forgiven for much, loved Jesus much and demonstrated it.

Does your love for Jesus show? Is it evident in your words and deeds? Whom are you most like—the host or the woman?

Begin with a prayer that expresses your love for Jesus, and then think about ways that you can show your love for Him today.

NO INVESTMENT, NO RETURN

Ruth 1–4, Luke 8:1–25 • *Key Verse: Luke 8:8*

What if you could be guaranteed that you would never lose money on any of your investments? You would jump at that opportunity! No losses, only gains.

If you find that deal, let me know. Until then, let me give you this tip. There is an investment opportunity that yields only gains, but it has nothing to do with money. Instead, it has everything to do with eternity.

In the parable of the sower, Jesus tells of a farmer who sowed seed. Some was lost, but "other seed fell on good soil. It came up and yielded a crop, a hundred times more than was sown" (v. 8).

When you "sow" the seed of the Word of God, some seed will not take root, but other seed will. Some, in a sense, will be lost. But this is an instance where your "losses" don't count against you. Your gains, though, are to your credit.

Still, the fact remains that if you do not sow, neither will happen. Jesus wants you to spread the Word, trusting Him for the results.

Where can you "sow" today? Is there a friend or acquaintance whom you should tell about Jesus?

STRENGTHENED THROUGH THE STORMS

1 Samuel 1–3, Luke 8:26–56 • *Key Verses: Luke 8:22–23*

God sometimes leads us into difficult situations for our good and His glory. Do you believe that? Perhaps not, but keep it in mind as you look at the account of Jesus calming the storm.

He had put His disciples "in harm's way," so to speak. Jesus instructed them to go to the other side of the lake. Did He know there was a storm coming? Of course He did. As Warren Wiersbe points out, "It was a part of the day's curriculum." Jesus can use a storm to teach.

The disciples' reaction was normal. They despaired. "We're going to drown!" they cried. Sometimes the storms of life fill us with despair as well.

It was then that Jesus demonstrated His power. In Mark it is recorded that He said, "Quiet! Be still!" And it was (Mark 4:39). He has the power to calm the storms.

The result was a sense of awe on the part of the disciples. What Jesus had just done helped develop their faith as they began to see Him as more than a man. He is the God-man whom the winds and the waves obey.

It is the same for us at times. God deliberately leads us into difficult situations. We may despair, but it is in the storms that He can demonstrate His power. Our faith is strengthened as we see Jesus working in our lives through our difficulties.

Ask God to help you learn the lessons He has for you, even the ones taught through difficult situations.

GOOD LUCK CHARM

1 Samuel 4–6, Luke 9:1–17 • *Key Verse: 1 Samuel 4:3*

Here's a short assignment. Do a study on the use of the word *luck* in the Bible. Let me make it easy for you—it isn't in the Bible. Most people like the idea of have "good luck," a force at work making things go well. Sometimes, though, it is "bad luck" that gets the blame for an undesirable turn in circumstances.

If only "luck" could be manipulated! Perhaps carrying a rabbit's foot would help. You do not have to look far to find examples of things people carry, things they do or don't do, or rituals they follow all in hopes of nudging luck to be good fortune.

That is essentially what Israel tried to do in a battle with the Philistines. They took the ark of God and treated it like a good luck charm. After a defeat they decided to "'bring the ark of the LORD's covenant from Shiloh, so that it may go with us and save us from the hand of our enemies'" (4:3).

At first, Israel was encouraged and the Philistines discouraged by this act. When the Philistines heard the cheering from Israel's camp they were afraid. "We're in trouble!" they said. "Woe to us! Who will deliver us from the hand of these mighty gods?" (vv. 7–8).

In the battle that followed, however, Israel was defeated and the ark captured. It didn't go as planned because God is not a good luck charm, something to help make things go well for us.

How do you regard God? Is your heart set on pleasing Him, or is your desire that He please you?

REJECTED

1 Samuel 7–9, Luke 9:18–36 • *Key Verse: 1 Samuel 8:7*

Rejection always causes us to ask "why?" Sometimes you are the one doing the rejecting and have to answer the question. What happens when you return something you've purchased to a store? Typically, a clerk will ask why you want to return the item. Or perhaps something is given back to you, such as a proposal at work that is turned down. We can learn lessons from rejection.

Israel wanted a change in leadership. Samuel was old, and his sons were not good candidates to succeed him. So the elders said, "Appoint a king to lead us" (8:5).

When Samuel heard the request he felt rejected. But God assured him that he was not the one being rejected. The people were rejecting God.

Why? Because they wanted to be like other nations and serve other gods (vv. 5, 8). Even after being warned of the dangers of this, the people still said, "We want a king over us. Then we will be like all the other nations" (vv. 19–20).

Was that a good reason to ask for a king? No, but it was a common one. God's way is often rejected not for a better way, but for a preferred way. The preferred way appeals to man and, just as with Israel, is more like the way of the world.

Israel later reaped the negative effects of this decision—a sure result of rejecting God. Listen to His Word and follow His way, because that is the only path to blessing.

Consider carefully your choices and ask if they lead you closer to or further away from God. Determine that your heart will be set to follow Him.

A TOO-COMMON SIN

1 Samuel 10–12, Luke 9:37–62 • *Key Verse: 1 Samuel 12:23*

Last words typically catch our attention. When we are hearing someone give a farewell, whether it is at retirement or when death is imminent, we listen more intently—and if we are the one speaking, our words are more carefully chosen.

The people of Israel had asked for a king and God granted their request. Now Samuel was giving his farewell speech. The people agreed that he was leaving his office blameless. Having said that, Samuel then warned them, reminding the nation of past failures in hopes that they would learn from their history and not repeat it. His encouragement for the days ahead focused on the people serving the Lord with all their hearts.

Then comes the surprising statement. There is a sin that he himself was determined not to commit, yet one that to this day is an all too-common sin. "'As for me, far be it from me that I should sin against the LORD by failing to pray for you'" (12:23).

Could it be that to pray less is to sin more? A failure to be a person of intercessory prayer is, in Samuel's words, a sin against the Lord. While there are many good and profitable emphases on prayer today, there is also a noticeable lessening of emphasis. Fewer churches gather for prayer, accommodating instead the trend to give God less time during the week.

Join Samuel in this determination. Remember to pray for others.

Write the names of three others for whom you should pray today. Now, pray for them.

RESULTS OR RELATIONSHIP?

1 Samuel 13–14, Luke 10:1–24 • Key Verse: Luke 10:20

I heard it said that we live in a society of calibration, always seeing how we measure up. No wonder we like numbers and statistics. Checking the numbers, whether they are the value of our home, income level or attendance figures, helps us know how we measure up compared with others.

One day I decided never again to ask other pastors about the size of their churches. It seems to be a staple of conversation, like talking about the weather. "So, how many attend your church?" Perhaps this question is asked from a good conscience, but it just as easily can be asked to see how one pastor measures up against another.

We all play the comparison game at times, whether we're comparing Beanie Baby collections, years on the job or our credit level.

The disciples came back from a preaching mission talking about the results. "Lord, even the demons submit to us in your name," they said (v. 17), but Jesus showed them what was more important. "Do not rejoice that the spirits submit to you," He said, "but rejoice that your names are written in heaven" (v. 20). More important than results is the relationship we have with Jesus.

Knowing how we measure up compared with others may be the underlying motivation for some of our conversations. Examine your heart. Is the comparison really that important? Look instead at what matters for eternity—your relationship with Jesus.

And in your ministry, leave tallying results up to God. He knows the real score.

Your greatest joy should be your salvation. Ask God to help you rejoice in that, determine to serve faithfully, and leave the results with Him.

THE LEXICON OF DISOBEDIENCE
1 Samuel 15–16, Luke 10:25–42 • *Key Verse: 1 Samuel 15:23*

Words fitly spoken are said to be like apples of gold. That familiar line stresses the importance of well-chosen words. Mark Twain said that the difference between the right word and the almost-right word is the difference between lightning and a lightning bug.

God chooses His words well. Careful attention should be paid to what He says and the words with which He says it. While the language of today seeks to minimize sin, God does not. It is striking to see the two bold statements found in 1 Samuel 15:23.

First, the open insurrection of rebellion is said to be the equivalent of "divination." People may call rebellion what they want, but God associates it with forms of spiritism and human sacrifice. When a person rebels against God, he is serving the one who is opposed to God. To rebel is to join forces with Satan.

Second, the pushy presumption called arrogance is linked to idolatry, the superstitious worship of household gods. An arrogant person refuses to submit to the commands of God and is in essence the worshiper of other gods.

The rebellious and arrogant person is following the path of a Satan-serving idolater—strong words that remind us how repulsive sin is to God.

Call sin what God calls it. His words are fitly spoken.

"Lord, help me see things as You see them so I can know what truly is sin. Keep me from the temptation to find other words for wrongful things, and help me to remember that renaming does not change wrong to right."

THE RELIANT HEART

1 Samuel 17–18, Luke 11:1–28 • *Key Verse: 1 Samuel 17:45*

Upon whom or what do you rely? In a time of financial challenge, do you check your wallet? When health concerns surface, is your physician the source of your confidence? During the downs that come between the ups at work, is your network or resume your source of comfort?

When facing a problem, the natural tendency is to look over our resources, abilities and connections and find in them the confidence needed to get through.

Israel tried that route when faced with a problem of giant proportions—Goliath. No one, not even the king, who was head and shoulders above all others, would face the champion of the Philistines. And then David came on the scene. His reliance was not on past victories, though he had them, nor on the armor that was made available to him, nor on the weapons he carried with him.

David relied on God. That does not mean that he did not use his skills, ones carefully honed while shepherding his father's sheep. It does mean that his confidence was not in self alone.

"You come against me with sword and spear and javelin, but I come against you in the name of the LORD Almighty," he said (17:45). David wanted all to know that "it is not by sword or spear that the LORD saves; for the battle is the LORD's" (v. 47). God gave a swift victory to the one who trusted Him.

Not all our difficulties will be short-lived. Still, our confidence must not be in self alone but in God.

Whatever you face today, remember to trust in God. Ask Him to help you through the challenge before you.

VENEER OR REAL?

1 Samuel 19–21, Luke 11:29–54 • *Key Verses: Luke 11:34–35*

It used to be said, "There's nothing like the real thing." We can't say that anymore because so many things are like the real thing. Put a little veneer over particle board and it can look like real wood. Creative manufacturing can make particles glued together look like solid wood, grain and all. The finished product looks like one thing on the outside, yet is another on the inside.

There is a word used to describe a person who is one thing on the outside and something different on the inside—*hypocrite.*

Jesus was concerned that we be like lights, shining forth the truth. He also was concerned that what we are on the outside is what we are on the inside. "When your eyes are good, your whole body also is full of light," He said. "See to it, then, that the light within you is not darkness" (vv. 34–35). He desires truth to be within and to show without.

Someone once said that it looks like the Pharisees have had the last laugh. Christians can be very concerned about the external, how they look, and give too little concern to the internal, which really is where they live.

Veneer is fine for furniture. But Christians are to be solid, not filled with darkness and a thin layer of light glued on the outside.

Are you veneer or the real thing?

"God, I want to be genuine before You, myself and others. Help me to be filled with Your light, and may it show."

SOMEONE TO LEAN ON

1 Samuel 22–24, Luke 12:1–31 • *Key Verse: 1 Samuel 23:16*

A popular song says, "Lean on me when you're not strong, and I'll be your friend, I'll help you carry on. For it won't be long till we're going to need somebody to lean on." At times we all realize the truth of those words: we need someone to be there for us, someone to lean on.

David was going through one of those times when a very special friend showed up. Saul had heard that David was in Keilah, so he headed that direction in pursuit. When David heard that Saul was coming, he asked God what to do. With the warning confirmed by God, David returned to the desert strongholds. A good first response! He went to God, as should we.

Then along came his close friend. Jonathan was the person David could lean on. Saul's son went to David "and helped him find strength in God" (23:16).

Notice two things. First, David had gone to God and God used a friend to help him. There will be times we need someone, and someone will need us to be that friend.

Second, Jonathan helped him find strength in God. The ultimate source of strength, the most-needed resource, is not human effort but God.

Just having, or being, someone to lean on is not enough. The strength we need and the encouragement we give must go beyond our abilities to God's resources. Through His Word and prayer, we can help others find their strength in God.

"I need to learn to lean on You, O God. Help me do that right now and throughout each day."

A HOLE IN THE POCKET

1 Samuel 25–26, Luke 12:32–59 • Key Verse: Luke 12:34

"If I win the lottery, I'll tithe." Ever hear someone say that? The words may change a bit from one get-rich-quick scheme to another, but the sentiment expressed stays the same.

Yet the truth is, the more a person earns, the less likely he is to give at least 10 percent. According to the Barna Organization, fewer than 10 percent of born-again Christian tithe 10 percent to their church. The people most likely to do this, in fact, are those who earn the least, and even that is not a high percentage. Only 8 percent of those making $20,000 or less tithe. And the percentages keep dropping as the income rises, to only 1 percent of those making $75,000 to $99,999. (After that the percentage of tithing does rise some.)

Still, it appears that the more one has, the less likely he is to tithe. You would think the opposite would be true. Surely the more one has, the easier it is to give. But that is not the case.

As one prospers, the heart can be affected, drawn away from heaven to earth, from that which is eternal to things that are temporary. Jesus' words strike at the heart of both the problem and the person: "Where your treasure is, there your heart will be also" (v. 34).

Want to check your heart? Check your checkbook. That book will have the evidence to confirm what holds the attention of your heart. Focus on making deposits in the bank of heaven.

Do a check of your checkbook. Does it reflect a life that gives to God?

WHAT SAUL SAW

1 Samuel 27–29, Luke 13:1–22 • *Key Verse: 1 Samuel 28:6–7*

A person can get a bit tongue-tied trying to tell what happened in 1 Samuel 28. Saul saw a seer because of what he had seen. When Saul saw what he saw, he sought a seer to see what the seer would say about what he saw.

That may seem like a ridiculous set of sentences when you are reading the Bible and having devotions, but they make a point. What Saul did was ridiculous, a mistake we should not make either.

The bottom line is that Saul was living by sight, not by faith. "When Saul saw the Philistine army, he was afraid; terror filled his heart" (28:5). His first response was to pray, but God did not answer. His next response shows that he was not seeking God as much as he was looking for help, no matter where it came from. "Find me a woman who is a medium, so I may go and inquire of her," he said (v. 7). It wasn't the first time that Saul's impatience got him into trouble. In 1 Samuel 13:11–12, he was rebuked by Samuel. His defense was, "When I saw . . . I thought."

Living by sight was a pattern with Saul. Living by faith was not. Yet living by faith is blessed by God. Living by sight is not.

How do you live? When God does not seem to answer quick enough for you, it is tempting to decide on the basis of what you see. Don't do it. Don't be like Saul, who let what he saw decide what he would do.

Going to God should not be your last resort but your first. Seek Him and stay away from those whose advice is not from His Word.

STRENGTH TRAINING

1 Samuel 30–31, Luke 13:23–35 • *Key Verse: 1 Samuel 30:6*

A key component of any successful athletic program is strength training. The willing team or performer must have not only ability but strength and endurance as well.

Sometimes we can find our strength stretched to the limit, leaving us wondering how we can continue. That must have been David's feeling when, after an extended time fleeing Saul and fighting the enemies of Israel, he came home to a devastating situation. Ziklag, the city where David and his men lived, had been destroyed by fire, the women and children taken captive. He and the men wept until they had no strength left to weep (30:4). The men even talked of stoning David (v. 6).

When physically and emotionally drained, "David found strength in the LORD his God" (v. 6). That was his best, if not the only effective, option.

The same is true for us. We find strength in the Lord by turning to His Word. In the Bible we read of His love for us, His promises given us and His instructions to us. We find strength in the Lord by turning to Him in prayer. Rather than hold onto our troubles, we can lay them before God, seeking the help we need at His throne. We also find strength in the Lord by turning to His people. Remember how Jonathan strengthened David in the Lord? Others can do the same for us as they remind us of and teach us from God's Word, holding our tired arms up in prayer as well.

Look to the Lord for your strength. He strengthened David and will do the same for you.

INVESTING WITH NO RETURN

*2 Samuel 1–2, **Luke 14:1–24** • Key Verses: Luke 14:13–14*

We always like to get something back from our investments. Money we put in the stock market is done so with the hope of gain. A gift sent to a client is given with the hope of gaining more business. Even a favor for a friend might be done with an eye on a future time when the favor will be returned. The unspoken mantra is, "What's in it for me?"

In the margin of my Bible next to verse 14 is written, "disinterested goodness." This verse exhorts us to invest with no hope of return, to do good without an eye on the immediate future. Jesus tells us to show hospitality to those who cannot return the favor, an act of goodness but a disinterested one. It is "disinterested" in the sense that it is not deposited with hopes of gaining something in return, like interest.

Is it really hospitality when we invite someone to our home in hopes of what we might gain from the time? Perhaps as we define *hospitality* it is, but it will not meet the standard of what Jesus set before us. He instructs us to reach out to the poor, the crippled, the lame, the blind (v. 13). God will reward us in eternity.

Until then, we should do unto others not because of what they may be able to do unto us, but simply because we should.

Think of something you can do today for someone who cannot repay— and do it.

STAY SALTY

2 Samuel 3–5, Luke 14:25–35 • *Key Verses: Luke 14:34–35*

Expiration dates are printed on just about everything nowadays, even on soda pop cans. One place you will not find an expiration date, however, is on salt. Ever hear anyone say, "This salt tastes old. It must not be very fresh"? Probably not. Salt never goes stale.

Jesus said, "Salt is good, but if it loses its saltiness, how can it be made salty again? It is fit neither for the soil nor for the manure pile; it is thrown out" (vv. 34–35). If there is no such thing as fresh or stale salt, how could Jesus say this?

There are two ways salt can lose its saltiness. One is by dilution, the other by pollution.

Put some salt in a glass and add water. Stir, taste, and then add more water. The more you dilute the salt, the less you will taste it. Soon it has no value as salt. Or, take some salt and add to it other things. Continue to mix in things, polluting the salt, and eventually you will not notice the salt. Its saltiness is lost to the pollution.

Followers of Jesus are to be the "salt of the earth" (Matt. 5:13), but our saltiness can be lost the same way. Our testimony can be so watered down that by dilution it loses its saltiness, or so much other stuff can come into our lives that our testimony is lost due to pollution.

Stay salty—that is what Jesus wants. Do not let into your life things that will dilute or pollute your testimony.

ANYTHING DOESN'T GO

2 Samuel 6–8, Luke 15:1–10 • *Key Verse: 2 Samuel 6:7*

The more we focus on doing what pleases us, the less we will please God. That truth applies to many things, including worship. How we worship God is not a matter of "anything goes." It especially is not to be done with an attitude of "I like it, so God must also." He has made it clear in His Word that not all worship is acceptable.

When David wanted to bring the ark to Jerusalem he made a mistake. He consulted the leaders of the army instead of God (1 Chron. 13:1; 15:13). The attempt to move the ark led to disaster. A good desire was done the wrong way, and it was unacceptable to God.

The Bible offers other notable examples of wrong worship, such as the golden calf incident in the Sinai and the unauthorized fire offered by Nadab and Abihu (Num. 3:4). Throughout the Book of Leviticus specific instruction is given regarding how God is to be worshiped.

Scriptural teaching on proper worship is not just an Old Testament emphasis either. Jesus strongly condemned the worship of the Pharisees, and a major portion of 1 Corinthians deals with worship. God dealt with those in Corinth for their abuse of the Lord's Supper, and three chapters, 12–14, focus on the exercise of spiritual gifts with an emphasis on how it affects the worship of the church.

Worship is important to God and should be important to us. It should be done in a way that pleases Him, not us. We will learn what proper worship is not by consulting others who share our opinions and tastes, but by going to God's Word.

Examine the Bible, and then examine your worship. It is not true that "anything goes."

THE HOOK

2 Samuel 9–11, Luke 15:11–32 • *Key Verse: 2 Samuel 11:2*

Many times what we see gets us into trouble. The apostle John noted that the lust of the eyes does not come from God but from the world (1 John 2:16). The children's chorus "Oh, be careful little eyes what you see" is advice well heeded. Even Job, with everything else he had to deal with, stated, "I made a covenant with my eyes not to look lustfully at a girl" (Job 31:1). He knew the danger and wrong that begins with a look.

Think of what lies ahead for David at this point. Turmoil will strike his family, including a rebellion against him as king. A baby will die. A murder will take place that is part of a cover-up. The earlier stages of the cover-up include getting a man drunk in hopes that he will have sex with his wife. Before all of this there was adultery.

Where did it all begin? With a look. "One evening David got up from his bed and walked around on the roof of the palace. From the roof he saw a woman bathing. The woman was very beautiful" (11:2).

It was the look that set the hook, and it was all downhill from there. He sent for Bathsheba and slept with her, and she conceived.

Sometimes we see something "accidentally." We were not looking for it; it just came into sight, as was possible in David's situation. The glance is not sin, but the gaze is.

Watch your eyes and watch what you watch, because the look can set the hook.

IF ONLY . . .

2 Samuel 12–13, Luke 16 • *Key Verse: Luke 16:29*

I always have trouble seeing the 3-D images in those pictures that look like nothing more than colorful patterns. You hold them at nose length, stare through them as you slowly move it away from your face and, *voila!*, the Statue of Liberty (or something like that) appears. Only once have I successfully seen the image. Some of my friends, more adept at staring through pictures, get frustrated that I don't see the hidden image. "If only you . . ." their futile attempts at advice begin.

Sometimes when trying to convince someone that Christianity is true, we think in "if-only" terms. "If only" Noah's ark were found, then people would believe. "If only" Sodom and Gomorrah were found or this miracle would happen or that thing would appear. We think that indisputable evidence would end unbelief.

Try this one: "If only someone would come back from the dead." Even that would fail. If a person will not listen to the Word of God, he will not be convinced even if someone rises from the dead.

That's what Jesus said. In the story of the rich man and Lazarus, Abraham answers the rich man's request to have someone go to his father's house to warn them. He says, "They have Moses and the Prophets; let them listen to them" (v. 29). He goes on to say that a person coming back from the grave will not make a difference when the Word is rejected.

Give people the Word of God. That is what will change them, not our evidences or our stories.

BAD INFLUENCE

2 Samuel 14–15, Luke 17:1–19 • *Key Verse: Luke 17:1*

Have you ever been influenced? Of course you have. If people weren't susceptible to being influenced, the entire advertising industry would collapse. Sometimes when filling out the registration card on a purchase you are asked, "Where did you hear about this product?" You then can choose from a list that includes everything from TV, magazines and newspapers to friends and family. The manufacturer wants to know what influences are working best because we all can be influenced.

God knows that and at times warns us against being influenced. Yet He also wants us to be a good influence and warns us against being a bad influence. Jesus said, "Things that cause people to sin are bound to come, but woe to that person through whom they come" (v. 1).

There's no doubt about what Jesus meant when He said that. We are surrounded by things that cause people to sin. You do not have to look long and hard to see that—and you probably shouldn't look so long and hard for such things! We live in a sin-cursed world, and the opportunities for sin surround us always.

Jesus also knew that some people influence others to sin. "Woe to that person," He said.

We think, *Yes, woe to that pornographer, that bar owner, that call girl,* but by thinking of only "big," obvious sins we miss the possibility that you and I can cause others to sin. We can encourage gossip, disrespect for those in authority, dissension in the church and a multitude of "smaller" but just as wrong sins.

Yes, woe to the pornographers, abortionists and bar owners, but woe also to us when we cause others to sin.

Think carefully about this: are there ways that you are influencing others to sin?

WHEN WE FAIL TO FORGIVE

2 Samuel 16–18, Luke 17:20–37 • *Key Verse: 2 Samuel 16:15*

One of the most grateful testimonies of the joy of forgiveness is Psalm 32, in which David expresses both the pain of unforgiven sin and the pleasure of forgiveness. He suffered greatly for his sins of adultery, abuse of power, cover-up and murder, all resulting from his lust of Bathsheba. Covering sin brings pain, but forgiveness is a joy.

In 2 Samuel 17 there is a subtle but striking contrast between the forgiven man, David, and the unforgiving man, Ahithophel. The first part of the contrast is obvious. David had sinned, repented and found forgiveness but suffered from the effects of his deed.

The second part is not as obvious. Ahithophel was David's best counselor, whose advice "was like that of one who inquires of God" (16:23). But when Absalom rebelled, Ahithophel changed sides. He became the counselor of the king's son.

The reason for his betrayal is found in the genealogies. In 2 Samuel 23:34 it is recorded that Ahithophel had a son, Eliam. In 2 Samuel 11:3 Eliam's daughter is mentioned—Bathsheba. David's adultery was with Ahithophel's granddaughter.

When the opportunity came, Ahithophel joined the rebellion against the adulterer who had murdered his granddaughter's husband, Uriah. While David had found forgiveness, Ahithophel had not forgiven. Sadly, it is possible to be forgiven by God but not by God's people.

Ultimately, Ahithophel's course led to suicide, while David died peacefully—a striking contrast between the forgiven and the unforgiving. And a pointed lesson, aimed at our hearts, when we fail to forgive.

Whom are you most like, the forgiven man or the unforgiving man? Ask God to help you be one who forgives.

RUN THE WHOLE RACE

2 Samuel 19–20, Luke 18:1–23 • *Key Verse: Luke 18:1*

When the starting gun is fired at the beginning of a marathon, it is anticipated that fewer runners will finish than will start. And that is not even considering those who one day decided to run a marathon and never even made it to the starting line. There is something about a long run that thins out the crowd.

That is true not only with running but other endurance events as well. Anything that involves keeping at it for the long haul will invariably have more at the beginning than at the end.

One of the individual "marathons" we are all called upon to run is prayer. To His disciples Jesus one day told a parable to show them that "they should always pray and not give up" (v. 1). You can't miss the point of the story because Luke tells us in the first verse what it is about.

The fact that Jesus told this parable means that we do at times fail at continuing to pray. We give up rather than keeping on. In His word, we "faint."

Runners talk about "hitting the wall." Physically and emotionally they come to a point where they just want to stop. The same happens to "pray-ers." We hit the wall and want to give up, to faint. But Jesus says, "Don't."

Being a person of prayer is not a matter of a quick sprint but staying in it for the long haul. Pray, keep praying, and don't stop.

Is there a request you no longer pray because you gave up? Start praying for it again right now.

MASADA

2 Samuel 21–22, Luke 18:24–43 • *Key Verse: 2 Samuel 22:2*

Near the Dead Sea in southern Israel is an immense flat-topped plateau called Masada. It is one of the most visited archeological sites in Israel today. A palace and fortress built by Herod the Great sits atop the plateau. While Herod built the palace that remains there today, Masada may have been a stronghold in David's day too. First Samuel 24:22 says that David and his men "went up to the stronghold." The Hebrew word translated "stronghold" is *Metsade*, the equivalent of Masada.

In 2 Samuel 22:2 David uses that word again as he writes, "The LORD is my rock, my fortress [Metsade] and my deliverer." When David wrote the word *Metsade*, describing God as his fortress, he may have been able to see an illustration of what that meant. He knew of the stronghold there by the Dead Sea, the one that he himself might have used as a place of safety. At times he may have contemplated the security his men felt as they occupied the top of the plateau.

Then when he wanted to describe the safety he felt in God, he used the same word. God was his Masada.

If you ever visit Masada, or even see pictures of this fortress, remember that God Himself is your Masada, a fortress that will stand against any onslaught.

"Thank you, God, for being my rock. Help me always remember that I find deliverance in You."

SOMETHING FOR NOTHING

2 Samuel 23–24, Luke 19:1–27 • *Key Verse: 2 Samuel 24:24*

Most people like to get something for nothing. The less it costs, the better.

The opposite is true as well. At times people try to give what costs them nothing. If it was free to begin with, it may seem priced just right to be a gift.

Consider the newlyweds who were impressed with the expense of the gift they received from friends who also were recently married. Newlyweds typically do not have that much to spend on gifts for others! It was indeed a nice gift. Then in the box they found a second gift card. Call it recycling, if you like, but the gift the friends had given was a gift they had received. The couple enjoyed the gift and the humor of the situation—and later found times when they also gave gifts that cost them little or nothing.

Giving something that costs us nothing may be a wise use of our resources, until we try to pass it off as a sacrifice given to God. We may think we retrieved the first gift card out of the box, but God knows. He knows the stinginess of our hearts and how in pride we sometimes try to make ourselves look generous.

David would have none of this type of giving. "I will not sacrifice to the LORD my God burnt offerings that cost me nothing" (24:24).

God wants us to acknowledge our dependence on Him and our worship of Him in our giving. It won't happen if all we do is give what costs us nothing.

At times we need to evaluate our giving. Today these verses remind us to think through again how we acknowledge God in our finances.

THE TRAGEDY OF THE MOMENT

1 Kings 1–2, Luke 19:28–48 • *Key Verse: Luke 19:41*

Two people can look at the same thing, at the same time, and see things differently. An old table in a dumpster looks like trash to one, a treasure to another. One set of fans at a championship game will see triumph, the others tragedy.

On the Mount of Olives that first Palm Sunday, two saw the same scene differently. The disciples saw the triumph of the moment, while Jesus saw the tragedy. "As he approached Jerusalem and saw the city, he wept over it" (v. 41). Jesus saw tragedy that day, not triumph.

The tragedy had three parts. First, the people wanted peace but did not know what would bring peace to them. True peace is found only in Jesus. Second, they did not realize the destruction they faced. A few years later Rome captured Jerusalem, killing more than 600,000 people and destroying the temple. Jesus also knew that all face judgment unless they receive the forgiveness He can give. Third, He wept because they did not "recognize the time of God's coming" (v. 44). God became a man and lived among us—Immanuel! Yet many did not recognize that and instead rejected Him. A few days after Palm Sunday the cries of "Hosanna!" became "Crucify him!"

Jesus wept because the people did not know peace, realize they faced destruction or recognize that He was God.

Do you have peace? It is found in Jesus. He saves us from sin's power and penalty.

Recognize who Jesus is and receive Him as your Savior today.

AUDIT?

1 Kings 3–5, **Luke 20:1–26** • *Key Verse: Luke 20:25*

Almost two weeks have passed since what is considered the second-most stressful day in the year for an American adult—April 15, tax day. (Number one on the list is going to the dentist.) Perhaps you would rather not think about either thing—words like "root canal" and "audit" are pretty scary.

What if an audit letter should arrive at your home addressed to you? Which word would best describe your reaction: "fear," "anxiety," "dread," "depression" or "all of the above"? Probably, if you are like most, the answer is "all of the above." What words would best describe the outcome of an audit: "no problems," "a few corrections" or "guilty"? You probably don't need an audit to tell you the answer to the second question.

If you did the right thing, what Jesus said to do, then you gave "to Caesar what is Caesar's" (v. 25). Just think how much less stress everyone would have if everyone obeyed God's Word as it applies to taxes.

Next, Jesus said to give "God what is God's." What if God were to audit you on this? Sales tax is added automatically to purchases. Income tax is deducted from our pay. One way or another, Caesar will get what is Caesar's. But God does not send tithe collection agents. He gives us His Word, the Bible, the work of the Holy Spirit and the witness of those who teach and testify of the joy of giving.

Some day we will give an account. Will you be able to say, "I gave to Caesar what is Caesar's and to God what is God's"?

ONE FOR YOU, TWO FOR ME

1 Kings 6–7, Luke 20:27–47 • Key Verse: 1 Kings 7:1

I watched with interest as the worker at the espresso machine careful-ly divided the hot chocolates I had ordered. Both had been made in one container, but now she was pouring it into two cups, one each for my daughters who were with me. After the fourth or fifth time of putting a little more into each cup, eyeing the levels intensely, looking to see that both had the exact same amount, I said, "Do you have a sister?"

"Yes, a twin," she replied as another small dollop was added, making both as equal as possible. She was so intent on her task, I figured she must have experience dividing things with a sibling!

When dividing something, it is typical to want the other to get no more than we do. But sometimes we divide things in a way to get more for ourselves and leave less for others.

The temple Solomon built for God was spectacular—quarried stone, cedar walls and gold-covered walls, rooms with rich ornamentation and furnishings. No expense was spared and no detail overlooked. It sat like a golden crown on Mount Moriah. Zion, the city of God, was a jewel glistening on the heights. It took seven years to build God's royal residence.

"It took Solomon thirteen years, however, to complete the construc-tion of his palace" (v. 1)—almost twice as long. Later, Haggai the prophet would point out that the people built their houses and neg-lected God's (Hag. 1:4).

Dividing hot chocolate is pretty minor, but the heart that will keep for self will even keep from God.

Watch your heart. Make sure it can give.

AT EASE WITH GREED

1 Kings 8–9, Luke 21:1–19 • *Key Verses: Luke 21:1–4*

It would seem that the more a person makes, the easier it would be to give. But that is not the case. Possessions have a way of possessing. A wealthy person may give a larger dollar amount but a proportionately smaller amount than a poor person.

God looks at the proportion, not the amount. It is within the grasp of every person to please God with his giving because He weighs the gift not in dollars but in sacrifice.

Jesus saw among those bringing their gifts to the temple a widow. Her offering was "two very small copper coins" (v. 2), worth very little. Yet she is the one He commended. She did not give a pittance out of her excess but gave excess out of her pittance.

Jesus is interested in the heart that gives, not the hands that have. He did not commend the rich for the size of their gifts but the widow for the size of her sacrifice.

With prosperity comes a peril. A person no longer has things, but things have a person.

Do a heart exam on yourself. Is it a heart that Jesus would commend or condemn?

FINISH WELL

1 Kings 10–11, Luke 21:20–38 • *Key Verse: 1 Kings 11:9*

Leith Anderson tells of a man named Kenneth Kruse, who "served the Lord faithfully in Africa for 25 years before returning to England, where he worked with the Scripture Gift Mission. He retired at age 65, and three years after the death of his wife, he returned to Africa at age 70 to resume missionary work there.

"Prior to leaving for the field, his son wrote him a letter in which he quoted Psalm 146:5: 'Happy is he that hath the God of Jacob for his help.'

"Kenneth responded with a letter containing a quote that should become an all-time Christian classic. He wrote, 'I think I would rather be a Jacob than a Solomon. Solomon started so promisingly but finished up so disastrously; but Jacob started so disastrously and finished up so promisingly.'"

Solomon did not finish well. He began with such great promise, rewarded by God with wisdom, riches and honor. It was his privilege to build the magnificent temple and to have his prayer answered for God's glory to dwell there. The blessings upon him and the nation were many, but at the end of his life, "his heart had turned away from the LORD" (11:9).

Finishing well is not automatic but is mandatory. As God gives you years on earth, give your years to God with a determination that you will finish well.

Commit yourself to finishing well. Perhaps a visual reminder, such as a card with the words "Finish Well" posted on the refrigerator or bathroom mirror, or used as a bookmark in your Bible, will challenge you to keep this commitment.

NO ONE ELSE TO BLAME

1 Kings 12–13, Luke 22:1–30 • *Key Verse: 1 Kings 13:26*

Guilty people have a tendency to shift the blame to others. Adam did it first: "The woman you put here with me—she gave me some fruit from the tree" (Gen. 3:12). He blamed God for giving him Eve and then blamed her for giving him the forbidden fruit. She learned the "blame game" from Adam and said, "The serpent deceived me" (v. 13).

But God didn't buy it. Shifting the blame didn't work. He already had said, "What is this *you* have done?" (emphasis mine). Then He spoke words of punishment to the serpent, Eve and Adam. Eve was punished for what she did, as was Adam and the serpent.

When we disobey God, we take the blame. No excuses or blame shifting will work.

"By the word of the LORD a man of God came from Judah to Bethel" to pronounce judgment against King Jeroboam (1 Kings 13:1). The man was commanded by the word of the Lord: "You must not eat bread or drink water or return by the way you came" (v. 9). So he did as he had been instructed, until an old prophet told him that an angel had given different instructions. But the old man was lying.

The man of God went home with the prophet, disobeying the Word of God. While they were sitting at the table the prophet then spoke the truth. Judgment would come because of the disobedience, and it did. The man died on his way home. He was judged for his disobedience, even though it was because of a lie told him.

The bottom line is that we cannot shift the blame. It didn't work in Genesis 3 or 1 Kings 13—and it doesn't work today.

"God, help me take responsibility for my actions, but especially help me live in obedience to Your Word so I do not need to take responsibility for wrong actions."

DRAWING STRENGTH FROM WEAKNESS

1 Kings 14–15, **Luke 22:31–46** • *Key Verse: Luke 22:32*

Have you ever benefited from someone telling you about a mistake he made? Perhaps he told you about a turn he missed, resulting in either getting lost or a longer trip. Maybe it was when he was installing new software on his computer. When he heard you were traveling to the same place or buying the same software, he passed on to you the "benefit" of his experience.

It's good to learn from mistakes, whether they are our mistakes or the mistakes of others. Actually, I prefer learning from the mistakes of others, and I don't recommend making mistakes just to see what can be learned from them!

What Peter was about to do went beyond a wrong turn or incorrect sequence on a software installation. He was about to deny that he knew Jesus. The Lord knew this would happen and that Peter would truly repent. He also knew that Peter would soon head off in the wrong direction and would have to be turned around. So, Jesus told Peter to be ready to help others learn from the mistake he was about to make.

We are not to make mistakes just to have a lesson to teach, but when they happen, we need to be concerned about others enough to teach them. We can be quick to give directions for trips and computers. We also need to be quick to teach lessons that are of eternal benefit.

Plan to succeed in your spiritual life. Plan also to pass on to others the benefit of your successes, and at times, your failures. When you do, you will be like Peter, in the positive sense, of helping strengthen your brothers.

"Lord, help me realize when I need to learn a lesson You have for me, and may I be ready to help others, strengthening them in their walk."

MISPLACING THE BLAME

1 Kings 16–18, Luke 22:47–71 • *Key Verse: 1 Kings 18:17*

As the story a couple of days ago illustrates, we do like to shift blame. Adam started it, Eve followed, and there's no telling how many others have done it.

There's one problem with blaming others, however: God knows who is to blame, and the longer we continue to live in denial, the longer it will be before we change directions, do what is right and learn the lessons God has for us.

Ahab was a blame shifter. God was punishing Israel with a long drought, which the prophet Elijah had announced. In the mind of Ahab the king, the drought was Elijah's fault. His "greeting" toward Elijah demonstrated his attitude: "Is that you, you troubler of Israel?" (18:17).

Elijah tossed the blame back squarely on Ahab's shoulders. "I have not made trouble for Israel," he said, "but you and your father's family have. You have abandoned the LORD's commands and have followed the Baals" (v. 18).

Since he couldn't shift the blame and didn't like the message, Ahab wanted to "shoot" the messenger, Elijah. What else was there to do?

Unfortunately, that is still done today. The faithful pastor may be pressured to leave the church because his messages are too pointed. The friend who counsels may be rejected because the truth hurts. The spouse may feel the tension because what he or she said is not what the other wanted to hear.

It's easier to call the other person "the troubler" when the real troublemaker is yourself. Don't be like Ahab. When the blame fits, accept responsibility, and then change.

Do you see yourself as others see you? Do you see your faults as God sees them? "Help me, God, to know the wrong in my life that I might do what is right instead."

LETDOWN

1 Kings 19–20, Luke 23:1–25 • *Key Verse: 1 Kings 19:4*

Once you reach the mountaintop, it's all downhill from there. While that is obviously true in a physical sense, it's also true emotionally. When we reach an emotional peak, the next step is downhill. The question is not if but how far down a person will go. And as we go down emotionally, it's easy for us to go down spiritually as well.

Consider Elijah. His mountaintop experience physically was on Mount Carmel. The 450 prophets of Baal posed a formidable lineup. Only Elijah stood on the Lord's side. But when the people saw the fire of the Lord fall, they cried, "The LORD—he is God!" (18:39).

Elijah was vindicated. The false prophets were defeated. Rain returned as the drought ended. And Elijah wished he were dead.

All it took was a threat from one woman, Jezebel, and the man who ran ahead of Ahab's chariot all the way to Jezreel headed south—way south—into the desert, where he sat down and wished that he were dead.

It doesn't seem possible. After a great victory, the prophet of God prayed, "Take my life" (19:4).

But it does make sense. Emotional peaks can be followed by emotional valleys, and when we are in the valley we are most susceptible to discouragement. It happened to Elijah, and it happens to us.

So be prepared. When on the mountaintop, remember that a valley will come next. Do not allow the letdown after a victory to become an occasion for discouragement.

"God, help me always to be strong—during the trials, the victories and the times of difficulty."

DO YOU KNOW ME?

*1 Kings 21–22, **Luke 23:26–56** • **Key Verse: Luke 23:47***

A credit card company used as an advertising campaign the line, "Do you know me?" Famous people were portrayed in normal settings as being unrecognized—until they pulled out their credit card. The name on the card gave them recognition. Without it, they supposedly were unknown.

The world did not recognize Jesus, according to the apostle John (John 1:10). People may have known His name and hometown, but still did not realize who He was. Jesus wept that first Palm Sunday because the people did not recognize the time of God's coming to them (Luke 19:44).

People were curious about Jesus. Crowds gathered to see Him wherever He went. At Jesus' trial, Herod hoped He would do a miracle, much like a person wanting to see a magic trick. Both Herod and Pilate asked Him questions about who He was—"Are you the king of the Jews?" Pilate asked (23:3).

Then came the cross and His death. The centurion who was there, a man who had undoubtedly witnessed many crucifixions, realized that this one was different. His reaction is amazing. "The centurion, seeing what had happened, praised God and said, 'Surely this was a righteous man'" (v. 47). Matthew and Mark quote him as saying, "This man was the Son of God."

The centurion's words contain a significant testimony. He recognized who Jesus truly was. He recognized that Jesus was not just a man but also the Son of God. The blessing of eternal life comes to those who recognize and receive Him as Lord.

Do you recognize Jesus as just a man, a great person of history, or as your Savior? If you know Him, thank Him for your salvation. If you do not, you can, like the centurion, confess Him as Lord.

HELP FOR THE HURTING HEART

2 Kings 1–3, Luke 24:1–35 • *Key Verse: Luke 24:32*

Nothing takes the wind out of our sails like discouragement. We get an idea in our heads, come up with some plans and take steps toward seeing a dream become a reality. Then, just when it starts to look good, something goes wrong. The more our hearts are in it, the more it hurts. And then discouragement sets in, leaving our minds in turmoil as we try to sort out things.

Try to imagine being a disciple, convinced that Jesus was a prophet, that He was one whose words and deeds were powerful before God and man. Add to that a hope He would redeem Israel. The wind is starting to fill the sail! Then He died. The seeming finality that death brings hits hard.

Confusion is added to the mix as some talk about angels they had seen and a body that is missing. No wonder these two disciples, when approached by Jesus, "stood still, their faces downcast" (v. 17). When the heart hurts, the head hangs, and theirs did.

Notice what Jesus did for them. He talked to them about the Bible, opening to their understanding the writings of Moses and the prophets, the Scriptures concerning Himself. As they listened, their hearts burned within them. The Word, spoken by the unrecognized resurrected Lord, rekindled the flame within their hearts.

When your heart is heavy, look to the Word of God. Don't just read it. Learn it and live it. As God's Word becomes fire in your heart, your life will change.

In times of discouragement where do you turn? Get into the Word. Find in it the encouragement you need that will heal your hurting heart.

LAST THING, FIRST THING

2 Kings 4–6, Luke 24:36–53 • *Key Verses: Luke 24:50–53*

Boiled down to its essential core, worship is a response. It is not an entertainment option we choose or an event we attend, but the essence of our lives as followers of Christ. Christ comes into our lives and we live out the remainder of our days in response to Him. He is, He acts; we respond, we worship.

The last thing Jesus did before returning to heaven was bless the disciples. Luke says that "while he was blessing them, he left them and was taken up into heaven" (v. 51). The blessing was the last thing. The first thing the disciples then did was worship Him.

That is the way we should live. Worship should be preeminent in our lives. This does not mean we must sit in a pew singing and praying, listening to preaching all day. It does mean that we live with an awareness of God, that we show how much we value Him in everything we say and do. For example, we are careful with our words because He tells us to be. When we do that it is an act of worship, because we are seeking to please Him. We are honest in our business dealings in the same way, for the same reason. And of course there are the times we devote solely to worship, singing His praises.

The last thing Jesus did on earth was bless the disciples, and the first thing they did was worship Him. Like the disciples, put worship first.

How well do you understand worship? As you read your Bible, look for the word, learn what the Bible says, and then live your life in response to God. "God, help me to desire to please You so my life may be an act of worship."

GUILTY SILENCE

2 Kings 7–9, John 1:1–28 • *Key Verse: 2 Kings 7:9*

Early one Saturday there was a knock on the door. The friend standing there asked, "What size suit do you wear?" I told him. He then said, "There's a garage sale two streets over and they are selling suits your size. You might want to check it out."

I did. And I bought five designer suits in excellent condition for $10 each! Only one needed any altering. My friend had brought good news.

Having good news is one thing; sharing it is another. If later my friend had said, "I should have told you about the garage sale near you," the news would not have been as good.

Getting a good deal on a suit is pretty minor compared to the good news God has given us—the good news of the Gospel. Knowing it and not sharing it is not right.

Four lepers understood that principle. The city of Samaria was under siege and the people expected to starve to death. These men decided to surrender to the enemy, since they figured they were going to die anyway.

When they got to the enemy camp, they found that God had caused the Arameans to flee, leaving behind everything. The lepers ate, drank and plundered. "Then they said to each other, 'We're not doing right. This is a day of good news and we are keeping it to ourselves'" (v. 9). Out of fear of punishment, they returned to the city and reported the good news.

We face a similar situation. Our city may not be under siege, but we have good news—Jesus saves! The principle remains: Having good news is one thing; sharing it is another. We have good news that we must tell others. When we keep it to ourselves, how will they hear?

What keeps you from telling others about Jesus? Decide right now whom you will share the Good News with, and pray for the strength to do it.

INCOMPLETE OBEDIENCE

2 Kings 10–12, John 1:29–51 • Key Verse: 2 Kings 12:3

"Done" can be a nice word. Sometimes I write the word "do" on a list and then later enjoy going back, adding two letters and making it "done." It's a nice word, if it stands alone. When it begins with "un" as in "undone" or is preceded by "needs to be" or "not quite," the word is not as nice. "Almost done" can be encouraging or discouraging. The "almost" can indicate that either it will soon be completed or that it remains incomplete.

Too often a job is incomplete. The finishing touches are undone. That happens with everything from home remodeling to sewing to yard work, and, unfortunately, with obedience. Our spiritual lives too often have areas of incomplete obedience.

Israel was given the Promised Land with specific instruction to get rid of all the idols and places of idolatry. Yet repeatedly in the Old Testament we read statements such as the one found in 2 Kings 12:3: "The high places, however, were not removed." The places that were allowed to remain often became an enticement, entrapping the people in false worship practices. That is why God wanted them removed, so they would not pull people into sin.

In a similar way, we can keep in our homes and lives things that God wants removed. We can do most of what God wants but stop short of getting it done completely. Our obedience is incomplete, not fully done, and Satan uses those things that remain undone to tempt and trap us.

Are there areas of your life where obedience is incomplete? Promise today to obey God fully, asking Him to help you see the things that need to be done.

IT USED TO BE A CHURCH

2 Kings 13–14, John 2 • *Key Verse: John 2:16*

The sign in the front lawn said, "For Sale by Owner." What made this particular for-sale item interesting is that it was a church! It made me think—just who was the owner of this building that had been called "the house of the Lord"?

Buildings that were built to house churches sometimes become restaurants, bookstores, antique shops, offices and other such things. The original purpose of the building has been replaced by a new purpose. The reasons vary. Sometimes a congregation outgrows its facility and relocates. Often, however, it's because of something far less positive—the death of the congregation. A group may begin with a good purpose but allow the purpose to be replaced with another, one that ultimately leads to demise.

Jesus confronted the people in the temple, challenging them with the statement, "How dare you turn my Father's house into a market!" (v. 16). When personal gain was more desired than worship, the temple became something other than what God intended.

As you study the Bible, read carefully to learn God's purposes for the Church. Recognize also the temptation to turn from His purposes to our pleasures. It happened in Jesus' day and it happens in ours.

Maybe that sign in the lawn of the church was telling the truth. The real owner was selling it because it no longer served His purpose.

"God, I know You love the Church and want it to bring glory to You. Help me learn from the Bible Your purposes and keep my desires in check. May You be pleased as we worship and serve You."

NEW BIRTH

2 Kings 15–16, John 3:1–18 • *Key Verse: John 3:3*

The bride and groom step up to the wedding cake holding a knife. They slice a piece from the top tier and lovingly "feed" a bite to each other, perhaps getting frosting on each other's face. In reality, the cake is a fake. The top layer is real, but everything else is cardboard, decorated with frosting. It looks so good on the outside, but inside is missing all the necessary ingredients.

A religious man came to see Jesus. The man looked so good on the outside. He was a leader, a teacher, a Pharisee named Nicodemus. If all that matters is what's on the outside, then this man had what it takes. He looked so right.

But Jesus knew what was on the inside. To this leader of the Jews He said, "I tell you the truth, no one can see the kingdom of God unless he is born again" (v. 3). Salvation is not just a matter of righteousness on the outside, but also of a right relationship with God on the inside.

Yes, we must live holy lives and do what is right, but a change on the inside is required. While many would have looked at Nicodemus and pronounced him righteous, Jesus looked and saw what was still need-ed—the new birth. To this man He would say those wonderful words, "For God so loved the world that he gave his one and only Son, that whoever believes in him shall not perish but have eternal life" (v. 16).

What are you on the inside—a born-again person? If so, thank God for your salvation. If not, why not right now receive Jesus as Savior?

TAUGHT TO WORSHIP

2 Kings 17–18, John 3:19–36 • *Key Verse: 2 Kings 17:28*

In a general sense, worship comes naturally to us. We do know how to worship—that is, to respond to someone or something with praise. We respond to a beautiful sunset, a tasty dessert or a winning team. Our struggle with worship comes when we worship God. Unfortunately, that worship does not come naturally.

When the king of Assyria resettled Samaria, the people did not worship the Lord and were judged by God for that. "So one of the priests who had been exiled from Samaria came to live in Bethel and taught them how to worship the LORD" (17:28). Worship did not come naturally, so the people had to be taught how.

But even with teaching, they failed to worship God correctly. Each group made its own gods and worshiped them also. "Even while these people were worshiping the LORD, they were serving their idols" (v. 41).

Genuine worship must be learned. It is not a matter of what we like but what God wants. He will not share worship with other gods.

Take the naturalness of worship but conform it to the Word. Direct your worship to God alone in the manner that pleases Him. He desires worship and seeks worshipers. And if you desire to be a worshiper who pleases Him, then learn to worship.

"God, I want to worship You in the way that pleases You. Help me to learn to become a worshiper who brings You joy."

WHAT GOD SEEKS

2 Kings 19–21, John 4:1–30 • Key Verse: John 4:23

There are few things that the Bible says God actively seeks. So if God seeks something, it must be important to Him and ought to be important to us. Luke 15 portrays God as seeking the lost. Lost people matter to God and should matter to us. God also seeks glory for Jesus, according to John 8:50, and in John 4 Jesus said that God is seeking worshipers.

The Samaritan woman raised a question about worship. Perhaps the conversation was uncomfortable, so she switched subjects. It could be that she realized Jesus could sort out the controversy between her people and the Jews. Either way, what He said about worship is instruction we also need to hear.

In this context Jesus spoke of "the kind of worshipers the Father seeks," those who worship in "spirit and truth" (v. 23). God is spirit. He cannot be worshiped as an image, nor is worship confined to a place. Truth is also a non-negotiable. The worshiper God seeks must worship in truth as it is revealed in the Word of God.

God is actively looking for people who will worship Him. Our challenge is to be the kind of disciple God wants. In seeking to please Him, we must be worshipers who worship Him in spirit and truth.

"God, are You pleased with my worship? Help me do more than just attend church. Help me give You, in spirit and in truth, the worship You desire."

WHAT MAKES GOD MAD

2 Kings 22–23, John 4:31–54 • *Key Verse: 2 Kings 22:13*

Has a friend ever said to you, "You know that makes me mad"? That person is speaking to you because you know him, and you know him well enough to realize what upsets him. You also know to avoid some topics for the simple reason that you don't want to make him mad.

God lets us know what angers Him. Israel needed to be reminded that God's anger burned against them because they had not "obeyed the words of this book" (22:13). The book was the one found by Hilkiah the high priest in the days of Josiah. It was the Book of the Law, the Word of God, which had long been discarded.

Josiah listened to the words of the Book of the Law. Immediately, "he tore his robes," which was a sign of great emotional distress (v. 11). Then he instructed the priest to ask God what they should do.

When God says, "You know this makes Me angry," it should affect how we act. This story teaches us that failure to obey His Word angers Him.

You have God's Word, and you read it. But do you obey it? The Lord's anger burns against us when we do not obey Him.

Ask God if there are specific things in your life that are wrong. If you know you are not being obedient, do not continue to anger God. Instead, repent, ask His forgiveness, and do what is right before Him.

WHAT REALLY MATTERS?

*2 Kings 24–25, **John 5:1–24** • Key Verses: John 5:16–17*

What's the big deal about an appendix anyway? I don't mean the one at the end of a book, but the one that sometimes is removed by a surgeon. It really isn't important and goes unnoticed until it becomes a pain.

Some "issues" that cry for attention are like an appendix. What's really important is overlooked and what's not is overemphasized. It happened in Jesus' day and it happens in ours.

The important thing Jesus did was heal a lame man, one who had been an invalid for 38 years. The man was waiting by the pool of Bethesda, hoping to be healed. And he was!

The Jews then persecuted Jesus because He healed on the Sabbath. What was important was overlooked—the man was healed. What was unimportant was overemphasized—observing the Sabbath the way the Jews thought it should be.

Jesus' defense was, "My Father is always at his work to this very day, and I, too, am working" (v. 17). That brought more criticism as He was accused of blasphemy, equating Himself with God.

Just think of all the emotional energy that could have been saved if the right thing had been emphasized: the lame man was healed.

Does what matters to you really matter to God? Is He as concerned about the traditions and practices that may characterize your Christian life? Now reverse the question. Does what matters to God really matter to you? Jesus healed people, even on the Sabbath, because He was doing what mattered to God.

Sometimes it's hard for us to see ourselves as clearly as others do. The next time there is some "issue" that is bothering you, ask a wise friend about it. Are you overemphasizing something unimportant?

THE LIFE OF DEATH

1 Chronicles 1–3, **John 5:25–47** • *Key Verse: John 5:25*

We are surrounded by death and reminders of it. In our homes may be pictures of family and friends who have died. Perhaps you were an heir and received an item that belonged to one of them, and that also reminds you of them and of the reality of death. Somewhere near where you live are both an undertaker and a cemetery. The sirens we hear—of ambulances rushing their passenger, rushing to beat death—rush only toward the inevitable. One day, if Jesus tarries, the obituary will be yours.

But in the midst of death's silence there is a voice, "'and those who hear will live'" (v. 25). It is the voice of Jesus, the Son of God, the One to whom God has granted "'to have life in himself'" (v. 26). All the dead will ultimately hear but not all will rise to live. Some "'will rise to be condemned'" (v. 29).

The reality of death makes us face the reality of life. Whether we will rise to live or to be condemned is decided now, in this life. Jesus said, "A time is coming and has now come" (v. 25). Salvation is for now, too, not just later. The "now-ness" of it begins when we hear His Word and believe.

Then death's reminders become reminders of life. We will breathe our last if Jesus does not come first. Our obituary will be written, printed, read and forgotten. The possessions precious to us will be passed on to others—but that will be of little concern to us because with death we live, eternally with Him.

"Father, help me see my time on earth as temporary and to be prepared to live eternally with You. May death not be feared or dreaded but accepted in Your time. And may I be comforted knowing that through Jesus I will rise to live."

THERE WILL BE A TEST!

1 Chronicles 4–6, John 6:1–21 • *Key Verses: 1 Chronicles 5:20, 25*

It has been said that the problem with the school of hard knocks is that the tests are given first. That's a hard way to learn—test first, lesson later. Paul, speaking particularly of the Old Testament, said that these things were "written to teach us" (Rom. 15:4). If only we would learn first, we might do better passing the tests.

In 1 Chronicles 5 we can learn from people who passed and then failed. It looked like they knew what to do but then forgot. The people were of the tribes of Reuben, Gad and half of Manasseh.

First they show us that trust in God can bring victory. "They were helped in fighting" by God "because they cried out to him . . . . He answered their prayers, because they trusted in him" (v. 20).

Then "they were unfaithful . . . and prostituted themselves" to other gods (v. 25). Just as trust in God can bring victory, so unfaithfulness can bring defeat. They paid a high price for their forgetfulness. God raised up an enemy who took them captive and carried them away into exile.

If you saw three people in front of you lose their money in a vending machine, would you put in your quarters? Hopefully not! Instead, you would learn from their example.

Learn from the examples of those who lived in Bible times. Trust can bring victory; unfaithfulness, defeat. Tests will come. All that remains is for you to show that you have learned—and pass the test.

As you read your Bible, look carefully for the lessons God has for you and apply them to your life. He did not give us the Bible just to increase our knowledge but to change the way we live.

I JUST WORK HERE

1 Chronicles 7–9, John 6:22–44 • Key Verse: John 6:38

"Don't ask me, I just work here" are words usually spoken by someone wanting to avoid responsibility, not as an expression of submission to authority. The obvious intent is to pass the buck, if not the blame, to someone higher up.

Actually, though, it could be a great statement of submission. If those words were said as an acknowledgment that the person is doing as told, it would reflect an obedient attitude, that of one who is submissive to whomever is in charge.

Unfortunately, we are more prone to sarcasm than submission. Yet God calls us to submission and gives us a model to follow—Jesus. He said, "I have come down from heaven not to do my will but to do the will of him who sent me" (v. 38).

Knowing what God wanted Him to do kept Jesus from getting sidetracked. The crowd wanted Him to feed them from now on. That was their will, but He would not submit to their desires because He was already submitted to the will of the Father. And it is clear that He not only knew God's will but was submitted to it and determined to carry it out.

There was no sarcasm in His voice as He said these words because they came from a submissive heart. What a contrast to the self-serving words of the crowd, who said, "Give us this bread" (v. 34). They were asking for what they wanted.

Do your words come from a submissive or a self-serving heart? When you pray, which matters most—your will or God's?

How serious are you when you pray, "Not my will, but Thine"? Look for submissiveness in your life. Can you find evidence of it in how you use your time, talents and finances? Read Ephesians 5:21. Do others see this verse in your relationships?

SAD ENDING

1 Chronicles 10–12, John 6:45–71
Key Verses: 1 Chronicles 10:13–14

"No statistic is more meaningless than the score at half time," a sports philosopher once said. There have been some miraculous comebacks, and being ahead at the half is no guarantee of a win.

What is true in sports is true in life. How a person is at life's "half time" is no guarantee of how he will be at the end. Jacob started disastrously but finished well, while the opposite was true with Solomon. Now add Saul to the latter list. At one point he looked good—so good that he stood out from the crowd, was chosen to be king and led the nation with the blessing of God.

The last half of his life, however, is remembered for its bitterness, the pursuit of David and a suicidal death. God's blessing turned to judgment. Saul's life had a sad ending for three reasons.

One, he was unfaithful to the Lord. God expects faithfulness of His people. Saul was not. Two, he did not keep the Word of the Lord. Obedience is to be a characteristic of the people of God. His became a life of disobedience. Three, he sought guidance from the wrong place and not from the Lord. As his kingdom was unraveling, Saul turned to a witch instead of to the Lord.

In two verses, 1 Chronicles 10:13–14, we are given an epitaph of sorts, an analysis of a life that began promisingly but ended disastrously. It ended that way not because of things beyond Saul's control but because of things he did not control. He could have remained faithful, kept the Word of the Lord and sought God's guidance, but he chose not to.

Some things are beyond our control. Concentrate on the things that are. Examine how you are doing on these three things: remaining faithful, keeping the Word of the Lord and seeking God's guidance.

OOPS!

1 Chronicles 13–15, John 7:1–27
Key Verses: 1 Chronicles 13:3, 15:13

Two familiar adages seemingly contradict each other. One is, "If at first you don't succeed, try, try again." The other is, "When all else fails, read the directions." Perhaps if we combined the two we'd have the best advice—something like, "Read the directions, and if you fail, read them again and try again." That's not as pithy as the other two, but it's certainly more practical.

David had the right idea but didn't read the directions. He said, "Let us bring the ark of our God back to us, for we did not inquire of it during the reign of Saul" (13:3). But David disobeyed God, and in the midst of a time of celebrating, God's anger burned against Uzzah for touching the ark, and He struck him down. The right thing was being done the wrong way.

Later David did try again—after reading the directions. He said, "We did not inquire of [God] about how to do it in the prescribed way" (15:13). This time the ark was successfully brought to Jerusalem.

David could have just tried and tried again. Or, when all else failed, he could have read the directions. The good news is that he did not get to the point of "all else failing." After one attempt, he read the directions.

Think of how much better it would have been if David had inquired of God first. God's anger would have been avoided, the ark would have been moved, and the celebration would not have ended in judgment.

God has given us "directions" for living—His Word, the Bible. Read the directions first and then follow them.

"God, help me to learn and live Your Word. Give me a heart to follow Your directions."

WHAT TO WEAR TO WORSHIP

1 Chronicles 16–18, John 7:28–53 • *Key Verse: 1 Chronicles 16:29*

Oh, the dilemma of what to wear! Clothing is more important to some than to others, but most of us have those times where we think, *What should I wear?* Dress at work may be a mandated uniform, an expectation of coat and tie, or the dreaded, because it might not be well defined, "corporate casual."

Have you ever thought about what to wear to worship? Times have changed. For some, shorts and sandals are fine, while others dress as if worship is impossible without a white shirt and tie.

One thing is essential to wear to worship, and that's holiness. David's psalm of thanks instructs us to "worship the LORD in the splendor of his holiness" (16:29). That phrase can mean several things. One is that God lives in the splendor of holiness and that we must worship Him there. Another is that He is holy so we must worship Him as holy.

But I think the primary meaning is that we, as worshipers, are to be garbed in holiness when we worship Him. We worship Him clothed in the splendor of holiness.

How do we put on the splendor of holiness? Holiness is not a matter of external dress but internal condition. It cannot be put on and put off like a comfortable sweater. You decide to live a life that is set apart to God, set apart from the world. Your life becomes one of holiness as you live out that decision.

Holiness is what God wants us to wear to worship. Put it on and remember that it is a splendid garment, one to wear and never remove.

Is holiness like a sweater to you, something to put on and take off depending on the temperature? It's not to be like that. Check what you are wearing. Is it holiness?

THE EASIEST WRONG TO CORRECT

1 Chronicles 19–21, John 8:1–27 • Key Verse: John 8:7

The easiest wrongs to identify and correct are those of others. By nature we are both faultfinders and fault avoiders. We can see the errors of others much more easily than our own and manage to expect change from them while finding excuses for ourselves.

When the Pharisees brought an immoral woman before Jesus, their intent was to pin Him on the horns of a dilemma. How could He, a friend of sinners, condemn her? How could He, a righteous man, fail to keep the Law? Their focus was on Jesus as they not only set but also sprung their trap.

Ever notice that the man involved in this act of adultery was not brought before Jesus? Perhaps the adultery itself was part of the setting of the trap and he was part of the plot, providing an opportunity to catch a woman in the act.

Then the unexpected occurred. Instead of answering their question, Jesus pinned the Pharisees with His statement, "If any one of you is without sin, let him be the first to throw a stone at her" (v. 7).

No stones were thrown. Their error was exposed. The faultfinders could not avoid their own faults. It is interesting that the first to leave were the older ones, men who knew there was no use denying their own sins.

Seeing the wrong in others is easy; seeing the wrong in ourselves is imperative. There are times when we confront others biblically regarding their sins. But we must always confront ourselves as well.

The psalmist prayed, "Search me, O God, and know my heart: test me and know my anxious thoughts. See if there is any offensive way in me, and lead me in the way everlasting" (Ps. 139:23–24). Pray that prayer now and often—especially when you are finding fault in others.

IS YOUR WORSHIP WORK?

1 Chronicles 22–24, John 8:28–59 • Key Verse: 1 Chronicles 22:19

People will stand in long lines this summer waiting for their turn to ride a roller coaster. After perhaps an hour or more, they will get their three minutes of thrill—or terror, as the case may be. At the end of the ride, some will immediately go back to the line and wait to ride again.

Amusement parks employ people whose responsibility it is to "test ride" the rides. Every day begins with hurtling along the tracks. No lines, just get in and go. What an enviable job! How great it must be to get to do that every day. For these workers, however, the roller coaster ride is just that—work. The thrill is gone; the ride is routine.

This happens in ministry also. We get so used to going to church, teaching Sunday school, singing in the choir, that ministry becomes a routine.

Worship was important to David, so he wanted to build the place that would be the center of worship. He made preparations for the temple to be built, assembling the workers and materials.

But worship is more than a building. It is an issue of the heart. To the workers David gave this additional instruction: "Now devote your heart and soul to seeking the LORD your God" (22:19). The work of our hands is important, but so is the worship of our hearts. The things we do must not become so routine that we lose the thrill of serving God.

Has your service of God become routine? Then it's time to "devote your heart and soul." That will involve a conscious effort to keep yourself from just going through the motions. Your service is to be an act of worship.

WHY?

1 Chronicles 25–27, **John 9:1–23** • *Key Verse: John 9:3*

Perhaps the most-oft asked question of God is "why?" Sometimes people ask it in an accusatory tone, as if they can demand of God an explanation for His actions. Other times it is the plaintive cry of a searching heart, one of pain or confusion. In the Bible we can find the answers to that question.

One day the disciples asked Jesus the "why" question. They thought they knew the answer and only wanted it refined. Why was this man blind? To the disciples, it was obvious the man was blind because of sin. So their question really was, "Who sinned?"

We need to let God answer the question, not give Him our answers. That became obvious when Jesus replied that "neither this man nor his parents sinned" (v. 3). Yes, there are times of suffering due to sin and its effects, but that is not always the answer. As Jesus explained, some suffering occurs so that "the work of God might be displayed." And in John 11:15, we're told that Lazarus' death happened "so that you may believe."

Our troubles can be times of testimony as Jesus works in our lives.

Instead of asking why, just pray. Ask God to use your troubles as a testimony so that your life will bring glory to Him and draw others to Jesus.

SPENDING SOMEONE ELSE'S MONEY

1 Chronicles 28–29, John 9:24–41 • *Key Verse: 1 Chronicles 29:16*

A credit card in the hands of a college student can be a dangerous thing when the name on the card is not his own, but dad's. With my permission—actually, by my instruction—my daughter and her fiancé had a nice meal at a restaurant near their college. When the bill came to the table, the credit card came out of the wallet. I later kidded my daughter, a former waitress, about the generous tip she left, also charged to my card.

I had no problem with her charging the meal, or even with the amount of the tip. It was what I had told her to do. And it illustrates a truth. It is easier to spend someone else's money than your own, especially when told to spend it. We know that, but sometimes we struggle to really do it.

You might be thinking, *I wouldn't have a problem doing that!* But perhaps you do. Everything you have belongs to God. It is all His— even your money. He tells us how to use His money, but sometimes we struggle spending His money the way He wants it spent.

David understood that, and it affected not only him but the people of Israel as they raised the money needed to build the temple. He even said, "As for all this abundance that we have provided for building you a temple for your Holy Name, it comes from your hand, and all of it belongs to you" (29:16).

When we realize that our money is really God's, then we will spend and give as God wants His money spent and given.

How do you view your finances and possessions? Does your checkbook reflect the heart of a faithful steward of God's resources? If not, refigure your budget today and give as God instructs.

A PRICELESS WORD PICTURE

2 Chronicles 1–3, John 10:1–23 • John 10:11

If a picture is worth a thousand words, then how much is a word picture worth? When it communicates the message Jesus has for us, it is of inestimable worth. A priceless word picture is found in John 10, that of the shepherd and his sheep.

Most of us have little experience with sheep. In fact, most of what we know is secondhand information gathered from lessons taught at church, maybe from Psalm 23. We are like sheep and Jesus is the Good Shepherd. We are the wanderers and He is the finder, keeper and protector.

Take this part of the word picture—a man dying, intentionally, for animals. Hard to imagine, yet it is the image that Jesus used to describe what He did on Calvary. Willingly, on purpose, the shepherd is described as one who "'lays down his life for the sheep'" (v. 11). Let those familiar words sink in for a minute. The Finder, Keeper and Protector of the wanderers died on purpose, with purpose, for us.

Death can be striking. It catches our attention, making us pause and reflect. The death of Jesus occurred nearly 2,000 years ago, but it should still catch our attention. We like to talk about salvation being free. That is true—but what was free to us came at tremendous cost. The price paid was the life of the Good Shepherd.

Quietly reflect on this tremendous truth—Christ died for you. Then thank Him for paying the price. You had a debt you could not pay, and He paid a debt He did not owe. "Thank You, Jesus."

THE PRESENCE OF GOD

2 Chronicles 4–6, John 10:24–42 • *Key Verses: 2 Chronicles 5:13–14*

On top of Mount Moriah in Jerusalem today stands one of the most beautiful buildings in the world, the Dome of the Rock. Even when seen from the distance as one looks across the Kidron Valley from the Mount of Olives, the glistening golden dome is a captivating sight. The building is a visual feast of mosaics and marble, a blending of circle and octagon with gold gilding. It is a Muslim holy site.

Somewhere on that mount stood the temple Solomon built. While the exact location is not known for certain, the general area is agreed upon. It is interesting to stand on the temple mount and reflect on the account found in these verses. There was a day when the glory of God so filled the temple that "the priests could not perform their service because of the cloud" (5:14).

God answered Solomon's prayer. While we sometimes sing of God's glory in our hymns and songs, Solomon and the people saw it displayed. The temple became the dwelling place of God's glory.

Today the temple is gone. God's glory has departed from there. But here's the compelling thought: the Bible tells us that our bodies are the temple of the Holy Spirit of God (1 Cor. 6:19). As believers in Jesus Christ, we are the dwelling place of His glory!

Solomon's temple showcased the glory of God. It was a place of great beauty and magnificence. We may not think of ourselves as being like that building, but we are! And, just as then, our bodies also must showcase the glory of God.

Is the glory of God evident in your life? As you look at how you live, think of what Solomon did, and determine to be a temple that brings glory to God.

PULLING AN ALL-NIGHTER

2 Chronicles 7–9, John 11:1–29 • *Key Verses: John 11:9–10*

The life of a college student includes eating a diet drawn from the four basic food groups—fast, frozen, microwave and pizza—and a time-management plan based on the "all-nighter." The assignment that is filed away under "I can do it later" one day becomes the assignment due tomorrow and really is done "later"—as in staying up until three or four o'clock in the morning. On every college campus lights burn late into the night as caffeine-energized minds try to get work done.

Isn't there a better way? Of course there is, but there is a great gulf between the ideal and reality. It would be much better for all of us if we used our time wisely.

Jesus used time wisely and sometimes confused His disciples in the process. When He heard that Lazarus was sick, He waited. Then when He said, "Let us go back to Judea" (v. 7), His disciples protested that the time was not right. At that point, Jesus gave them a lesson on using time wisely—do what God wants, when He wants it.

"Are there not twelve hours of daylight?" Jesus asked (v. 9). The person who walks in the daylight will not stumble, but the person who walks in the dark will. It makes sense to use the right time to do the right things.

Jesus worked on the Father's schedule. He neither rushed ahead by going to Bethany too soon, nor did He lag behind by going when it was too late. Knowing what God wanted done and when to do it was the guiding principle of time management for Jesus. It should be for us as well.

Are other demands keeping you from doing what God wants? If you know things that God wants that you are not getting accomplished, examine the guiding principle for how you use your time.

DU JOUR CHRISTIANITY

2 Chronicles 10–12, John 11:30–57
Key Verses: 2 Chronicles 11:16, 12:1

Restaurant menus sometimes include a "soup du jour." A little French makes the soup prepared for that day sound like something extra special. It is special in that it was made for that day, but that is the extent of its distinctiveness. Adding the French words for "of the day" make it sound nice, but it is still only temporary.

That is fine with soup but not with commitment. We too often live as if it is sufficient to have commitment du jour, the amount needed or wanted for today, when what is needed is commitment for life.

In the Bible we find repeated examples of commitment du jour. When Rehoboam became king, he immediately fortified Judah. The priests and Levites rallied to him and they were followed by "those from every tribe of Israel who set their hearts on seeking the LORD" (v. 16). For three years they "strengthened the kingdom of Judah and supported Rehoboam, . . . walking in the ways of David and Solomon during this time" (v. 17).

But the next chapter presents a different picture. "After Rehoboam's position as king was established and he had become strong, he and all Israel with him abandoned the law of the LORD" (12:1). The crisis passed and commitment waned—a sad pattern that continues even today.

Make sure that the commitments you make are ones that last.

"God, help me strengthen my commitments. May I not waver but continue to be steadfast in my Christian life."

THE LONG HAUL

2 Chronicles 13–14, John 12:1–26 • *Key Verse: 2 Chronicles 13:10*

The familiar phrase "in it for the long haul" is sometimes used in regards to investing. Day traders are people who buy and sell stocks in a way that focuses on short-term gain rather than long-term. Some investment counselors advise against that and recommend investing for the long haul. Let the money stay and gain over the years rather than by the minute.

Our commitment to God is to be for that proverbial long haul and not a thing of the moment or for the crisis du jour. Once we receive Jesus as Savior, we need to focus our hearts on life-long discipleship, not wavering but continuing in our commitment.

When the people in Judah abandoned the Law of the Lord, God dealt with them in a way that got their attention. The attack of Shishak, king of Egypt, was humbling. Then when Israel, under the leadership of Jeroboam, attacked Rehoboam's successor, Abijah, God gave Judah the victory.

What had changed? They were once again committed to God. Abijah said to the armies from the north, "As for us, the LORD is our God, and we have not forsaken him" (13:10).

Each of us should be able to say, at any point in our life, that we have not forsaken God. We are to be committed for the long haul.

Asa, the next king, also did right. He acknowledged that "the land is still ours, because we have sought the LORD our God" (14:7). As they remained faithful, God blessed.

God's blessing is desirable, but to receive it, our commitment is necessary.

You cannot live on yesterday's obedience. Pray that today you will be faithful, and remind yourself to pray this prayer daily.

CHECK ENGINE LIGHT

2 Chronicles 15–16, John 12:27–50 • *Key Verse: 2 Chronicles 15:4*

Some people fastidiously maintain their vehicles, doing all the right things on schedule. They change the oil every 3,000 miles, rotate the tires and check the brake pads. They even follow the inspection guide in their owner's manual, going to the dealership at the prescribed times—"mileage milestones" for preventative car care.

The rest of us wait for the check engine light to come on. There's nothing like the red glow on the dashboard to encourage us to build our relationship with a mechanic! And we wince when asked, "When was the last time you . . . ?" Our typical answer is, "I was meaning to take care of that just the other day."

When something goes wrong, we seek help; when things are fine, we don't. We may live that way in regard to our cars, but we should not in our relationship with the Lord.

When Asa was king of Judah, the prophet told him, "The LORD is with you when you are with him. If you seek him, he will be found by you, but if you forsake him, he will forsake you" (15:2). That is plain enough—but ignored. It was "'in their distress [that] they turned to the LORD'" (v. 4).

Sadly, we are more prone to turn to the Lord in a time of distress than any other time. God desires that we always look to Him, in good times and in bad, as well as all times in between. If today is a day of distress for you, turn to Him. He will not reject you. Then, make it the habit of your life. Don't wait for the "check engine light" to come on first.

If you have an urgent need, pray about it right now. And if there is nothing pressing, pray right now that God would help you always to turn to Him whatever the day might bring.

HOW LOW WILL YOU GO?

2 Chronicles 17–18, John 13:1–20 • *Key Verses: John 13:14–15*

Ever see a candy wrapper on the floor of the lobby at church? Probably, and if not there, maybe you saw one left on a pew, along with the discarded bulletin from the service.

Did you ever pick up the candy wrapper and throw it away, or did you leave it for someone else? If you left it, could it be that you did not stoop to pick up someone else's trash because it was "beneath you"?

We can assess our pride by considering the question of what we will or will not do in various situations. In a sense, a candy wrapper is an easy test. It gets harder when it's a used tissue on the floor, or a church workday when you are assigned to clean toilets. How "servant" our servant heart is will be revealed by where we draw the line in what we will do.

The disciples served their Master but drew the line at washing feet. It was a mealtime, where provision had been made to attend to this lowest of servant tasks, but not a single disciple moved to pick up the basin and towel. It probably did not take long to establish that no one was going to do what obviously should be done.

Then Jesus wrapped a towel around His waist, poured water into a basin and began to wash His disciples' feet. What they would not stoop to do, He did. "I have set you an example," He said (v. 15).

Examples are set to follow. The candy wrapper you see next Sunday at church is a test. How low will you go to serve your Master?

Pride is a danger that must be carefully watched. Ask yourself, "What is beneath me?" and then ask the Holy Spirit to bring it to your mind again, especially at a time when it is not just a question but a genuine test of pride.

LOGO WEAR

*2 Chronicles 19–20, **John 13:21–38** • **Key Verses: John 13:34–35***

A current marketing trend is stores that sell only logo wear. Want a hat that has a favorite team name on it? You can get it there—as well as shirts, pants, socks, pens, pencils, posters, Beanie Babies . . . you get the picture. We like to let others know our favorite teams, schools, vacation spots and hobbies by becoming a walking billboard. We proclaim our loves.

While we proclaim our loves, Jesus wants our love to proclaim. Specifically, He said that by our love for one another "all men will know that you are my disciples" (v. 35). The logo wear of the disciple of Christ is love.

Read carefully, though. Jesus said that we are to love as He has loved us (v. 34). The definition of love does not come from the latest popular movie or song on the radio but from the example set by Jesus. In Ephesians 5:25–32, Paul detailed Christ's love for us:

1. His is a sacrificial love—He gave himself up for us (v. 25).

2. His is a purifying love—He did that to make the Church holy (v. 26).

3. His is a caring love—just as we take care of our bodies, He takes care of us (v. 29).

4. His is an unending love—like God intended for husbands and wives, united permanently, a union that illustrates the union of Christ and the Church (vv. 31–32).

It's easy to put on a hat with a favorite team logo to let people know we are fans. But it is vital that our lives be a logo, stamped indelibly with the trademark of a disciple—love for one another. And not just any love, but a love patterned after the love of Christ.

Does your love for others show enough that you are recognized as a disciple?

CERTAINTY IN UNCERTAIN TIMES

2 Chronicles 21–22, John 14 • *Key Verse: John 14:1*

Sometimes our hearts can feel like waves tossed in the wind. The word *troubled,* found in verse 1, can be defined that way, as if Jesus were saying to His disciples, "Don't let your hearts be like wind-tossed waves."

That is easier said than done. Troubled hearts need more than the admonition "don't." They need reasons. The hope of heaven is a cure for troubled hearts. To comfort their troubled hearts, Jesus taught the disciples three things about heaven.

First, heaven is a place. It is the dwelling place of God, angels and the redeemed, not an imagined place.

Second, it is a prepared place—prepared by Jesus, for us! He is there now preparing a place for us, an abiding place, a "mansion" as some translations put it.

Third, the presence of Christ is there. He promises to return for us, and we look forward to a glorious reunion, one that will be eternal as we dwell in heaven, the place He has prepared for us and will take us to.

Do not lose heart. Do not allow your heart to be tossed about by winds of despair. Believe in Christ. Believe in heaven, and let not your heart be troubled. Jesus did not promise an untroubled life but a peaceful heart, and it comes from an eternal perspective that sees heaven as home and knows how to get there from here.

Remember that this world is temporary. One day all of these things will be gone. Ask God to use the hope of heaven to calm your heart.

REPEATED REMINDERS

2 Chronicles 23–24, John 15 • *Key Verses: 2 Chronicles 24:17–19*

The last time someone said to me, "How many times do I need to remind you?" I replied, "At least one more time." Some lessons seem to stick easier than others—and if repetition really does aid learning, we ought to be geniuses by now.

Occasionally we have opportunity to learn from the mistakes of others. Perhaps you are trying to get to another part of town and know that construction is affecting traffic, so you ask someone who recently drove through it. A quick call might alert you to potential problems, and you can avoid making the same mistake.

The Bible is filled with mistakes—not errors, but the mistakes of people. A recurring one is starting well but finishing poorly. Joash is yet another example of that. He started well under the tutelage of Jehoiada the priest, who made a covenant that "he and the people and the king would be the LORD's people" (23:16). As king, Joash ordered the repair of the temple. He started well.

But then the day came that "they abandoned the temple of the LORD," who sent prophets "to bring them back to him, and though they testified against them, they would not listen" (vv. 18–19). The result was judgment. Joash was lying in bed, recovering from wounds suffered in battle, when he was murdered. Another account of one who started well but ended poorly.

How will your account be written? Determine to finish well.

It's a morbid thought, but if your obituary were written today, would it say that you finished well? Ask God to help you stay true to His Word and finish well.

A TEST ON PRIDE

2 Chronicles 25–27, John 16 • *Key Verse: 2 Chronicles 26:16*

Human nature has a strong and strange capacity for self-delusion. We err in our assessment of ourselves—usually by overrating ourselves or our importance. At the heart of this problem is pride, a problem we all face at times.

King Uzziah was powerful but "his pride led to his downfall" (v. 16). Humanly speaking, his accomplishments were great, but his attachment to them was even greater. He became so proud that he was unfaithful to the Lord, doing what was not allowed of even the king. He was not permitted to take the place of a priest to burn incense on the altar in the temple. God judged him and he died of leprosy, living the final days of his life in quarantine, in a separate house, excluded from the temple.

Pride can affect our judgment and our attitude, and ultimately lead to a fall. It is a peril to avoid.

How can you tell if pride is a problem in your heart? Answer these questions to help you examine yourself.

1. What is beneath you? Are there things you will not do because you are "above" them?

2. Who is beneath you? With whom will you speak or not speak? Do you look down on some because they don't measure up in one way or another?

3. How do you expect to be treated? Do you need to be recognized, credited, coddled?

A proud person knows what is beneath him, looks down on others and expects special treatment. To the extent these things describe you, ask God to help you overcome pride.

Read carefully and reflect on the questions asked in today's devotional. They can help you discern if you have a problem with pride.

NO, I HAVEN'T BEEN SICK

2 Chronicles 28–29, **John 17** • *Key Verse: John 17:13*

A cartoon showed two people sitting next to each other on a bus. It was obvious that the man was answering a question asked by the woman next to him. There was nothing unusual about her appearance, but his caught my eye. He looked thin, with a gray complexion and hollow cheeks. His suit was black, worn with a white shirt and thin black tie. With his hands folded on his lap and his shoulders slouched, he gave the impression of one both weak and meek.

The question posed by the woman was not in the cartoon, only the man's answer: "No, ma'am, I haven't been sick. I'm a minister."

That cartoon played off people's conception of what ministers are like—pale, weak, meek, sickly. The humor, as often is the case, is truth thinly veiled. Christianity suffers at times from an image problem. We have conveyed the image of the character in the cartoon rather than the reality Christ wants for us.

In what is truly "the Lord's prayer," Jesus said, "I say these things while I am still in the world, so that they may have the full measure of my joy within them" (v. 13). When we have the full measure of His joy in us, we will not be mistaken for sick people.

A Christian has no guarantee that trouble will never come or illness will never strike. Some days we look ill because we are! But nothing should ever rob us of that inner joy that comes from Jesus and is not dependent upon our circumstances.

Do people see joy in you? Think about what you say, how you say it and in what way you say it. It could be that your focus is off Jesus and your joy is lost. "God, help me have the full measure of Your joy within me."

"NEVERTHELESS, SOME . . ."

2 Chronicles 30–31, John 18:1–18
Key Verses: 2 Chronicles 30:10–11

Where were you on December 31, 1999, as midnight approached? Preparations for the infamous Y2K bug varied—from building bunkers to ignoring the warnings. Responses to the forecasts of Y2K-related problems were both extremes and everything in between, but it basically came down to one of two. Either you did something or nothing. Some heard the warnings and heeded them, while others chose to laugh them off.

Long before computers were even conceived of, a letter went out and was met with the same basic responses—people scorned and ridiculed the message, but some listened. The message was from King Hezekiah, calling the people of Israel to return to the Lord. He wrote, "Do not be stiff-necked, as your fathers were; submit to the LORD. Come to the sanctuary, which he has consecrated forever. Serve the LORD your God, so that his fierce anger will turn away from you" (30:8).

Return, yield, serve—a needed message for a people who as a nation had become unfaithful to the Lord.

The people scorned and ridiculed the messengers. Sounds like today. The message of God is not always received. But notice verse 11: "Nevertheless, some . . . humbled themselves and went to Jerusalem." Thank God for the "some."

Hezekiah's message is of eternal significance and so much more important than the Y2K warning. How do you respond to the Word of God? Are you part of the "scorners" or one of the "some"?

God didn't give us His Word just to increase our knowledge but to affect the way we live. If it is going to change you, you must be open to hearing the message. Determine to be one of the "some." Hear and heed His Word.

SCIENCE PROJECT

2 Chronicles 32–33, John 18:19–40
Key Verses: 2 Chronicles 32:7–8

One of the most dreaded days in the life of parents is when their elementary-aged child brings home a piece of paper that reads, "Science project." Truth in advertising laws should apply and the assignment be called what it is: "Parent/Child Cooperative Homework Assignment." What has been given to the child to do inevitably requires parental involvement.

The thing to avoid is either extreme. If it is done totally by the child, the project will probably not meet the teacher's expectation. If it is done totally by the parent, that's obviously unacceptable. In between is the holy grail of homework: parental involvement and student participation. It is a "both/and," not an "either/or," situation.

The challenges we face in life should be approached with a "both/and" mentality. But in this case, the two parts of meeting the challenge are not parent and child but you and God.

In Hezekiah's day, Sennacherib, king of Assyria, invaded. Hezekiah prepared to be attacked. The water supply was secured, the walls repaired, towers built and weapons and shields manufactured. That was his part.

The other part of the defense was God's. "There is a greater power with us than with him," Hezekiah said of Sennacherib. "With him is only the arm of flesh, but with us is the LORD our God to help us and to fight our battles" (32:7–8).

"Either/or" was not enough. The people did not rely just on the "arm of flesh" or just on God. It was "both/and." They prepared and trusted God—an early "Praise the Lord and pass the ammunition" approach, which needs to be our approach. Work and pray.

Do you trust just in what you can do, forgetting God? Or do you sit back waiting for God to do it all? Determine to live in balance, not with an "either/or" mind-set but "both/and." Work and pray.

WARNING IGNORED

2 Chronicles 34–36, John 19:1–22
Key Verses: 2 Chronicles 36:15–18

Perhaps it is the result of lawsuits that we have so many warning labels today. They are found on coffee cups at fast-food restaurants, batting helmets, side-view mirrors on cars—everywhere, it seems, except on credit cards, one place where they are probably most needed!

Familiarity does breed contempt, and the overuse of the word *warning* has resulted in chronic disregard of the word. Still, there are times that warnings are needed and should be heeded, such as when a tornado is sighted. Going out with a camcorder to film a tornado is not wise. Going to the basement is.

God gives warnings to us in His Word. He also tells us about people who did the unwise thing, choosing to ignore and even ridicule the warning. The closing chapter of 2 Chronicles is sad as it tells of the fall of Jerusalem, an event that occurred after God's messengers were ignored.

The messengers of God came to the people "again and again, because he had pity on his people . . . . But they mocked God's messengers, despised his words and scoffed at his prophets" (vv. 15–16). Judgment came as God handed His people over to the Babylonians.

The Bible tells us how to live as disciples of Christ. In it are instructions and warnings along with examples from which we learn valuable lessons. We need to read the Word, learn the Word and live the Word, putting into practice the principles God gives us.

Reading your Bible is only the beginning of what God wants. You also must learn what it teaches and then live it. When you read and learn, do you then live it?

A BRIGHT SPOT

Ezra 1–2, John 19:23–42 • *Key Verses: Ezra 1:5–6*

The morning newspaper is not typically encouraging reading for the start of the day, and neither is the evening news for the end of the day! Yet sprinkled among the stories of crimes and severe weather are bits and pieces of encouragement. Sometimes we can read the repeated stories of failure by God's people and miss the words telling of their successes. The Book of Ezra begins with an encouraging note.

God was at work not only in the hearts of His people but also in the heart of the king. Cyrus was moved to do what would fulfill the Word of the Lord. He decided to send back to Jerusalem some of the people living in captivity so the temple of God could be rebuilt. God at work in the events of man is an encouragement!

He was at work also in the hearts of His own people, moving them to go and build the temple. The king was making it possible, but he needed workers who were willing to make the journey and do the work. Again, it is encouraging to see God at work, this time in the hearts of His people.

One other encouraging note here. As the workers prepared to go, their neighbors assisted them by providing silver and gold, goods and livestock, and valuable gifts (v. 6). Cyrus would also send along things taken from the temple by Nebuchadnezzar, but what an encouragement that people would give what they had to help.

Be encouraged as you see God at work. Look for examples and thank Him for the evidence that people are responding to the moving of His Spirit. Also, be an encourager. You may be able to help—financially, physically, spiritually or emotionally—someone who is serving God.

THE FORK IN THE ROAD

Ezra 3–5, John 20 • *Key Verses: John 20:21–22*

"When you come to a fork in the road," Yogi Berra said, "take it." Not the most coherent piece of advice, but possibly one of the most realistic. We do come to forks in the road of life and often do not know which path to take. What we know is that we cannot stay there.

The disciples came to a fork in the road when Jesus died, and they couldn't stay there. Already they were locking the doors for fear of the Jews. Then came the news and their run to the tomb—Jesus was alive! So they gathered in a room with the door locked as they stood at their latest "fork." And Jesus met them there.

At that place He gave them three things:

1. Peace. He pronounced a blessing of peace on the disciples.

2. Push. He pushed them toward the fork of His choosing when He said, "I am sending you" (v. 21).

3. Presence. He told them to receive the Holy Spirit, the Comforter who would be with them as they went, bringing them inner peace.

Jesus had brought them to that fork in the road. They were there by His design, and the path of His choosing now lay before them. With His peace they were to go forth, accompanied by the Holy Spirit.

Have you ever sensed that you were standing at a fork of God's design? It may seem safer to stay at the fork in the road, but Jesus promises you peace and will give you a push, sending you along the road of His choosing in the presence of the Holy Spirit.

Have you been stalling? Perhaps God has brought you to a decision point where you need to take a next step. Don't hesitate to go where He is leading you. Remember, He gives you peace and the presence of the Spirit.

PRECEDENT'S DETRIMENT

Ezra 6–8, John 21 • *Key Verse: John 21:22*

Ever hear of the "law of unintended consequences"? It's the idea that sometimes there are consequences that were neither intended nor expected. Sometimes that happens with establishing precedents. Something is done once and becomes the benchmark by which other similar things are done. Precedents are feared by those who inadvertently set them and revered by those who want to use them. They can be positive in effect but often are not.

When we focus on precedents, we may get sidetracked, leaving undone the important things. Jesus did not want that to happen to His disciples. These weren't His exact words, but his message in John 21:19 and 22 was, "Don't get sidetracked by how someone else is treated."

Jesus gave Peter an indication of "the kind of death by which [he] would glorify God" (v. 19). Then He said what really mattered: "Follow Me." But Peter got sidetracked. Was Jesus setting a precedent here? "Lord, what about him?" Peter asked of John (v. 21).

Immediately, Jesus brought Peter back to what was important. Peter did not need to wonder about how John would die but did need to remember that he must follow Jesus. True to human nature, a rumor then began to spread among the disciples about John not dying. That was not the intended consequence, but a needed reminder that we can get so curious about how others are treated that we miss what is important.

Follow Jesus and don't get sidetracked. That is what is most important.

We can easily get sidetracked wondering about other people and what God might be doing in their lives. Instead of wondering about others, we need to focus on these simple words of Jesus: "Follow Me."

PART OF THE CROWD

Ezra 9–10, Acts 1 • *Key Verse: Acts 1:14*

In today's passages are two scenes of prayer: one at a time of confession, the other at what must have been a time of confusion. Both remind us that while we should often have times of private prayer, we also need times of praying with others.

The people in Ezra's day were enjoying the blessing of God's good hand upon them. Then they became aware of a sin that needed to be addressed. Ezra's prayer is a powerful statement of confession before God—no excuses or pulling punches, no requests mingled in, just confession. Most people like to confess in private, but at times we need to confess as a group before God.

The disciples had experienced a veritable blitz of contrasting emotions. Jesus died and was buried. Sadness. He arose! Amazement. He ministered with them for another 50 days. Excitement. They were instructed to wait to receive the Holy Spirit. Anticipation. He ascended into heaven. Confusion. What next?

What better recourse than to pray? But notice that the disciples "joined together constantly in prayer, *along with* the women and Mary the mother of Jesus, and his brothers" (v. 14, emphasis mine). Yes, they could have prayed alone, but they did not. They established the practice of praying together, one that became a characteristic of the early church (Acts 2:42).

We do not live the Christian life in isolation but in community. We are to be people who pray alone and pray with others.

If you want to establish a closer relationship with others, pray with them regularly and often. You will find that the closer you draw to God, the closer you will draw to one another.

A MODEL TO FOLLOW

Nehemiah 1–3, Acts 2:1–21 • *Key Verse: Nehemiah 1:11*

You can make a career out of writing instructions. People need them for all kinds of things—assembling, installing, using and replacing. Sometimes we need pictures to go with the words. To know what to do is good. To be told what to do is good also. But to be shown what to do can really help!

We can talk about the importance of "having devotions," but still we wonder how to have them. The words in Nehemiah 1 provide a picture, a model to follow. It is not the only way but is an excellent pattern.

Notice that Nehemiah worshiped as he spoke of the awesomeness of God (v. 5). Thus, our devotional times should include worship as well as what followed: confession (vv. 6–7). Nehemiah confessed without offering any excuses. We, likewise, should regularly make sure the slate is clean before God. Yes, our sins are forgiven when we receive Christ as Savior, but God desires that we confess those wrongs we do after becoming His children too.

Nehemiah's devotional life also reveals that he knew the Word of God. In verse 8 he cited what God said to Moses. Do you read the Word regularly, consistently?

Finally, after worship, confession and recalling the Word, Nehemiah presented his request. Too often our requests can be the entirety of our praying, yet we find many examples in the Bible where worship, confession and reading the Word preceded the request.

So, how do we "do" devotions? Nehemiah gives us a model to follow.

If you are using this devotional guide regularly, then you are spending time in the Word. That's great! Keep some paper with this guide and make a prayer list. Include on that list praises and thanksgivings to God. Remember also to keep the slate clean—confess. And ask, but keep a balance. Don't just be an asker. Be a pray-er.

BACK TO THE FUTURE

Nehemiah 4–6, Acts 2:22–47 • *Key Verse: Acts 2:42*

What we learn from the past can help us prepare for the future. God has given us the Bible to tell us how to be saved and how to live as His people. It is very important that we learn to live as part of the community of believers, in fellowship with others as part of the church. In Acts we are given a picture of the first church, and it is a model for us to follow. When we look at it we are in one sense going back, but as we learn and follow this model, we are looking to the future.

The first church was devoted to very specific things: teaching, fellowship, communion and prayer. Together, they learned the Word, remembered what Jesus had done and prayed. These were the hallmarks of the first-century church and should be of the last-century church, whenever that may be.

Notice also that they were together both in the temple courts and in homes. The large-group gatherings and small-group ones provided a balance in their experience and increased their accountability.

Among other reasons, we need large-group worship and fellowship to remind us that we are part of something much greater than ourselves and to give testimony to others that the church is alive. And in small groups, the instruction can be more specific, we can be held accountable to one another, and we can more effectively minister to others in the Body of Christ.

What is your involvement with others in the Body of Christ? Follow the example of the first church and be devoted as they were to learning the Word, fellowshipping, remembering Christ's work and praying.

THE PERSON FOR THE JOB

Nehemiah 7–9, Acts 3 • *Key Verse: Nehemiah 7:2*

"Who ya gonna call?" became a catch phrase back in the 1980s. Both the question and its intended answer came out of popular culture but hit on a basic need. When you need something done, who are you "gonna call"? And from the world of advertising came the slogan, "When it absolutely, positively has to get there . . . " From both movies and Madison Avenue, a basic need was recognized—the need for being able to trust that the job will get done. In particular, it is knowing whom you can trust.

When the wall was completed, Nehemiah knew that the job was not done. There was more to restoring the city of Jerusalem than just putting the pieces back together. He needed to put someone in charge of the city, to see that things were run the way they should be. He chose his brother Hanani, along with Hananiah, the commander of the citadel. Nehemiah knew his brother's ability and he also knew two things about Hananiah that made him the right choice.

First, Hananiah was a man of integrity. When someone is a person of integrity, he can be trusted. There is no deceit or acceptance of wrongdoing in such a person.

Second, Hananiah feared God more than most men do. For many people, the opposite is true: they fear man more than God. But Hananiah kept it in the right order. He was more concerned about what God thought than what other men thought. That perspective would keep him a person of integrity.

Hananiah is an example of what every one of us should be—people of integrity who fear God.

Are there any weaknesses in your life, areas that you hope no one learns about? Today you can take the first step in strengthening your integrity. If you really fear God, you will not want any wrong in your life.

PUT IT IN WRITING

Nehemiah 10–11, Acts 4:1–22 • *Key Verse: Nehemiah 10:29*

Every time you sign a credit card receipt, you are signing a legally binding contract. The wording of the contract states simply that you agree to pay the debt. Putting something in writing carries more weight than a verbal agreement.

Imagine putting in writing and signing your commitment to God. The people of Jerusalem did that; they made a binding agreement, put it in writing and sealed it (9:38). What they agreed to should challenge us to be so committed in the following areas:

Separation. The promise not to intermarry was not a prejudice against the people but a commitment to be separated from the world and unto God.

Sabbath. The determination not to buy and sell on the Sabbath was a return to obedience. One day in seven was to be set aside, as God had commanded.

Support. They also promised to support the house of God. This was a commitment to giving their finances, which also was a return to obedience.

Each of these commitments is significant in and of itself. But the people put their commitment in writing, signed it and sealed it before God. They were serious about these things!

The next time you make a commitment to God, make it a contract. Write it out, date it and sign it. Then keep it in your Bible so that periodically you will review it to see how well you are keeping your commitment.

Have you been slack in one of your commitments? Perhaps it is your commitment to read your Bible, to support God's work or to tell others about Jesus. Write a contract, renew your commitment and keep it before God.

AGREED

Nehemiah 12–13, Acts 4:23–37 • *Key Verse: Acts 4:32*

It doesn't take too many percentage points above 50 for an election to be considered a landslide. When the vote totals edge closer to 60 than 50 percent, politicians talk about the mandate they have and how the people have spoken. Really? More than half the voters may have agreed, but not much more than half.

Consider this description of agreement: "All the believers were one in heart and mind" (v. 32). We're not talking a simply majority here, but unanimity of consent that was both felt and known, of heart and mind.

The evidence for this is indisputable. Stronger than a recorded vote is the demonstration of unity that extended to their attitude toward personal possessions. Among the things that can be a source of division within a local church are the issues that relate to material things—such as how the congregation uses it money, what it buys, how much it pays the pastor or which missionaries it supports.

The early church gives us a model of unity we can follow. It did not come about by political maneuvering but by the Word, prayer and the power of the Holy Spirit (v. 31). Those are the things that characterized the activities of the church.

If you want unity in your church, emphasize the Word, prayer and the power of the Holy Spirit.

Unity in your church begins with you. Be in the Word, pray and allow the Spirit to work in your life. Be the first person of unity and see how God can work in your church.

PUBLIC FAITH

Esther 1–2, Acts 5:1–21 • *Acts 5:12–14*

A growing trend in sports is for athletes from opposing teams to gather after the game, kneel and pray. What began as the practice of a few players on one team has spread to other sports, from the ranks of pros down to prep athletes.

A simple act becomes a public confession of faith. Some players refuse to join in, even though they may "respect them" for their faith. Others are drawn to the circle of prayer because they desire a relationship—not just with other athletes, but with Jesus Christ. When they commit themselves to Jesus and join the circle of prayer, they join the people of God as well.

This happened in the Book of Acts too. "The believers used to meet together in Solomon's Colonnade" (v. 12). That was the public arena for them. This simple act became a confession of faith. Yet "no one else dared joined them, even though they were highly regarded by the people" (v. 13). They were respected for what they did. "Nevertheless, more and more men and women believed in the Lord" (v. 14). Others did join as they committed their lives to Jesus.

Our simple acts, done in public, can be used to bring others to Jesus.

Does your commitment to Christ show? Perhaps praying before a meal in a restaurant will be the testimony that touches another. Maybe you can join or lead a group in prayer after a game. Even the regularity of your church attendance can tell others that Jesus matters to you. But remember to follow up your lifestyle with the verbal word of testimony. Help others come to Christ by how you live and what you say.

BREAK THE SILENCE

Esther 3–5, Acts 5:22–42 • *Key Verse: Esther 4:14*

"Silence is golden," but in truth there are times when silence is anything but valuable. In fact, it can be quite costly. Imagine walking by a house and seeing through a window that the family inside is enjoying a quiet evening at home. You walk on in silence, leaving them undisturbed. That is good silence.

But what if you see a fire smoldering on the roof and realize that they are unaware? Would your silence be "golden" or costly?

Esther was in a position to make a difference if she would break the silence and speak, but she feared approaching the king (4:11). She had her excuses. Her uncle Mordecai did not counter all her reasons but laid out before it the price of silence. Her failure to speak out would be costly, costing at the minimum her life as well as that of her family.

Then he said, "And who knows but that you have come to royal position for such a time as this?" (v. 14). With that verbal push from her uncle, Esther began to take the steps that would ultimately spare the life of not only herself and her family but of her people.

We can engage in golden silence and guilty silence. There will be times when we are in the "right place at the right time" and must make a crucial decision: either we speak or remain silent. Far too often we fail. Fearing man, we remain silent when we should fear God more and speak.

When did you last speak to someone about Jesus? Yesterday's reading challenged us to be living testimonies. Today's focuses our attention on what we say. Is there someone who has seen your testimony but now needs to hear it?

DELEGATION

Esther 6–8, Acts 6 • *Key Verses: Acts 6:2–4*

If you want something done, ask a busy person. Why? Because busy people are used to getting things done. Some people never seem to get anything done, while others clip along at jet speed, accomplishing task after task. There is a problem with this, however. Things might get done, but is the person still doing the important things?

The Twelve were very busy men. Their responsibilities included distributing food daily to the widows. That was a good thing to do, but the job had grown so large that two negative things were happening. One is that they were unable to keep up with all the widows who had need. The other is that they were neglecting prayer and the ministry of the Word.

Something had to change. Getting others to help with the work was the solution. Other godly men were enlisted to take over this important work so the Twelve could give their attention to prayer and the ministry of the Word.

There are two things that a pastor cannot delegate to someone else to do: prayer and the ministry of the Word. The principle of delegation remains. Others can do "material" ministries, allowing pastors time for "spiritual" ministries. Both are important, and neither is to be neglected. But while one can be delegated, the other cannot.

What are you doing to allow your pastor to have time for prayer and ministry of the Word? Your "material" ministry allows for his "spiritual" ministry. The time you take is actually time you give.

BOUGHT BY BELIEF

Esther 9–10, Acts 7:1–21 • **Key Verse: Acts 7:5**

An engagement ring is tangible evidence of a promise. Words can be cheap, but the price of a ring placed on the finger carries more weight than just that of the stone. It says, "I will marry you." We like tangible evidences, but it takes more faith to believe when no evidence is given.

God gave great promises to Abraham—a nation, and a land for that nation to occupy. At the time Abraham did not have any children, nor had God given him any land. A promise with no evidence, yet Abraham believed.

In time a son was born. Isaac became the father of Jacob, and Jacob became the father of the 12 patriarchs, and ultimately a great nation resulted. God kept His promise.

But when Abraham died, all he owned of the Promised Land was a grave—and he paid for it himself. Yet he believed God. That is why he bought a burial plot in the land promised to him. He knew that one day the land would be given to him and his descendants. Ultimately God gave the Promised Land to the nation descended from Abraham. God kept His promise.

God still keeps His promises—perhaps not in our timing or according to our wishes, but He does keep them. Sometimes we have material or physical evidence for those promises, but often we do not. What we do have is His Word, which He calls on us to believe, just as Abraham did. The question is never, "Will God do what He says?" but, "Will we believe?"

"God, help me be like Abraham, not expecting or demanding evidences now. Help me believe, trusting You for the 'right now' and the right way to fulfill Your promises to me, Your child."

THE MOST PITIABLE WORSHIPER

Job 1–2, Acts 7:22–43 • *Key Verses: Job 1:20–21*

Worship on Sunday is one thing, but it can be quite a different thing on Monday, especially if things are not going well. On Sundays we gather with other believers to sing, praise, pray and preach. The time together may be uplifting and encouraging. We walk out of the service remembering the words of the psalmist who said, "I rejoiced with those who said to me, 'Let us go to the house of the LORD'" (Ps. 122:1).

But life is not always lived in Sunday-morning experiences. Sometimes it is difficult, and worship seems like something far away, almost inappropriate for the circumstances. If this is true of you, then there is a problem with your understanding of worship, because we are to live lives of worship in the good times and the bad.

Job worshiped in spite of the loss of family, livestock and servants. Four messengers arrived one after another, detailing the marauders who stole and killed, the "fire of God" that had fallen from the sky, and the storm that collapsed the house, killing his children. Job's response is instructive: he worshiped (1:20–21).

When things are going well, it is easy, even natural, to praise God. When things are going so-so, we may still worship, but it is another story to talk about worship on the heels of disaster.

In the *Disciple's Study Bible* it says, "The praiseworthiness of God does not depend on our circumstances. Job praised God not for his circumstances, but for God's unchanging and inherent worth." Job demonstrated that worship centers on God, who He is and what He does, not on man and what he wants.

Can you join Job in worship? Perhaps today you are struggling with difficulties or insurmountable problems. You may feel like a modern-day Job! Whatever the circumstances, praise and worship God.

HEMMED IN

Job 3–4, Acts 7:44–60 • *Key Verse: Job 3:23*

Among the words a child learns first are *no* and *why*—two words that indicate a predisposition to do one's own will and not the will of another. Children learn to say "no" very early. The one-word question comes a little later. The child looks at the parent and asks, "Why?" In essence he is saying, "What you ask does not fit my plans."

Sometimes we ask God the same question, looking toward heaven and saying in our hearts, if not with our lips as well, "Why?" Job did the same thing, although with more than one word. His why questions are spelled out in detail, and in chapter 3 he came as close as he ever would to cursing God. Instead, he asked a series of rhetorical questions.

"Why is life given to a man whose way is hidden, whom God has hedged in?" he asked (v. 23). Tough question! He felt hemmed in, but no longer by God's protection. Instead, he felt hemmed in by trouble. The way was hidden to him, made no sense to him, and no way out was apparent to him. So he asked, "Why?"

Job never would get his question answered. Instead, God demonstrated His glory to Job and he was so affected by it that he repented, regretting that he asked why in the first place (42:6).

At times we all feel hemmed in and wonder why. In those times we must trust that God is sovereign, faithfully in control.

Trust can be difficult, especially when things don't make sense. But they make sense to God. Ask Him to help you trust even when you want to ask why.

DRINKING POISON

Job 5–7, Acts 8:1–25 • *Key Verses: Acts 8:21–23*

Stephen Harnock once observed, "Bitterness is like drinking poison and waiting for the other person to die." It would be comical if it were not so tragically true.

Simon the Sorcerer wanted to do what the apostles were doing, so he offered to buy the giftedness they had from the Holy Spirit. Peter was quick to answer, discounting completely the idea that anyone can buy the gift of God with money.

But Peter saw deeper. He saw that Simon's heart was not right before God. In it was bitterness and captivity to sin.

Why bitterness? Bitterness begins with dislike, and Simon disliked the apostles because they could do what he could not. He disliked them even more when they refused his offer. His bitterness intensified when his way was rejected totally and completely by Peter. This brings us to the core of bitterness—wanting for self what others have and resenting them for having it.

Bitterness is like an unpleasant taste in the mouth, but it is so much deeper than a taste. It comes from within, from the heart. The Bible warns us against allowing bitterness to develop. We can prevent it from taking root when we effectively deal with our pride and covetousness. But as long as we seek to serve self, we provide the seed bed for bitterness to grow.

Ask God to help you determine if there is anyone toward whom you are bitter. If there is, ask for His forgiveness, and make right your relationship with that person.

I OBJECT!

Job 8–10, Acts 8:26–40 • Key Verses: Acts 8:32–33

My family and I walked through the areas at the state fair where young people had brought their livestock for competition. Many of the sheep we saw were not the picturesque ones, round with fluffy white wool, but sheared completely. We watched as some sheep went through the shearing process. They were brought in, sheared and sent out. No word of protest was offered.

Isaiah the prophet described Jesus in that way. Christ stood before His accusers and did not speak a word of defense. He was "'led like a sheep to the slaughter, and as a lamb before the shearer is silent, so he did not open his mouth'" (8:32).

We would protest if accused falsely, like Jesus was. That is what confused the Ethiopian eunuch. He read these verses from Isaiah and did not understand about whom the prophet was talking. God brought Philip to the eunuch. He began with that passage and told him "the good news about Jesus" (v. 35).

It is good news, the best of news, that Jesus would die without objection. He committed no sin nor owed no debt, yet like a sheep to the slaughter, a lamb before the shearer, He stood silently.

The eunuch's response was to receive Christ and identify with Jesus in baptism. He heard and received the good news that Jesus so willingly died that we might live.

We also can live if we receive Christ. It is good that you are reading the Bible, but understand that salvation is not received through good works but by faith in Jesus.

Have you received the Lamb of God as your Savior? He alone can take away the penalty of your sin because He died in your place. If you have not done so, today ask Him to forgive your sins and save you.

WHY?

Job 11–13, Acts 9:1–21 • *Key Verses: Job 13:20–22*

I've often heard people ask, "Is it all right to ask God 'why'?" People ask that question because they want to do just that, to ask God why.

What is the answer? Well, we know that Job did. Not just in this passage but in others he raised the subject. He said, "'He is not a man like me that I might answer him, that we might confront each other in court. If only there were someone to arbitrate between us, to lay his hand upon us both . . . . Then I would speak up without fear of him'" (9:32–33, 35). And most of chapter 3 records Job asking why.

To ask is one thing; to accuse is another. Sometimes the why question is more an accusation than an inquiry. Without a doubt, we are not to be people who accuse God. If our asking is a way of calling God to give an accounting for what He has done, then that is wrong. God does not have to give an answer to us.

So consider why you want to ask God the why question. If it is to get Him to give you a satisfactory answer, then the answer is no, it is not right to ask why. If, on the other hand, you are trying to understand what God is doing so you can learn what He is teaching and accomplish what He wishes, then it is permissible. We may pray, "God, help me to understand," but remember that you are not in a position to demand an answer.

Examine your heart before you ask why. Remember, He is God and you're not. And whether you ask or not, remember to trust Him and obey.

WILLING TO TAKE A RISK

Job 14–16, Acts 9:22–43 • Key Verses: Acts 9:26–27

Friendship is a wonderful gift that we can give to one another, a gift that can build up if given but destroy if withheld. One can only wonder how many people have been lost to the cause of Christ because others withheld the encouragement that comes with friendship.

Saul was a scary figure in the midst of the congregation in Damascus. For one, there was his past reputation, a persecutor of believers. For another, there was his powerful intellect, baffling the Jews by proving that Jesus is the Christ. Even while suspicion ran high, Saul grew more and more powerful.

Then he had to escape those who plotted to kill him. He traveled to Jerusalem and "tried to join the disciples, but they were all afraid of him, not believing that he really was a disciple" (v. 26). They all stayed away from him, except Barnabas. He came alongside Saul, listened to his story and defended him before the apostles. After that Saul was able to stay with the disciples and move about freely, speaking boldly in the name of the Lord. The brothers who feared Saul became his protectors when the Jews tried to kill him.

What brought about the change? The friendship of one man, Barnabas. He was willing to take the risk, to get to know Saul and speak to his defense. Later, Barnabas and Saul were sent by the church at Antioch to be the first missionaries. How different the story of the early church might have been if not for Barnabas!

Look around you at church. Do you see anyone new who needs a friend? Perhaps your greeting and help can make the difference between that person feeling welcomed or not. God only knows the difference you can make if you, like Barnabas, take a risk.

RIGHT OR WRONG?

Job 17–19, Acts 10:1–23 • *Key Verse: Acts 10:15*

Opinions vary as to what is right and what is wrong. We all have our ideas on the subject. The only problem is what we say is right may be wrong, and our wrongs may be right. That's not too reassuring, is it?

Peter definitely had an idea of right and wrong—and was wrong about it. God was preparing him to go to the home of a Gentile named Cornelius, something Peter would consider wrong. God had to convince Peter otherwise and did it with a vision involving what food was acceptable to a man like Peter.

God gave Peter a vision of various animals and instructed him to "kill and eat" (v. 13). He refused. The voice then said to him, "Do not call anything impure that God has made clean" (v. 15). Three times this happened, leaving Peter wondering what was going on. Then there was the knock at the door, men looking for him to take him to Cornelius. Before the vision, Peter would have refused. Now he knew his specific instruction was to go with the men.

What made the difference in Peter's thinking? Knowing God's Word on the matter.

The same thing will make the difference in our thinking. We are not to decide right and wrong on the basis of what we think but on what the Bible teaches.

Learn what the Bible teaches with a submissive heart, surrendering your opinions to the Word. Ask God to help you see things as He sees them, understanding what truly is right and wrong according to Him.

BARRIERS REMOVED

Job 20–21, Acts 10:24–48 • *Key Verse: Acts 10:28*

Often people are divided. At sporting events, fans root for opposing teams. When there is an election, voters choose candidates from opposing political parties. Even at the airport, travelers approaching the ticket counter find a line for first-class passengers and a much longer line for everyone else.

These divisions are acceptable in their own way, but other divisions are not. People are divided by prejudices that may be racial, sexual, cultural or even geographical. One of the sharpest of those in biblical times was the division between Jews and Gentiles.

God addressed this division very directly in a vision for Peter. When Peter was asked to go to the home of Cornelius, a Gentile, God knew he would not go. God had to break down Peter's prejudice. And he got the message—"God has shown me that I should not call any man impure or unclean" (v. 28).

Later Paul would write that Jesus "has destroyed the barrier, the dividing wall of hostility" (Eph. 2:14) and that "there is neither Jew nor Greek, slave nor free, male nor female, for you are all one in Christ Jesus" (Gal. 3:28).

Think again about the Samaritan woman. When Jesus spoke to her, He ignored religious, racial and sexual prejudices along with the disdain others showed her because of her immorality. He ignored these to give her the message of salvation.

We, too, must remove the barriers that keep us from reaching others and fellowshipping with those who are part of the Body of Christ.

Prejudice is a sin that can get deeply ingrained. Sometimes we do not notice that the words or phrases we use, even the jokes we tell, can indicate its presence. Examine your heart and ask God to help you remove all barriers between yourself and others in Christ.

CALLED ON THE CARPET

Job 22–24, Acts 11 • *Key Verse: Acts 11:17*

Reaching across the barriers of prejudice will probably be noticed—and questioned. Staying with the familiar is comfortable; changing is not. If the barriers are long-standing ones, then change is that much harder and that much more resisted.

Peter stepped across the line, in the minds of some, when he went into the home of a Gentile, Cornelius. "The circumcised believers criticized him" (v. 2), and Peter was called on the carpet to explain his actions.

He explained everything to them, vision and all, along with his own reluctance. Then he said, "The Spirit told me to have no hesitation about going with them" (v. 12). He told his critics that the Holy Spirit came on those Gentiles just as He had come on them. Peter concluded by saying, "So if God gave them the same gift as he gave us, who believed in the Lord Jesus Christ, who was I to think that I could oppose God?" (v. 17).

That ended the discussion. Instead of continuing to criticize him, they praised God that even the Gentiles were being given repentance unto life. They realized that the Gospel is for all, not just some.

We need to remember that all people need Jesus, no matter what their race, social standing, morals or anything else. And Jesus can make us one.

"God, help me examine my heart and show me if there are any others toward whom I harbor wrong feelings. May I see all as needing Jesus and see all who know Jesus as my brothers and sisters in Christ."

CONTINUED FAITH

Job 25–27, Acts 12 • *Key Verses: Job 27:2–4*

Three of the easiest words to utter are, "I give up." Often they are said when expectations are not met; you expected something, didn't get it, tried, but finally gave up. That happens with things like service at a restaurant, or information on a software problem, or with trying to get something repaired. But it should never be said in regard to God.

If ever someone had reason to say regarding God, "I give up," it would have been Job. But he did not. Instead he said, "As surely as God lives . . ." (27:2). Though difficult to utter, those words are among the most important ones a person can ever say. They comprise the most solemn oath a person can make, and in Job's case demonstrated his continued faith despite his circumstances.

Job could have given up. He even mentioned the bitterness that he had tasted, the justice he had been denied—both from God. Still, though, he began his statements with an oath that called upon God. Even in the hardest of circumstances, Job's faith in God continued.

Faith is easier when things are going well. We more readily acknowledge God in our words when we can see His blessing on us. But faith is not for just the good times; it's for all times.

Is your faith staying strong all the time, or does it ebb and flow like the tide, depending on how good things seem to be going? God is good, all the time. And our faith in Him is to be strong, all the time.

WISDOM'S BEGINNING

Job 28–29, Acts 13:1–25 • Key Verse: Job 29:28

I heard about a road in Africa that had a very difficult curve in it. What made the curve so challenging was the fact that you really didn't see how hard it was until you were right on it. A series of warning signs was posted but ignored. It just didn't look like that big of a deal until it was too late. Even the last of the warning signs did not slow some drivers, though it said, "You've been warned!"

A similar statement is found several times in the Bible that links the "fear of the Lord" with wisdom. In essence it says, "You've been told!"

The wisdom the Bible talks about is not the same as a high SAT score or straight A's in school. It is skill in living. The person who can take the instruction found in God's Word and apply it to his life is a wise person.

Wisdom is then linked with fear of the Lord. This kind of fear does not result in living in terror of God but having a reverence for Him. When we truly revere Him, we submit to Him and obey His commands. We should fear being irreverent or disobedient, but not in a way that sends us cowering in the corners, hiding from God. Biblical fear is responding obediently to God, choosing to do what He wants.

"God, help me to recognize my need to properly fear You. May I then see that my life, when it is one of obedience, is one of wisdom."

THE EYE COVENANT

Job 30–31, Acts 13:26–52 • *Key Verse: Job 31:1*

You have heard the old saying, "Beauty is in the eye of the beholder." Perhaps an appropriate updated version would be, "Beauty is too often in the eye of the beholder." We live in a visually stimulating age. Gone the way of dinosaurs are black-and-white photographs. Today, graphics and photos are full-color, eye-catching and often sexy.

Mankind has always struggled with lust, especially lust of the eyes. A beautiful woman named Bathsheba caught David's eye, and that first glance became a lustful gaze. Immorality was the result. Jesus condemned lust in the Sermon on the Mount, saying the person who lusts is committing adultery in his heart (Matt. 5:28).

As Job wrote in his own defense, listing sins he knew he didn't commit, he began by mentioning what he had done to avoid lustful looking. He made a covenant with his eyes "not to look lustfully at a girl." While some say, "What's the harm in looking?" Job knew that it was wrong. The look can set the hook, and it's downhill from there.

Sex sells, so ads are full of sensual images. Television programs and movies are full of sexual themes. Clothes are made to be enticing. We cannot escape seductive images, but we can covenant not to look at them.

Are you careful about what you view? Job's words are forceful for men especially. When your eye strays for a second look, remember what Job said. And determine right now to enter into the same covenant.

THE MODEL MISSION STATEMENT

Job 32–33, Acts 14 • Key Verses: Acts 14:21–23

A recent business trend has been that of writing a mission statement—a concise paragraph stating in a memorable way the purpose of a business or organization. Added to it might be some objectives and an explanation of how those objectives will be accomplished. Churches also use written mission statements as a way of focusing their efforts. The difference is that a church should draw all these things from the Bible.

Acts 14:21–23 could provide the framework for a church's mission statement. Luke's report on the ministry of Paul and Barnabas highlights three crucial aspects of their work. They were:

1. Evangelizing. "They . . . won a large number of disciples" (v. 21).

2. Edifying. ". . . strengthening the disciples and encouraging them to remain true to the faith" (v. 22).

3. Establishing. "Paul and Barnabas appointed elders for them in each church and, with prayer and fasting, committed them to the Lord" (v. 23).

What they did then, we must do now. These three objectives must be central to every church's mission. We need to be reaching people for Jesus, discipling them and helping the local church develop. There are other things to consider, but without a doubt these are core commitments for the church.

If your church is writing a mission statement, or already has one, are these three items incorporated in it? And are you involved in seeing these objectives accomplished?

Evaluate what you are doing. If you and your church are not seeking to accomplish these objectives, commit today to making the needed changes so that you are on God's mission.

OLD HABITS DIE HARD

Job 34–35, Acts 15:1–21 • *Key Verse: Acts 15:9*

Old habits die hard, but it seems at times as if old habits hardly die. Habits are called such for good reason—they are so ingrained that we do them without thinking. Sometimes a habit is not a matter of what we do but what we think.

God showed Peter that he was to go to the house of Cornelius, even though it meant going into the home of a Gentile. Avoiding contact with Gentiles was one of those habits that would die hard, or hardly die, so Peter had to explain his actions (Acts 11:1–18).

Even after acknowledging that it was of God that Gentiles were granted repentance unto life (11:18), the church struggled with accepting Gentiles into their midst. At the meeting in Jerusalem held to discuss the situation, Peter said that God "made no distinction between us and them, for he purified their hearts by faith" (15:9). He also pointed out that their attempts to put "a yoke" on the necks of the Gentiles was actually a way of putting God to the test. Still, it remained a problem, one Paul later would address as he wrote of the oneness we have in Christ (see Eph. 2:14).

Of all people, we in the Body of Christ should accept all others, regardless of race, social standing, nationality or finances. As the saying goes, the ground at the foot of Christ's cross is level, so no one is above anyone else.

In your heart do you accept all others who know Christ as your brother or sister? If you struggle with prejudice, ask Jesus to help you see people as He sees them. He does not classify us by color.

WHERE SELDOM IS HEARD . . .

Job 36–37, Acts 15:22–41 • *Key Verse: Acts 15:32*

Can you finish this line from an old song: "Where seldom is heard…"?
The answer is "a discouraging word." The song, "Home on the
Range," paints a picture of an idyllic place where even the words said
are seldom discouraging. If only song lyrics and reality matched! Far
too often home, work, school and even church are places where seldom is heard an encouraging word. We know how much we appreciate encouraging words; the question to consider is if our own words
are encouraging.

The early church had a problem. They met, discussed it and handed
down a decision that was then communicated to the churches by a
hand-carried letter. It was sent with Paul and Barnabas, who were
accompanied by Judas and Silas. Sometimes problems in a church are
due to decisions—who makes them, how they are made or what they
are. This one had the potential of stirring the issue rather than settling it. What tipped the scales toward settling it were the encouraging words that were spoken.

Luke called it an "encouraging message" (v. 31). Also, Judas and Silas
"said much to encourage and strengthen the brothers" (v. 32). The
response of the church was to send off the brothers "with the blessing
of peace" (v. 33).

Instead of merely dismissing the difficulty, church leaders resolved it,
with encouraging words, and the church was strengthened and
blessed. Now that's an encouraging word!

*Think about the words you say, especially when there is a disagreement.
Next time, use encouraging words, ones that will build up, not tear
down. Aim to not only settle the issue but to do so in a way that
strengthens those involved.*

SENSITIVE?

Job 38–40, Acts 16:1–21 • Key Verses: Acts 16:9–10

A sure way to end an argument is to say, "I believe it is God's will." Who can argue with that? Even Peter used it when he said in his defense, "Who was I to think that I could oppose God?" (Acts 11:17).

Sensitivity to the leading of God in our lives is important. Paul and those traveling with him demonstrated such in Acts 16:6–10. In those verses we find these phrases: "kept by the Holy Spirit from preaching," "the Spirit of Jesus would not allow them to" and "concluding that God had called us." Paul obviously was attuned spiritually to the unseen reality of God's moving in his life. And he was obedient; he did what he believed God wanted him to do.

The verses do not say he followed his feelings. One of the dangers of the spiritual life is confusing feelings with the leading of the Spirit. There is a huge difference—one is right, the other wrong. Discerning the difference should be a significant concern to us.

Feelings can often lead us to accomplish our will, while leading directs us to God's will. Perhaps we best begin sorting feelings from leadings by honestly examining our motivation. Upon close review, it may become evident that what we are calling God's will is actually our want. Yes, there can be times when what we want is God's will as well. Yet this may be a significant test, helping us discern the difference between His will and our wants.

"God, help me not only to pray, 'Not my will but Thine,' but also to know clearly the difference."

OOPS!

Job 41–42, Acts 16:22–40 • *Key Verses: Job 42:5–6*

Have you ever wished you could take back what you said? Probably the question isn't if you ever did that but how often you have—or how recently! Some of us have "foot-shaped mouths," the result from too often putting our foot in our mouth.

That may have been how Job felt when he said, "I despise myself" (42:6). He wished he could take it back. Not only did he despise himself, but he also repented "in dust and ashes." That indicates more than a bit of embarrassment.

What brought him to this point of humility was the response to his questioning of God. He had spoken presumptuous words, ones that were more than a searching for reasons behind his suffering. They were directed to God.

God had heard and He responded, but not with answers to Job's questions. Instead, God fired back a sequence of unanswerable questions, questions that made Job realize how great God is and how insignificant in comparison is man. "Surely I spoke of things I did not understand, things too wonderful for me to know," Job said (v. 3). No wonder he despised himself and repented in such a dramatic fashion.

There are times we want to ask God why? Trying to make sense of the struggles in life is a natural response. We err, though, when our questioning turns into demanding of God an answer. We, the created ones, have no right to call on the Creator to account for His actions.

There will be times when we want to ask God why. Ask God to help you be only a seeker, one trying to understand. Pray for the grace and wisdom needed to keep from questioning God about His actions, His motives and His plans.

CARRY YOUR BIBLE

Psalms 1–3, Acts 17:1–15 • Key Verse: Acts 17:11

In the church I attended as a young person we had a name for the sound of Bible pages turning. So many people had the same Bible that the collective rustling sound was called "the Scofield shuffle." Instead of the text, the pastor could have announced the page number!

Appearances can be deceiving. Not everyone who has a Bible reads it or obeys it. Still, people using their Bibles in church can indicate the spiritual quality of a congregation. If the people do not see the need for bringing their Bibles or have no desire to do so, it undoubtedly is a weak church.

Many churches have a class called "Berean." Some even choose that name for their church. It is an often-used name because of the spiritual quality of the believers in Berea. "They received the message with great eagerness and examined the Scriptures every day to see if what Paul said was true" (v. 11). Today we might say, "They carried and used their Bibles!" But there was more to it than that. They looked carefully at the Word, following the messages of Paul and verifying what he preached. And they did this daily.

To be spiritually strong, we must read, learn and live the Word. To be a strong church, the same is necessary. Use your Bible!

Ask God to help you keep up the practice of reading His Word daily. Pray also that as you read you will learn, and that you will put into practice what you learn.

THE SOFT SIDE OF A BOARD

Psalms 4–6, Acts 17:16–34 • *Key Verse: Psalm 4:8*

When he wanted to let me know how little trouble he had sleeping, a friend would say, "I could sleep on the soft side of a board." For others, though, the agony of insomnia is real. We can have trouble both falling and staying asleep, especially when wrestling with a problem. Difficulties can deny us a good night of rest.

Then we read a verse like Psalm 4:8: "I will lie down and sleep in peace." "Well, good for David," we say. "It must be nice to be king, having all your needs met, living in the lap of luxury, snoozing away the night."

But then we look closer. Verse 1 says, "Give me relief from my distress." This was not a time of calm in David's life. Perhaps it was when he was fleeing from his own son, Absalom. Whatever it was, David's distress did not disrupt his sleep—and therein lies the challenge for us.

Why do we let stress rob us of our rest? Sleep aids may only mask the pain. For David, the only "sleeping pill" was prayer. Read this psalm again carefully. Look for the words *prayer, trust, joy, gladness* and *peace*. David's sleep came as he rested not on the best mattress in the kingdom, but in God, "for you alone, O LORD, make me dwell in safety" (v. 8).

The next time you are struggling to sleep, read Psalm 4 and ask God to help you turn over your problems to Him.

LONG-TIME FRIENDS, SHORT-TIME ACQUAINTANCES

Psalms 7–9, Acts 18 • *Key Verse: Psalm 9:10*

To the casual observer, the wedding party looked typical. The bride wore white; her groom stood tall next to her. The bridal party had the usual complement of bridesmaids, groomsmen, a matron of honor, best man, flower girl and ring bearer. But there was an interesting difference—nearly everyone in the group was a close relative.

Over the years the bride and groom had observed that people eventually lose track of their "close" friends from college days, but one will always have his family. So they chose to make their wedding a family affair. Friends may come and go, they reasoned, but family stays.

As you think of former friends, perhaps ones that left you feeling deserted, consider this praise David gave to God: "You, LORD, have never forsaken those who seek you" (9:10). Knowing that God would be his forever friend, David also wrote, "Those who know your name will trust in you." In God's faithfulness we find comfort, and since He never forsakes us, we can trust in Him.

David wrote those words in a time of difficulty. He recognized that the Lord is a refuge, a stronghold in times of trouble, and in those times his trust was in God. Is yours?

Is there some difficulty in your life? Do you feel alone? Remember, God will never forsake you. Ask Him to help you experience the peace that comes when you truly trust in Him.

WHO ARE YOU?

Psalms 10–12, Acts 19:1–20 • *Key Verse: Acts 19:15*

If you are a "nominal Christian"—that is, you live the Christian life in name only—the devil probably will not bother you much. Why should he? You are little or no threat to him. But when you determine to be a fully devoted follower of Christ, living out the truth of God, seeking to impact others with the Gospel message, then brace yourself. You will be known.

If it weren't for the reality of demonic opposition, this account would almost be humorous. Paul's ministry in Ephesus included those who tried to copy him. Like him, they wanted to drive out evil spirits and tried to do so by invoking the name of Jesus. "In the name of Jesus, whom Paul preaches," they would say (v. 13).

Well, one day the sons of Sceva got more than they bargained for. The demons answered them, saying, "Jesus I know, and I know about Paul, but who are you?" (v. 15). Then they were literally beaten up by the possessed man.

Notice whom the demons knew or knew about. They knew Jesus and knew about Paul. But Sceva's sons were unknown to them. The demons did not know those who were not really seeking to serve Christ.

Sometimes we wonder if anyone notices what we do for Christ. Rejoice that God knows! And stick close to Him, because it may be that some of the attention that comes your way may challenge you to the core of your commitment.

"Father, help me stay close to You and draw from You the strength I need to resist the devil. May the shield of faith extinguish all the flaming arrows of the evil one."

ADMIT ONE

Psalms 13–15, Acts 19:21–41 • Key Verse: Psalm 15:1

Two friends who minister in Asia have had special opportunities to meet visiting dignitaries. A few years ago when Prince Charles was visiting the country, the wife received an invitation to a reception. More recently it was the husband's turn when he was invited to a dinner given for President Clinton.

Neither event was "open for the public." Both required a special invitation and security clearance, more so with the second than the first. There were other U.S. citizens in the country, but the door was open only to certain ones.

David asked, "LORD, who may dwell in your sanctuary?" While there were many in Israel, he realized that close fellowship with God was open only to certain ones. Having asked the question, he then answered it. The rest of the psalm is a description of a godly person. Read the psalm again and notice the following:

Their walk is blameless (v. 2).

The words are truthful (v. 2).

They respect and honor those who fear God (v. 4).

They keep their word (v. 4).

They help others with their money and do not accept bribes (v. 5).

The godly person is then described as being very stable, "never shaken" (v. 5).

Our salvation is not based on what we do. We are saved through faith in Jesus. But how we live as a disciple does affect the closeness of our fellowship with God. The godly person enjoys the closest fellowship and experiences a stability that God gives to those whose lives match the one described in Psalm 15.

Do you exhibit the traits of a godly person? Ask God to help you evaluate your walk, your words, whom you honor and your attitude toward money.

GRAVE ROBBER

Psalms 16–17, Acts 20:1–16 • Key Verse: Psalm 16:10

Archeologists sometimes uncover less than they hope for when digging because someone else got there first—namely, grave robbers. Artifacts that can help us understand past civilizations may be disturbed or the burial site looted. Both groups seek the items made with precious metals or gemstones, but for different reasons.

In Psalm 16 we read about a type of grave robber. This one robs the grave of death itself. David believed that even death could not rob him of life because eternal life is found in God.

The ultimate fulfillment of Psalm 16:10 was in Christ. Note the carefulness of the wording. "You will not abandon me to the grave." It does not say, "death." Jesus did die, but He was not abandoned to the grave.

"Nor will you let your Holy One see decay." Consider this carefully. With death comes decay—unless the grave is robbed, by God. God robbed the grave of Jesus not with crowbars, shovels and picks but by His awesome Resurrection power. Jesus truly died, but He did not remain dead. Jesus truly lives, bodily! The promise of Psalm 16 was fulfilled in every aspect when Jesus arose.

Unless Jesus returns first, you will die. Your body will be in a grave, and one day that grave will be robbed—of death. "The dead in Christ will rise first," Paul said (1 Thess. 4:16).

Jesus has conquered death and sin. If you have received Him as Savior, rest assured that life on this earth is temporary and that God will give you permanent life with Him. Thank God now for the wonderful gift of eternal life.

HYPOCRISY IS SKIN DEEP

Psalms 18–19, Acts 20:17–38 • Key Verse: Psalm 19:14

Ever wonder what another person is thinking? We may try to figure it out by what he does or how he looks, but the best thing is to listen to what he says—or at least you would think so. The fact is, someone may say one thing but not appear to mean it. We prefer that what a person thinks in his heart is the same as what he says. Anything else is hypocrisy, which is skin deep. Integrity comes from the depths of the heart.

To develop integrity begin with the prayer of Psalm 19:14: "May the words of my mouth and the meditation of my heart be pleasing in your sight, O LORD, my Rock and my Redeemer." Think about how this prayer, lived out, would keep you from hypocrisy and make you a person of integrity.

First, God knows when your words and your heart match and when they don't. He wants both to be the same; anything else is unacceptable to Him. Second, a person of integrity is the same on the inside as on the outside. Third, when we please God, our words and meditations will match. And since we want to please God all the time, our words and meditations will match all the time. The result will be integrity before God and man. And God will be pleased.

So, what are you thinking? Does it match what you are saying?

Integrity is an important character trait for the child of God. Are you known as a person of integrity? Begin with the prayer of Psalm 19, and live these words.

TORN AWAY

Psalms 20–22, Acts 21:1–17 • *Key Verse: Acts 21:1*

"And when they had sung a hymn, they went out," our pastor would say as the communion service concluded. And then we would sing the hymn "Blest Be the Tie That Binds." Nothing more clearly communicates our oneness in Christ as the Lord's Supper. Sadly, though, the family of God at times appears dysfunctional, even splintered.

The closeness Paul had with the church at Ephesus was indicated by the tears, hugs, kisses and grief evident as they accompanied him to the ship (Acts 20:37–38). Emotions ran high. The opening verse of the next chapter paints a powerful word picture: "After we had torn ourselves away from them . . . ."

Torn. Like two things glued together and then ripped apart. The separation is difficult, and the tearing is not clean as bits of pieces, held fast by the glue, are ripped and remain attached. Paul's break from the Ephesians was not a clean one. Their hearts were so attached to one another that saying good-bye was extremely painful.

It can be painful just to read about it. It's painful as we think of the agony the church felt knowing they would never see Paul again. It's also painful if it reminds us of the final farewells we've had to make.

And then there is a third kind of pain—the pain of never expecting an emotional farewell because our relationships with others are already fractured.

Are you experiencing close fellowship, or are your relationships broken? Jesus wants oneness in His Body, the Church. Are you a promoter or destroyer?

GOD'S WELFARE PROGRAM

Psalms 23–25, Acts 21:18–40 • *Key Verse: Psalm 23:1*

How much more change can we take? We have information overload, wireless communication that reaches everywhere and unbelievable stress. And the only change on the horizon is more change of the same kind—more information, expanded communication, all taking its emotional toil. What used to be the promise of the future causes us sometimes to brace ourselves, wondering how we will find our way through the maze.

David said, "The LORD is my shepherd." Silencing the incessant ring of the cell phone, slowing the pace of microprocessors, filtering out the Internet downloads is this calming, comforting, memorable statement. This is God's program for our welfare.

The Lord . . . none other than God Himself

is . . . a present, on-going reality

my . . . first-person singular, personal, possessive, mine

Shepherd . . . one who cares for, provides for and protects.

Say it aloud: "The Lord is my Shepherd." Each part carries special meaning, so say it repeatedly, changing the emphasis. "THE LORD is my shepherd." "The Lord is MY shepherd." "The Lord is my SHEPHERD." No matter which part is emphasized, the blessing is superb. And when all the parts are emphasized, we then experience God's welfare program: He shepherds us.

The cell phone will still ring, the information will still bombard us, the pace will be warp speed. But in the midst of it all, the child of God can stand calmly knowing that God cares, provides, protects. The "mantra" for survival is thousands of years old—"The Lord is my shepherd."

Say this truth slowly and let each part sink in. Then thank God. With the assurance that the Lord is your shepherd, rest in that truth.

THE BLESSING OF A BLAMELESS LIFE

Psalms 26–28, Acts 22 • Key Verses: Psalm 26:2–3

A candidate stepped out of the race and another stepped in to take his place. What was called a battle of titans now took on a different flavor. A relatively unknown candidate was now on the ballot against the well-known one. Unfair? Not really, the political analysts speculated. In fact, it became a much more difficult campaign for the well-known person. You see, there was plenty of mud to sling about the previous opponent, but nothing bad was known about the newcomer. Oh, the value of a blameless life when in a race for office!

Of far greater value is the blessing of a life that is considered blameless by God. David knew that blessing when he wrote this psalm. He even invited examination by the deity Himself. His actions, he was confident, would withstand the scrutiny.

The list in Psalm 26:4–8 is not exhaustive but is representative of the actions found—or not found—in the blameless life. They are good to review, reflect upon, remember and emulate. We should desire to be blameless in the sight of God and man. Lists like this help us evaluate ourselves.

Of course, David was not without sin. But the intent of his heart was to do the will of God, whom he trusted without wavering.

We do sin, but our lives must be focused on living to please God. Make no excuses. Repent. Change. Seek to live a blameless life.

If you were running for office, what mud would your opponent find to sling at you? When you answer that question, you will have a list of the areas in which you are not blameless. Determine to remove all such things from your life.

A CLEAR CONSCIENCE

Psalms 29–30, Acts 23:1–15 • *Key Verse: Acts 23:1*

Similar to the proverbial "satisfaction of a job well done" is the experience of being able "to look them straight in the eye." There is something about unblinking eye contact that communicates both truthfulness and determination. When we know we are right, we will stand up straight, look the other person in the eye and say, "I know I am right." To do that in regard to our job or payments made or obligations kept is important, but all of these pale in comparison to being able to say, "I have fulfilled my duty to God."

Paul did all of the above. He looked his accusers, the Sanhedrin, in the eye and said, with truthfulness and determination, "I have fulfilled my duty to God in all good conscience to this day" (v. 1). He knew he had done right, and not even the authority of this group would make him back down.

Often we look at this verse and think in terms of the confrontation between Paul and his accusers but overlook the insight it gives into Paul's character. He knew he had done what God wanted—and could look anyone straight in the eye and say so. His conscience was clear before God and man. It was the testimony of what truly was "a life well lived."

Knowing and doing the will of God is the great aspiration of a Christian's life, but far too often we just fit it in around what we want to do instead. If you were put on the defensive like Paul, what statement could you make? Do you live in such a way that you could say, "I have fulfilled my duty to God"?

THE PATH

Psalms 31–32, Acts 23:16–35 • Key Verse: Psalm 32:5

Someone once said, "Better the world on the shoulder like Atlas, than God's hand on the heart like David." This statement was in reference to Psalm 32:4, where David wrote, "Your hand was heavy upon me." He described that experience with words of pain—bones wasting away, groaning all day long, strength sapped. All of these phrases contrast sharply with the opening verses of the psalm, which describe the pleasure of forgiveness. David could write personally about both the pleasure and the pain. He also could write of the path that takes one from God's heavy hand to His blessing.

David had sinned, covered it up and experienced the pain that results. God sent His prophet Nathan to confront David and put him on the path to forgiveness. David took the needed steps. He acknowledged his sin to God.

We, too, must admit our sins to ourselves and to God. David confessed his transgressions, which goes beyond saying, "Yeah, I did wrong," to saying, "I see that I sinned." There is a difference in attitude between admission and confession. The difference is seen especially in the outcome. God forgives the one who truly confesses.

To the reader David says, "Do not be like the horse or the mule, which have no understanding" (v. 9). To state it bluntly, "Don't be like a dumb animal." At times God does put the bit and bridle in our mouths, but it is far better to heed His Word than wait for His rebuke. Choose to take the path that takes you out of the pain of unforgiven sin and returns you to the pleasure of forgiveness.

David hid his sin for a long time, a time he described in painful terms. Are you experiencing God's heavy hand upon you? Right now you can confess your sin, receive forgiveness and know again the pleasure of forgiveness.

EXTERNAL INFLUENCES

Psalms 33–34, Acts 24 • *Key Verse: Acts 24:16*

There is nothing like seeing a highway patrolman in the rearview mirror to get a person to drive the speed limit—or even a few miles under, just in case the speedometer is off a bit. When the internal moral compass is off a few degrees, an external influence, such as the sight of a patrol car, can set us straight again. God has given us "influencers" that can keep us doing right. Paul mentioned them in his defense before Felix.

"I strive always to keep my conscience clear before God and man," he said (v. 16). Before that he named the things that kept him on track to a clear conscience. He worshiped God, living his life in response to Him. Who God is, what He says and what He does affected Paul's life. He believed God's Word. "I believe everything that agrees with the Law and that is written in the Prophets," Paul said (v. 14). His was not a vague spirituality, but a commitment to living out biblical truth. And he had an eternal perspective. There is more to life than this world. There is a resurrection of both the righteous and the wicked. Knowing this also affected the way Paul lived.

His worship of God, belief in the Word and eternal perspective kept Paul on the right track. This trio of "influencers" needs to be ingrained in us as well and affect the way we live.

What keeps you from getting off track? Each of the influences that Paul mentioned is powerful, but together they are even more potent. Worship God. Live His Word. Think of eternity.

TOPICS OF CONVERSATION

Psalms 35–36, Acts 25 • *Key Verse: Psalm 35:28*

Weather probably tops the list, followed by sports and perhaps something in the news as typical topics of conversation. It's so easy to bring up these subjects. But do we really need another person to verify that it is hot today?

If these three are probably among the most common topics of conversation, what might be toward the bottom of the list? Our failures would probably make that list. Not too often do we bring them up in a conversation. "Let me tell you about how I messed up yesterday" is not an oft-used conversation starter. Also toward the bottom of the list might be these two: God's righteousness and praise.

David said, "My tongue will speak of your righteousness and of your praises all day long" (35:28). Does that mean David never commented on the weather or talked about current events? No, but it does mean that the subjects of God's righteousness and praise were not absent from his conversation, as they are often missing from ours. We can go days without praising God and telling others about Him. Here's how to change that:

1. Read the Bible, especially the Psalms, where we so often find God praised.

2. Make a conscious effort to remember not only what you have read but what you have experienced of God's goodness and greatness.

3. Repeat these things to others. Look for opportunities to speak of God's righteousness and praise.

Take this as an assignment for today. Decide on one specific thing about God or something to praise Him for, and determine to tell that to at least one person you talk to today.

SHORT AND TO THE POINT

Psalms 37–39, Acts 26 • *Key Verses: Psalm 37:3–5*

"Don't beat around the bush—get to the point" is the sentiment of some of us. We prefer concise, straight answers, not wordy explanations or instructions.

David got right to the point in Psalm 37. "Trust in the LORD" (v. 3). "Delight yourself in the LORD" (v. 4). "Commit your way to the LORD" (v. 5). "Be still before the LORD" (v. 7). In a beautiful simplicity, these statements say all we need to know and do.

Trust. Whatever our situation or circumstances, we need to have an abiding confidence in God.

Delight. Our heart's affections need to be set on the Lord, learning to find our joy and delight in Him.

Commit. We need to determine that our life will be lived the way He wants it lived.

Be still. It is almost impossible to hear God while running, especially with the noise and confusion that so often crowds in on us. We need the still times.

Could more be said about these things? Of course. Occasionally we need the point driven home, explained, illustrated and applied.

Yet there remains in the simplicity of these statements straightforward communication that catches our eyes, our ears and hopefully our minds and hearts so that we trust, delight, commit and remain still, experiencing the blessing of God.

Read the rest of Psalm 37. What other phrases like these catch your attention? Highlight or underline them in your Bible.

DEPRESSION RELIEF

Psalms 40–42, Acts 27:1–26 • *Key Verse: Psalm 42:5*

Depression has been called "the common cold of the mind." Many people experience it in varying degrees; some are only mildly affected on occasion, while others are caught in a downward spiral of increasing hopelessness. Whereas some things can be fixed quite easily, a downcast soul resists the quick fix. Yet we must never lose sight of the fact that there is hope.

The psalmist described such times as making him feel like a deer panting for water, desperately needing it. His food had been his tears, and even his memories of worship had almost a taunting effect as he remembered how it used to be. Notice what he did to address and change his situation.

First, he asked himself why he was downcast. When we know why, we can deal with the cause and not just experience the effect.

Second, he did remember—not just the good days past, but he remembered God. He focused his mind to dwell on God, to hear His songs in the night.

Third, he put his hope in God, a hope so certain that he knew the day would come when he would "yet praise him" (42:5).

The difficult days do come, the times when our soul feels parched. The cause may be complex and the cure evasive, but don't lose hope. Think through why, remember God, and determine to place your hope completely, without wavering, in God.

The praise song from this psalm is a beautiful reminder of why we should turn to God when feeling downcast. Perhaps today you need to do that. Ask God to help you understand why you are downcast, remember Him, and put your trust in Him alone.

WHEN GOD SLEEPS

Psalms 43–45, Acts 27:27–44 • Key Verses: Psalm 44:23–24

Nothing is quite as unsettling as the phone ringing in the middle of the night. You pick up the receiver, hoping it is a wrong number, irritated if it is, angered if it's a prank, but anxious as its sound jars you from your sleep. Remember the times you have been on the other end of those calls, when you were the one dialing a family member or friend because you needed them right then? Perhaps you even whispered, "Wake up, please wake up," as the phone was ringing. "Wake up. I need you."

There was a time when Israel felt as if God were asleep and they needed Him. The cry of the people was, "Awake, O Lord! Why do you sleep? Rouse yourself! Do not reject us forever" (44:23). It was a difficult time for them, not one that made sense in any respect, and it seemed that God was sleeping.

Now, God does not sleep. The Bible tells us that (Ps. 121:4). Still, there are times when it feels like He does, times when we want to rouse Him, like the ringing phone does us.

It's easy to read the Psalms and focus on the praises, skipping over the pains. In the Psalms we find the full range of human emotion, the highs and the lows. This psalm is written from the depths. The people felt rejected, disgraced—for no apparent reason. It felt like God had gone asleep.

Yet their hope did not waver. They continued to cry out to Him, the One who would redeem them because of His unfailing love.

In the dark times we may lack light to see our way clearly. The eyes of faith, though, will always be fixed on God. Pray that He will help you see Him clearly. Trust in His unfailing love even in the most difficult of times.

HITTING THE PAUSE BUTTON

Psalms 46–48, Acts 28 • *Key Verse: Psalm 46:10*

"Fast" and "faster" describe life today. Fast food picked up at the drive-through window. Computer processors and increased bandwidth for Internet access so information can flow even faster. Even our suitcases have wheels. Our lives are stuck on fast forward.

God says, "Be still."

"Is He kidding? Me, be still? Not with my schedule!"

We are on a mad dash, moving too quickly for our own good, particularly our own spiritual good. We want Him to be for us "our refuge and strength, an ever-present help in trouble" (46:1), like one of those flat tire repair kits where you can plug the leak and inflate the tire with an aerosol spray can. No jack, no lug wrench, no wrestling a tire off, just a fast fix. If only God were like that—convenient, accessible, requiring no dirtying of the hands, quickly fixing the flats so we can keep on speeding down the road.

"Be still," He says, and for good reason—"and know that I am God" (v. 10).

You may recognize your neighbor because you see his face as you drive by, but you will not really know him until you stop, get out of the car and spend time with him. Relationships are not built by a wave but a handshake, not by running past but by stopping to talk. What is true about getting to know our neighbor is true about getting to know God.

Do you take time to be still? Daily Bible reading, devotions and individual and corporate worship all require time and flourish as we are still. Be still. Get to know God better.

A HEALTHY SELF-IMAGE

Psalms 49–50, Romans 1 • *Key Verse: Romans 1:1*

These days, people never tire debating the importance of our self-image. We are told to understand what formed our self-image, to consider how as parents we shape a child's self-image, to help others with their self-image, to be concerned whether or not we have a healthy self-image . . . and the list goes on.

How do you view yourself? Now compare your self-image to how Paul viewed himself. He viewed himself as a servant—literally, a slave. He belonged without reservation to Jesus. He viewed himself as an apostle, one who had been sent. His life's work was to do what God sent him to accomplish as one appointed by God. He viewed himself as set apart specifically for the ministry of the Gospel, the good news of salvation in Jesus.

How he viewed himself affected what he did. Viewing himself as a servant affected his attitude toward God and others. What he did and why he did it was affected by understanding himself as one sent. Being set apart affected his aspirations, what he hoped to accomplish.

So with all this talk of self-image, we need to view ourselves like Paul, who saw himself from God's perspective. God formed his self-image. Accepting what God wanted in his life enabled Paul to truly be what God wanted him to be.

Do you see yourself as a servant, sent and set apart? The temptation is to be in control of your own life when instead you need to recognize that Jesus is Lord. Ask God to help you be what He wants you to be.

ROBBED

Psalms 51–53, Romans 2 • *Key Verse: Psalm 51:12*

We have a constitutionally guaranteed right to the pursuit of happiness. Notice, however, that the right is not to happiness but to the pursuit of it. Many people seem to miss that fine line of distinction. They live as if happiness is a right and nothing should ever stand in the way of their having it.

What God gives us is not temporary happiness, something dependent upon the current situation, experiences, possessions, activities or feelings. He gives us joy, an abiding inner sense of well-being that is not dependent upon anything other than our relationship with Him. The biggest difference between happiness and joy is that happiness is temporary and dependent on other things, while joy is permanent, coming from our relationship with God. The one comes and goes while the other stays—unless we allow ourselves to be robbed of our joy.

David was robbed and wanted his joy restored. The robber was himself—specifically, his sin. Covering up his sin instead of confessing it brought pain into his life, the result of God at work bringing David to the point of repentance.

Psalm 51 is David's prayer of repentance. Finally, he confessed. Now he would find relief and joy.

Joy is not a right but a blessing. It is not fleeting like happiness, but we can be robbed of it. Joy can be restored, however, when we repent before God, crying out like David, "Restore to me the joy of your salvation" (v. 12).

Do you have joy? If something in your life has robbed you of it, follow the example of David. Read again Psalm 51, praying it as your own prayer before God.

LOSING WEIGHT

Psalms 54–56, Romans 3 • *Key Verse: Psalm 55:22*

Disappointments, difficulties and the pains of life can weigh heavily upon us. That is why we use the word *burden* to describe them. Psalm 55 is the prayer of a burdened man, one that is written for our benefit.

David's burdens included the especially painful one of verses 12 and 13. His close friend with whom he had worshiped had become his enemy. It may have been Ahithophel, grandfather of Bathsheba, who joined the rebellion of Absalom. Not only did David fear the effective counsel Ahithophel could give against him, but he also felt the pain of a lost friendship.

The burdens were heavy ones, each capable of feeling weighty alone. Together, they were more than enough for any man to bear.

As much as we might want to just dump our difficulties and escape, that isn't an option. David tells us how to lose the weight. "Cast your cares on the LORD" (v. 22). God's plan does not allow for us to be destroyed but to be sustained. But we must do our part; we must lay our burden on Jesus. He will sustain us.

Laying our burden on Jesus does not mean losing all responsibility. There still may be things we must do. It does not mean immediate escape. The reality of the burden may continue. It does mean, however, that the load is shifted in such a way that we now look at the burden differently. Yes, it is ours, but Jesus is bearing it.

Learn to cast your cares on God. Pray that He will sustain you, and don't worry. When the worry starts up again, start praying again, asking God to help you give Him the burden.

BANKING ON THE RIGHT THING

Psalms 57–59, **Romans 4** • **Key Verse: Romans 4:3**

It was hard for the Jewish people in Paul's day to understand that their special covenant relationship with God was insufficient to save them. Even today many Jewish people believe that they are automatically a part of God's family and need no personal salvation.

But the apostle Paul, who was himself Jewish, warned his fellow countrymen that it was not Abraham's works or his circumcision but his faith that brought him to God.

Paul quotes Genesis 15:6 as proof. God told Abraham that the stars of heaven would not exceed the number of his descendants. But Abraham had no descendants; he was childless. Still, he "believed in the LORD, and he credited it to him as righteousness" (Gen. 15:6). Abraham believed God's promise and God credited Abraham's faith as righteousness.

That's the way it is with us as well. We are not saved by who we are or by any rite such as circumcision or baptism. We are saved by faith alone in Christ alone.

If you are banking on anything other than Christ's death at Calvary to pay the penalty for your sin, you're banking on the wrong thing. Have faith in Jesus' death in your behalf, and let God credit that faith to your account as righteousness. It's the only way to be saved.

"Lord, I believe that Jesus Christ died in my place, paying the penalty for my sin. I have faith that that is all You require for my salvation. Thank You for crediting my faith as if it were actual righteousness and for saving me."

THE HOPE OF SPRING

*Psalms 60–62, **Romans 5** • **Key Verses: Romans 5:1–2***

Ray Stedman tells of a friend who lived in the Midwest. He lived in the country, and one stormy morning, in the dead of winter, he looked out his window and saw the mailman drive up and leave something in his mailbox. Wanting to see what it was, he dressed warmly and went out into the bitter cold. With the snow swirling about him, he walked about a quarter of a mile down the lane to where the mailbox was located. He opened the mailbox, and to his disappointment saw that all that was there was a seed catalog. But he opened it and began to thumb through it.

There is nothing like a seed catalog to capture the beauty and brilliance of flowers and vegetables. As he stood there in the snow, suddenly he felt as though spring had come. He could taste the crunch of a cucumber and smell the fragrance of those red roses and feel the juice of a red-ripe tomato running down his chin. It seemed as though winter faded for the moment and he was caught up in the beauty of spring and summer. Hope stirred within him!

The hope for the Christian goes far beyond a summer garden to eternity. The joy within our heart far surpasses that of a man looking at a seed catalog, because "we rejoice in the hope of the glory of God" (v. 2).

"God, help me look beyond today and look forward to eternity. I may struggle now but have hope. Help me find the rejoicing that comes from the hope I have in You."

FREED FROM SIN

Psalms 63–65, Romans 6 • *Key Verses: Romans 6:22–23*

A remarkable fact about Romans 6:23 is often missed—this verse was written to believers. We often use it to tell others about God's gift of salvation, but Paul wrote it to the church. Too often the meaning of the text is missed because we think only in terms of how it applies to others. In this chapter, Paul is telling us how to say no to sin. One reason is found in these verses. We have been set free and are no longer a slave to sin.

In the past, the master we served was sin. Paul makes it clear that we were slaves to sin but have been set free by Christ. Our Master now is God.

The penalty for sin, the former service, is death. Now, the believer's outlook is to life.

Before it was a "wage" that was earned. We were destined to receive what we deserved. Now it is a gift received, undeserved but freely given. Sin pays us what we earn, which is death, but God gives us what we need, which is life.

Paul wrote these words to the Christian as an encouragement not to sin. The chapter begins with a stirring call for us not to continue sinning.

Why keep living like a slave to sin? There is no good reason to. Instead, we should live like people who have received the greatest gift ever given, the gift of eternal life.

"God, help me to turn away from sin and turn to holiness. Help me see sin as You see it and understand that in Christ I am free from the penalty and power of sin."

AT EASE IN ZION

Psalms 66–67, Romans 7 • Key Verse: Psalm 66:10

We prefer being at ease in Zion. It's nice to sit on padded pews in air-conditioned auditoriums. Our version of "life is hard" comes in the form of a street being closed for widening. We complain over being inconvenienced when the work is being done for our convenience! We're at ease in Zion, blessed, enjoying the good life.

Then one day the plug is pulled. A doctor's grim expression belies the test results. *Downsizing* is not just a word found in a book on business trends but in a note in the pay envelope. Your accountant calls; the ink in his pen is red. You reach for the motion sickness pills because your boat is now rocking. Life is no longer smooth sailing.

There are times when God rocks our boat, and with a good purpose. He wants to test us so that we will emerge from the experience better. The imagery the psalmist used is that of the process for refining silver. Silver is heated to the point of melting so the impurities float to the surface. Then they are skimmed off, leaving better-quality silver, a more pure metal.

God at times tests us to remove the wrong and the unnecessary from our lives. We may find that these tests increase our praying, strengthen our faith and cause us to reorder our priorities. The result is a better-quality Christian, one who has been tested and strengthened.

Times of difficulty are tough. Don't try to escape them. Instead, learn the lesson(s) God may have for you in those times. Ask Him to give you the wisdom to know what He is teaching you.

MIND MATTERS

*Psalms 68–69, **Romans 8:1–21** • Key Verse: Romans 8:5*

Sometimes our minds are like dry ground, rutted by erosion, with grooves that channel the water that runs over it. Mentally, we always seem to follow the same grooves. We get into a particular way of thinking, perhaps seeing only what we want to see or thinking about only what we want to think about. Events, values and memories are forced into the same grooves, cutting them even deeper.

Paul used different imagery to describe the mental rut. He wrote that for some people, their minds are set on the sinful nature. Since their minds are set that way, they live their lives according to the sinful nature. In contrast, Paul wrote, "Those who live in accordance with the Spirit have their minds set on what the Spirit desires" (v. 5). If our disposition is toward the things of the Spirit, our lives will show it.

In exasperation, someone may rebuke us with the words, "What were you thinking about?" That's a theologically astute question! It strikes at the heart of our actions, our mind-set.

Through your waking hours, your mind absorbs an overwhelming amount of information. Like water over the ground, it will channel into the mental grooves of your mind-set. Your preoccupation must be the things of the Spirit.

What preoccupies your thinking? Your mental grid must be spiritually oriented. Focus your thinking on the Word of God. Then, your mental pathways will develop a mind that is set on the Spirit.

SECURE IN NOTHING

*Psalms 70–71, **Romans 8:22–39** • Key Verse: Romans 8:31*

The newspaper reminds us of the uncertainty of life. Things happen that are unexpected, tides turn, fortunes shift, lives end. One of the basic needs of humans is a sense of security, yet the events of the day remind us of the insecurity that comes from the uncertainties of life. We just don't know what's next. That's why we turn to the Bible. In it we find reasons to feel secure. We are secure knowing that:

- His purpose will not be frustrated. Since God is for us, none can be against us (v. 31).

- His generosity will not be quenched. Since He has not spared His Son, God will withhold nothing in taking care of us (v. 32).

- His forgiveness will not be canceled. No prosecution can succeed, since God our Judge has already justified us (vv. 33–34).

- His love will not be severed. God has revealed it in Christ, and nothing, even the ten powerful items listed here, will separate us from Christ's love (vv. 35–36).

While most people look for security in something, the Christian finds it in nothing. Nothing can frustrate God's purpose. Nothing can quench His generosity. Nothing can cancel His forgiveness. Nothing can sever His love from us.

Nothing can change the fact that, as Ruth Harms Calkin put it, "None of these nor all of them heaped together can budge the fact that I am dearly loved, completely forgiven and forever free through Jesus Christ."

God holds us in the palm of His steady hand. We are secure—secure in these "nothings."

Read again each of the verses listed, noting how each teaches us these truths. Then read aloud these words: "Nothing can frustrate God's purpose, quench His generosity, cancel His forgiveness and sever His love from us." Now smile! What joy is found in "nothing."

EYES RIGHT

Psalms 72–73, Romans 9:1–15 • *Key Verses: Psalm 73:2–3*

When the parking lot of our church was slippery due to snow, ice or a combination thereof, often at the end of the service I would remind people of Paul's admonition in 1 Corinthians 10:12: "Let him that thinketh he standeth take heed lest he fall" (KJV). A little overconfidence is a dangerous thing when walking on ice. Another reason we slip is because we get distracted. A friend says, "Hi," we take our eyes off the pavement, begin to wave back and, well, you get the picture. Worse yet, the pain from our fall seems greater when someone else has witnessed our unceremoniously landing.

Literally, not watching how we walk can result in a physical fall. Figuratively, the same is true. If we do not keep our "eyes right," we can slip spiritually. Carelessness and a momentary distraction, either one or both together, can result in a fall.

Asaph, the writer of Psalm 73, reminds us of that truth in words of testimony. "My feet had almost slipped . . . . For I envied the arrogant when I saw the prosperity of the wicked."

Life does not give us a smooth track for walking. Our struggles can be compounded as our eyes wander and we get distracted by the apparent ease and prosperity of the ungodly. Then we slip.

We can keep from slipping by focusing our attention on Jesus and how He wants us to live. We look not for the ease of this world but the reward of the world to come.

Godliness with contentment is great gain, according to Paul (1 Tim. 6:6). He also said, "I have learned to be content whatever the circumstances" (Phil. 4:11). Ask God to help you be contented, not envious.

BOOTSTRAPS CAN'T HELP

*Psalms 74–76, **Romans 9:16–33** • Key Verses: Romans 9:30–32*

We sometimes describe a person who has accomplished much on his own as one who has pulled himself up by his bootstraps. Though today it might be hard to visualize what a bootstrap is, we nevertheless understand what this phrase means. It speaks of working hard, doing yourself what is needed rather than asking or expecting someone else to do it for you. It is being self-reliant, independent, self-sufficient.

Bootstraps remain a powerful aspect of our mind-set and philosophy. Unfortunately, this belief spills over into the way people understand God and their relationship to Him. Many think that the way to heaven is to live a life sufficiently meritorious so that their good deeds outweigh their bad, and on that basis they earn or achieve eternal life.

Romans 9 destroys any hope that salvation is something a person can earn or deserves. The first part of the chapter emphasizes God's work in our salvation. It is only by God's mercy that any of us are saved. Then the focus turns from God's sovereignty to man's responsibility.

To the surprise of the Jews, Paul wrote of the salvation of the Gentiles, obtained by faith. Also to their surprise, he spoke of the Jews' failure of not obtaining righteousness. They could not gain by works what others received by faith. The difference between those who obtain salvation and those who do not is the difference between faith and effort.

The bottom line is Jesus. Faith in Him, not our effort, saves.

Are you a bootstrap kind of Christian, hoping what you have done will be enough to get you into heaven? You can't get to heaven by your works, only by faith in Jesus. Today, give up the bootstraps and receive the Savior's work on your behalf.

CALL ON HIS NAME

*Psalms 77–78, **Romans 10** • **Key Verse: Romans 10:13***

If anyone could have achieved salvation by his own efforts, it was Martin Luther. In 1505, when he was 21, he abandoned his career in law and entered the monastery, but not to study theology. His motive was to save his soul.

He gave himself rigorously to the prescribed ways to find God. He fasted, prayed, devoted himself to menial work and practiced penance. In his quest for salvation, he confessed his sins, even the most trivial ones, for hours on end until his superiors, wearied of his exercise, ordered him to stop until he committed some sin worth confessing! He was the most exemplary of monks, yet had no peace.

Luther tried to satisfy God's demand for righteousness through good works. *But what works?* he thought. *What works can come from a heart like mine? How can I stand before the holiness of my Judge with works polluted in their very source?*

It was not until John Staupitz set him to studying the Bible that Luther realized what the difficulty was. He was trying to earn salvation by works, when the righteousness needed was not human but divine. He then understood that "'everyone who calls on the name of the Lord will be saved'" (v. 13).

Luther learned to stop working for righteous. Salvation is a gift received by faith, given by God to everyone who calls on His name.

Perhaps Luther's example will help you see if you are like him, trying to work your way into heaven. Salvation can't be obtained that way. It can be received only by calling on the name of the Lord.

HARD OF HEARING

Psalms 79–80, Romans 11:1–18 • *Key Verses: Romans 11:7–8*

Ever hear of "selective hearing loss"? I don't know if the condition is medically valid, but at times I have seen it. Here is what it looks like: A person hears some things but not others. What he hears is not due to volume or clarity but want. He hears what he wants to hear and tunes out the rest—selective hearing loss.

Now, have you ever heard of "spiritual hearing loss"? Again, it's not a diagnosis found in medical texts, but it is in the Bible. And while we may smile at "selective hearing loss," there is nothing humorous about "spiritual hearing loss." Here is what it looks like: If anyone hears the truth and does not respond to it, the time may come when he will be incapable of responding.

Jesus spoke of it when He said, "'They hardly hear with their ears, and they have closed their eyes'" (Matt. 13:15). Paul wrote of it here in Romans 11:7–8. What he says about hardening should be sobering to all, for the principle is universal. Those who reject God's grace, trying instead to work their way into heaven, thinking they can make themselves righteous, may one day be incapable of responding to the free gift of salvation. Faith in Christ is sufficient; man's substitutes for faith are insufficient.

It is good that you are reading the Bible daily. But remember that what makes a person a Christian is not his good deeds but faith in Christ. Keep reading, but be sure you have received Christ. "Spiritual hearing loss" is a sobering truth. If you have not done so yet, respond today to God's grace.

FROM THEOLOGY TO DOXOLOGY

*Psalms 81–83, **Romans 11:19–36*** • ***Key Verses: Romans 11:33–36***

The first verse of Romans 12 says, "Therefore." What Paul says next flows out of the first 11 chapters. You cannot rightly understand and practice Romans 12:1 if you do not consider Romans 1–11. The first chapters teach us about God; the concluding ones about serving Him. When we look not just for chapter divisions but flow of thought, we find that the bridge between the doctrinal and practical parts of the book is a doxology.

The opening chapters of Romans are theology, explaining our belief about God. The concluding verses of chapter 11 are doxology, our praise of God that leads up to the great "therefore" of chapter 12. The concluding chapters focus on our devotion to God, our serving Him.

What can we learn from this bridge? First, consider that there can be no doxology without theology. If we do not know God and know about Him, then we cannot rightly praise Him. We cannot worship an unknown god—and knowing God brings worship.

Second, consider that devotion to God and serving Him flow out of theology and doxology. If we know God and praise Him, we will serve Him. God does not want devotion without theology or without doxology. To serve not knowing and not praising is not acceptable.

Third, realize that all three are equally important. We must know, praise and serve God.

The real conclusion to the first 11 chapters is not 11:33–36. It is 12:1, a truth obscured by what is possibly the worst chapter break in the Bible, because we too easily separate theology from life.

What we know affects how we live. We need to read and learn the Word and then live it. Don't be content with either an undevotional theology or an untheological devotion. Read the Word and live it.

MAKE THE MARK

*Psalms 84–86, **Romans 12** • Key Verses: Romans 12:1–2*

In his commentary on Romans, Ray Stedman tells the following story. "Many years ago a man was walking through Union Station in Chicago. It was busy and crowded. He had been thinking of what he might do with his life. It suddenly dawned on him the only logical thing he could do with his life, since it belonged to God and had been redeemed by the Lord, was to give it to Him and ask Him to use it.

"Right in the midst of the crowd he stopped and drew a little mark with his toe. Then he stood on the mark and said, 'Lord, here I am, I am Yours. The rest of my life, whatever You want me to do, if You will show me and convince me what You want, I will do it. The attitudes You want me to have, I will have. As I study and read Your Word, I will try to carry out what You tell me to do, and think the way You tell me to think. Here I am, Lord; do with my life as You want.'

"That commitment service in Union Station in Chicago was known only by this man and God. But God picked that man up and began to use him in remarkable ways. He has traveled the world and touched hundreds of lives because God used him."

That story embodies the significance of Romans 12:1–2, a text that takes the step beyond doctrine and doxology to duty. We are called to make a decisive commitment to God.

Like the man in the train station, have you ever made that mark? If you have, then stay by the mark, stay committed. If you have wandered from the mark, get back to it. And if you never have made it, then right now pray and make the mark.

WHEN THERE IS NO RELIEF

Psalms 87–88, Romans 13 • *Key Verse: Psalm 88:1*

The words "and they lived happily ever after" are usually found at the end of fairy tales. We read the last line of the story, sigh at the nice ending, close the book and return to the reality of a world without fairy-tale endings. The truth is, sometimes life is fine, and sometimes it isn't. Sometimes problems get solved, and sometimes they don't. *Hopeless* should not be found in the Christian's vocabulary because we do have hope in Christ. It's not an "I hope so" hope but a certain hope. Still, there are times when hope dims.

Psalm 88 is a prayer that begins simply enough: "O LORD, the God who saves me, day and night I cry out before you." We read on expecting to find the usual—God hears, God saves, the psalmist praises. But not this time. Instead we find ourselves reading the saddest of the psalms. Notice all the times the writer speaks of death. He writes not of the death of others but of feeling as if he is about to join the dead. His situation is so dismal that his closest friend is the darkness (v. 18).

There is no "happily ever after" to this story. The psalm is not a fairy tale but a tale of real life. Sometimes our situations will look hopeless. We feel like we are about to die. Our prayers seem to go unanswered.

So what then? We do what we find in verse 1. We pray and keep praying. This psalm calls us to a higher faith, one that continues when the darkness closes in on us.

The next psalm begins with words of hope, but until we get out of the dark times, we must keep praying. Are any ongoing situations weighing you down today? Don't give up. Ask God for the continued faith you need to trust Him.

TWO PRIORITIES

*Psalms 89–90, **Romans 14** • Key Verse: Romans 14:19*

Some of the most difficult disagreements are over what is considered right or wrong. The Bible is very clear on some things, but not on others; hence, the disagreements. We call these issues "gray areas." How to handle the gray areas must be an important subject since Paul not only discussed it in this chapter and part of the next, but also devoted three chapters to it in 1 Corinthians (8–10).

Gray areas were a problem in the first-century church and will be a problem in the last-century church. We will always have areas in which we do not agree as to what is right and wrong.

So Paul gave us two priorities to carry into these discussions. First, "make very effort to do what leads to peace" (v. 19). "Make every effort" speaks of the seriousness we have in this regard. Our efforts are to be directed toward peace. We are better at being divisive, getting our way, making our point, when instead we should be pushing hardest toward peace.

Second, our efforts should build others up, not tear them down. And we should do it in such a way that we benefit as well. Our efforts must be directed toward "mutual edification." We should come out of the discussion better, not bitter.

So the next time you get into one of those gray-area discussions, think about this: Are you working for peace, and are you and the others both growing through this?

We can be so convinced in our minds that there is no room for disagreement. But disagreements will come. Ask God to help you always be a person of peace and edification. Then ask if there is someone with whom you are right now not at peace. Plan your efforts to bring peace and build up each other.

GOD'S SECRET PLACE

Psalms 91–93, Romans 15:1–13 • Key Verse: Psalm 91:1

Did you have a secret hideout when you were a child? A place where you could go to feel safe and protected? Mine was in the woods behind our house, beside a bubbling brook.

God has a secret place too. It's called God's pavilion, the place under His wings—God's hiding place. Psalm 27:5 promises, "For in the day of trouble he will keep me safe in his dwelling; he will hide me in the shelter of his tabernacle and set me high upon a rock."

The more I learn about God's secret place, the more I am convinced that it's not a place at all—it's a person. Jesus Christ is our secret place. He is our shelter in the time of storm, our shield and buckler, the One under whose wings we take refuge. He said, "Remain in me, and I will remain in you. No branch can bear fruit by itself; it must remain in the vine. Neither can you bear fruit unless you remain in me. I am the vine; you are the branches. If a man remains in me and I in him, he will bear much fruit; apart from me you can do nothing" (John 15:4–5).

Are you looking for God's special hiding place today? Are you in need of some encouragement and nourishment from Him? The answer is to find God's secret place and live there. The answer is to find Jesus Christ.

"Lord, give me the courage to live in You today, and not just run to You when I am in trouble. Help me to find peace and shelter in You, and give me strength from the true Vine, Jesus Christ."

BALANCED WORSHIP

Psalms 94–96, Romans 15:14–33 • *Key Verses: Psalm 95:1, 6*

Do you have a preferred "style" of worship? In some churches only a piano and organ are allowed for accompaniment, and if it isn't in the hymnal, it isn't sung. In other churches the drummer sits behind a Plexiglas wall so as to not overpower the band. Whatever the instruments used, some people prefer a quieter, contemplative service while others are attracted to a more lively celebratory style.

Which is right? Neither and both.

Neither is right if it is all a person experiences. If every worship time is contemplation, or every worship time is celebration, that is not right. What is modeled in the Bible, which is the right arbitrator of such discussions, is a balance of reverent celebration and reverent contemplation. It may seem that hand clapping and knee bending don't mix, but they do when we have a biblical balance in our worship.

The words of contemplative worship are found in a popular praise song: "Come, let us worship and bow down, let us kneel before the Lord, our God, our Maker." It is a quiet, reflective song, with words from Psalm 95.

But the psalm begins with, "Come, let us sing for joy to the LORD; let us shout aloud to the Rock, our salvation." Those are the words of celebration. Sing and shout aloud!

Psalm 95 calls us to both contemplation and celebration. Our life of worship is lived not at the extremes. It is not to be an "either/or" but a "both/and" balance.

Consider your time of worship. Do you at times sing and shout aloud in celebration? Do you at times also bow down and kneel? If you are doing only what you prefer, remember, God wants us to be worshipers who both celebrate and contemplate.

HANDSHAKES AND HUGS

*Psalms 97–99, **Romans 16** • Key Verse: **Romans 16:16***

When we hear the word *church*, if we think only of a building, we miss the point. The word does apply to a church building; in reality the church is people. Actually, if you take the people out of the building, it is no longer even a church building. As Paul concluded his letter to the saints in Rome, he gave them a powerful reminder of the truth about the community of believers. A careful reading of the chapter reveals:

1. The church is people who are diverse (vv. 3–16). In this list we find diversity in race (Jewish and Gentile), in rank (slaves and free) and gender (nine of the 27 are women). Paul evidently thought highly of them all!

2. The church is people who are united. Paul spoke of his "sisters" and "brothers" and called them "beloved." Then there are the fellow workers and fellow sufferers. Six times he referred to meeting in houses. The essence of the church is its unity, since it is the one and only community in the world in which Christ has broken down all the dividing walls.

3. The church should be a place of handshakes and hugs (v. 16). In Paul's day, the holy kiss was a visible and tangible gesture of greeting. It was more than a formality; it was an expression of fellowship and of love for others.

There is diversity in the Body of Christ, but by His work He has brought us together. That unity should be obvious and genuine. Church should be a place of handshakes and hugs.

Do you struggle in your relationships with other believers? Consider what Paul did. He commended the believers, recognized the differences but realized that we are one in Christ. Recognize this truth and live it. Learn to love others in Christ.

RESOLUTIONS

Psalms 100–102, 1 Corinthians 1 • Key Verses: Psalm 101:2–3

As we approach December 31 every year, we start to think about making New Year's resolutions, some of which we keep well into the next day! Far too often our resolutions are far too short-lived. Some people find it more beneficial to make their resolutions for only that day and then to renew them each day. Their morning begins with a recitation of what they are determined to do or not do. The decisions are lived one day at a time.

Psalm 101 sounds like a New Year's resolution, but it isn't. The intentions expressed in these verses were not to be followed only for a day or two but for life.

In a resolute way, David stated his "objectives." These included a blameless walk, a guarding of his eyes, a perspective that rejects wrong and embraces right, and an intolerance for deceitfulness.

Read again this psalm and identify David's statements of resolution, such as, "I will walk in my house with blameless heart" (v. 2). Then think about how that applies to your life. The next one may be easier. "I will set before my eyes no vile thing" (v. 3). This affects what you watch on TV, the magazines you read and the books you buy.

If Psalm 101 describes how you want to live, make it your daily resolution. Determine that this is how you will live today and every day.

To help this become your resolution, print the words of Psalm 101 on a piece of paper and post it where you will see it every day. Then read it, aloud even, daily. Renew your resolution every day.

UNDESERVED TREATMENT

Psalms 103–104, 1 Corinthians 2 • Key Verses: Psalm 103:10–12

"It's just not fair," we sometimes say, perhaps not thinking too clearly about what we are saying. If someone is being fair toward us, he is following a standard of what is right and proper, not giving consideration to anything or anyone else. We want to be treated fairly—or at least we think we do. Typically, the standard by which we decide if something is "fair" is one of our own perspective. It is our attempt to get what we think we deserve.

We should be thankful that God does not give us what we deserve but instead gives us what we don't. David said in Psalm 103:10 that God "does not treat us as our sins deserve." The reason He doesn't is forgiveness. He removes our transgressions from us, separating them from us at an incalculable distance.

Consider how far east is from west. If you go north far enough, you will reach the North Pole. It's all south from there. Or go south far enough and you will encounter the South Pole. One more step and you are headed north. North and south really are next to each other. But go east and you will never reach an east pole. Same is true with the west. East is not just a step away from west. They are not even "poles apart."

Verse 12 is a vivid image of forgiveness: as far as east is from the west. God has removed our transgressions farther than we can imagine.

Thank God for forgiveness! Thank Him that He did not give you what you deserve.

ADVICE AVALANCHE

Psalms 105–106, 1 Corinthians 3 • *Key Verse: Psalm 105:4*

Your newspaper probably includes a daily advice column, or perhaps two or three. There are the old standbys of Ann Landers and Dear Abby, along with others, some local, some syndicated. Need advice on your car? Listen to *Car Talk* on National Public Radio. For home decorating, a slew of television and radio programs is available, along with Web sites that include video clips on specific topics of interest. Self-help books abound, some capitalizing on our frustrations and feelings of ignorance, as seen in titles like *HTML 4 Dummies*.

So many voices, so many solutions. And we haven't even mentioned self-help groups, support groups, networks, workshops, seminars and infomercials. Where do you start?

Always start at the same place—and it is not the library, the book-store, the talk show, the newspaper or the neighbor. "Look to the LORD and his strength; seek his face always" (105:4).

As the psalmist continues, he reminds us of some of God's great works. "Remember the wonders he has done, his miracles, and the judgments he pronounced" (v. 5). In particular he tells of how the Lord worked in bringing the people of Israel out of Egypt. They were "few in number," he writes, but they left Egypt "laden with silver and gold" (v. 37). God kept His word. He protected and provided for His people. And He gave them the land He promised them. Praise the Lord!

Some of today's advisors may have good advice, but start every day, every endeavor, by looking to the Lord, to His strength, seeking His face.

"God, help me to put You at the top of the list of my advisors. May I always start with You when looking for the help and strength I need."

STAYING FOCUSED

Psalms 107–109, 1 Corinthians 4 • *Key Verses: 1 Corinthians 4:1–2*

My daughter came home from an overnight stay at a friend's house with a latch hook rug she had made. Her friend's mother had taught the girls how to do latch hook. The process involved attaching pieces of yarn to a plastic grid using a hook. Various colored pieces were placed so that the picture of a cartoon character was evident. Such talent!

Yes, it did take talent, but mostly the picture was the result of following the instructions and the pattern printed on the grid. The more the girls stayed focused on those two things, the better their rugs looked.

It's the same with life. The better we follow the instructions and the pattern God has given us, the better our lives will be.

Paul helps us stay focused by reminding us of who we are and what we are to do: we are servants who have been entrusted by God to accomplish His will. It's so easy to lose that focus. We typically have an "I" problem. When we look at things with our "I," what God wants is not so clearly seen. It is also hard for an "I" to be a servant. Yet that is exactly what we are—servants who are to be faithful stewards.

Remember that a steward is a manager, not an owner. God entrusts things into our care. What He, the Owner, then requires of us, the manager, is that we be faithful. That is the pattern for our lives, the one that we must keep in focus.

Do you have an "I" problem? It really is easy to see how things get out of focus. Ask God to help you stay focused on His pattern, determining to serve as a faithful steward.

REACH FOR THE LIGHT

Psalms 110–112, 1 Corinthians 5 • *Key Verse: Psalm 112:4*

Occasionally I will notice my youngest daughter playing with a flashlight—with my flashlight, to be precise. I'm not being possessive, but when I see her doing that I get concerned. "When you are done," I say, "be sure to put it back where it belongs."

You see, I have a set place for that flashlight. It's a place where I can find it in the dark. If the power goes off, I want at least enough light to keep from stubbing my toe on my way to find matches and candles. I want to be able to reach my hand out and find the flashlight.

I find it interesting that God used the imagery of light in the dark as one of the blessings He has for us. "Even in darkness light dawns for the upright" (112:4). Obviously, the psalmist was not speaking of literal darkness but used it as a metaphor, a vivid one that brings to mind the dark times of life. In those dark times we need and want light. Like a dad reaching out for the flashlight, we can reach out and know with even greater certainty that the Source of light will be there.

If this is a dark time for you, look to God for the light you need. Ask Him to help you find His light, which will lead you through that darkness.

TWO TESTS

*Psalms 113–115, **1 Corinthians 6** • **Key Verse: 1 Corinthians 6:12***

We live in an "anything goes" world, and sometimes it seems as if everything has gone! Occasionally we need the Bible to jerk us back to reality, biblical reality. It is the same for the child of God as it was for you as a child of your parents. Remember how sometimes they told you no? Anything didn't go, and it still doesn't.

If God says clearly that something is wrong, then it is wrong. There's no use asking because the answer is no.

Then there are all the other things, the ones the Bible neither says are wrong nor right. We usually call these "gray areas." Paul gives us two important things to remember.

First, even if something may be allowed, ask yourself if it is beneficial for you. Some things can be like the weights mentioned in Hebrews 12:1, the things that hinder us in the Christian life. They are not wrong, but they don't help.

Second, don't let anything control you. Paul teaches us that we are to be controlled by the Spirit—nothing else. We can be controlled not only by addictive substances but by addictive activities. Habits, compulsions, foods and so much more can control a person. Paul says to us by his example and teaching that we must "not be mastered by anything" (v. 12).

This verse gives us two tests to use in deciding what we will do or not do. In any area that Scripture does not clearly address, ask yourself these questions: Is it beneficial? Will it control me?

Anything does go, but some things should go! Ask God to help you see if there are things in your life that are not beneficial to you or that control you.

SEXUAL PURITY

*Psalms 116–118, **1 Corinthians 7:1–19***
Key Verses: 1 Corinthians 7:2–3

In a world of extremes, Paul brings balance. He addresses in this chapter one of the significant subjects of life—sex. In a few verses he details for us what God intends in regard to this topic.

Abstinence is God's will for the unmarried. Paul, who was himself single, did not view singleness negatively, but he did view sexual immorality that way. Believers should not be in a hurry to marry according to verse 1.

In the marital relationship each partner is to meet the needs of the other. It is not a one-sided arrangement. The only limitation is this: sex is reserved for the married. God puts no limitations on a husband and wife. The only exception is when a couple mutually agrees to a limited time of celibacy for the purpose of devoting themselves to a concentrated time of prayer.

We need to realize that singleness is not wrong, nor is the single person "second class" in any respect. In regard to sex, however, the single person must live according to God's standard of abstinence. That is contrary to the ways of our society, but it conforms to the will of God.

For the married, God has given clear instruction. Sex within marriage is good. Keep it there. That is His will.

The Word of God is clear regarding sexual purity. We need to be just as clear in our commitment to it. If you are single, ask God to help you maintain a life of abstinence. If you are married, ask God to make your relationship with your spouse one of fulfillment and blessing.

THE BLESSING OF THE BIBLE

Psalm 119:1–88, 1 Corinthians 7:20–40 • *Key Verse: Psalm 119:1*

What is your view of the Bible? One answer that may come to mind is, "It's the Word of God." That's a good beginning of an answer. "Only a good beginning?" you might ask. Yes, because there is so much more that should come to mind. Psalm 119 helps us see the Bible as the Word of God in a fuller way.

If you have not done it before, notice how many of the verses in this passage mention the Word of God. In almost every verse our attention is drawn specifically to some aspect of the Word. Go through the psalm and underline the words that refer to the Bible. Eight different Hebrew words are used. They are translated as "law," "statutes," "precepts," "commands," "commandments," "decrees," "word" and "promise."

Notice, though, how the psalm begins. It speaks of the blessing of the blameless, those "who walk according to the law of the LORD."

There is a blessing in knowing and doing what the Bible teaches. To have that blessing we must read the Word, learn the Word and live the Word. Only one out of eight people who read the Bible say it affects how they live. God didn't give us His Word just to increase our knowledge but to affect our lives. The writer of this psalm understood that. He found the blessing that comes from reading and obeying.

This psalm calls us to obedience and faith. Ask God to help you have the same attitude about His Word that the psalmist did.

COOK OUT

Psalm 119:89–176, 1 Corinthians 8 • *Key Verse: 1 Corinthians 8:13*

My family enjoys cooking out on the grill. We have been known to brush off the snow and fire it up on days that most people stay indoors. I'll tramp out into the snow, tend to the meat and tramp back into the house. There is nothing like the smell and taste of a grilled dinner.

I think of a nicely cooked steak on my plate every time I read 1 Corinthians 8:13. Paul, who understood Christian liberty, wrote extensively on the subject and lived it in the context of the first-century church, said he would never eat meat again if it would cause another brother to fall into sin.

That is absolutely amazing to me. First, I'm amazed that he would give up eating meat! I think of what a sacrifice that would be and wonder whether or not I could do the same. Second, Paul knew he had rights, which he discussed in the next chapter, but he was willing to set them aside. We tend instead to insist on our rights. Third, it is simply amazing to see how concerned Paul was for the spiritual welfare of others. More important than a nicely grilled steak was the well-being of others. His focus was not on himself.

Are you concerned about others, enough to give up something that you enjoy, something that is not a sin? Paul is an amazing example of one who did not live for self but for others.

We can have an extended discussion of what is right, wrong or gray and in the process lose sight of what Paul was saying. He was concerned for others. Are you? Is there anything you absolutely would not give up if you knew it caused another to sin?

"I'D LOVE TO GO!"

Psalms 120–122, 1 Corinthians 9 • *Key Verse: Psalm 122:1*

Have you ever received an invitation that you didn't want? Perhaps you had planned to play golf that afternoon but instead were sitting in a pew waiting for the wedding to begin. Have you ever not received an invitation that you wanted? Undoubtedly! Someone tells you he has an extra ticket to the big game, you have the day free, and you want to go badly. Then he heads off, saying, "I need to find someone to go with me." You are in agony.

Then there is the time you get an invitation you want. It does happen, occasionally. Think about your reaction when that happens. "Sounds great! I'd love to go."

Three scenarios: invited but didn't want to go, wanted to go but not invited, wanted to go and invited. Three responses: dread going, disappointed not going, and ecstatic about going.

Which of those three responses would match yours if you received this invitation: "Let us go to the house of the Lord"? Since it is an invitation, one response is eliminated, that of disappointed not going. So, two answers are left, and only one of them is right.

Can you honestly say that you would be ecstatic? Or would your real response be closer to dread? This is pretty convicting, isn't it? It makes us consider our attitude toward worship.

Psalm 122 is one of the pilgrimage psalms, sung as the people traveled to Jerusalem for one of the annual feasts. This one expresses deep joy at the thought of being called to travel to the house of the Lord. That invitation should always bring rejoicing.

Do you share the psalmist David's heart for worship? Ask God to help you come to worship with rejoicing.

THE EYES OF SLAVES

Psalms 123–125, 1 Corinthians 10:1–18 • *Key Verse: Psalm 123:2*

There probably has been a time when you could not get the attention of your waiter or waitress at a restaurant. Maybe you needed another napkin or wanted a refill of your coffee or just wanted the check. You probably began with a slight wave of the hand, not wanting to be too distracting to others. Then your hand started moving a little higher in hopes of catching the eye. Finally, you wave like you're waving to a friend on the other side of the stadium!

Some members of the wait staff seem to catch the slightest signal. A glance into your coffee cup and they are there anticipating that you are about to ask for a refill. Your child spills his drink and before you signal the need for an additional napkin, they arrive at your table with an ample supply. They are more observant than an auctioneer who can catch a bid off the raising of an eyebrow.

Today's key verse reminds me of these waiters: "As the eyes of slaves look to the hand of their master . . . ." They watch, wanting to serve well, trying to please, anticipating what they should do next.

However, this verse isn't about others, but about us: ". . . so our eyes look to the LORD our God." It isn't about what we should expect when we go out to eat but how we should live as the servants of God. The slightest indication of what He desires should be sufficient to catch our attention.

Does God have to "wave big" to catch your attention, or are you attentive to His signals? Pray that today you will be more aware of what He wills so you can serve Him better.

FOR THE GOOD OF OTHERS

Psalms 126–128, 1 Corinthians 10:19–33
Key Verse: 1 Corinthians 10:24

Sometimes we get so focused on what we want that we lose sight of what God wants. He not only wants us to consider whether or not something is beneficial for us but also whether it is good for others.

The emphasis on self can distort our view of others. When self occupies our vision, it becomes difficult to set aside what we want or what we think is acceptable. Yet Paul repeatedly reminds us that we do not live for ourselves only. We are part of the community of believers and must consider how our actions affect others.

"Nobody should seek his own good, but the good of others" (v. 24). Paul is not talking about good things we can do for others but how we must consider the effect our actions will have on others. It is not just a matter of saying, "This is right for me." It is even more than deciding something is edifying. This verse commands an added dimension to our decision making—how will what I do affect others, and will it be for their good?

"God, help me think about how what I do affects others. Give me a heart that desires to do what will be good for them, not just what pleases myself."

WEANED OR FUSSY?

Psalms 129–131, 1 Corinthians 11:1–16 • *Key Verse: Psalm 131:2*

I sometimes humorously talk about things that sound true but are not. My list of "accepted lies" includes "one size fits all." Another one that parents of newborns especially understand is "sleeps like a baby." In reality, that means waking every couple of hours and demanding to be fed. Babies can be fussy and demanding at anytime, day or night.

Among the challenges of parenting are teething and weaning. It is a blessing when the child no longer has sore gums and is no longer so demanding in his or her attachment to the mother when hungry. It is a blessing when babies truly sleep like a baby!

Christians are to be like a weaned baby, still and quiet. Our souls are to have a calmness that is like a sleeping baby's. So often, though, we are like the unweaned child, demanding immediate relief for our discomfort. We fuss while waiting for God to be the immediate provider of the warm milk that will allow us to go back to undisturbed sleep.

Even my teenagers at times wonder if they are going to be fed, especially when we are traveling. I sometimes say to them, "We haven't let you starve yet!" in hopes that they will quiet down. "Relax. Trust me to feed you" is what I'm really telling them.

God wants us to trust Him, to be still and quiet our souls. We need to be like a weaned child, resting confidently that He will take care of us.

Look over your prayer list. Do the personal requests sound like a weaned child or a fussy baby? Be still and quiet your soul. Sleep like a baby, not like a fussy newborn.

SELF-EXAMINATION

Psalms 132–134; 1 Corinthians 11:17–34
Key Verse: 1 Corinthians 11:28

Socrates once said, "The unexamined life is not worth living." By that he meant that we must not take things for granted but investigate everything to see if it has a ring of truth.

The apostle Paul said much the same to the Corinthian believers. Apparently the Corinthian Christians were abusing the sanctity of the Lord's Table. They were gorging themselves at the communal meal; some were even getting drunk. Then, still wallowing in their unrepentant sin, these believers were partaking of the Lord's Supper. Paul warned, "A man ought to examine himself before he eats of the bread and drinks of the cup" (1 Cor. 11:28).

Self-examination is good for all of us. We need to keep short accounts with God. Daily we should ask, "Is what I'm doing today pleasing to God?" We should even ask, "Does what I do give evidence of my salvation?" Paul wrote, "Examine yourselves to see whether you are in the faith; test yourselves" (2 Cor. 13:5). When we keep short accounts with God it prevents that ugly sin build-up that stains so many Christians' lives.

Take a close look—at yourself. Would you be comfortable knowing the Lord Jesus is examining your life closely? He is, you know. We all should do the same.

"Father, I want You to examine my life, but first let me take a hard look and clear away any clutter I find there. Give me the courage to daily check my life for the ring of truth—Your truth."

GOD'S CHOICES ARE RIGHT CHOICES

Psalms 135–136, 1 Corinthians 12 • *Key Verse: 1 Corinthians 12:18*

Have you ever wanted to be someone else? Have you wanted to handle a basketball like Michael Jordan or hit a baseball like Mark McGwire? Do you feel like you got the short end of the stick when it comes to gifts and talents? If so, cheer up. God has good news for you.

The Corinthian congregation was made up of very diverse people. In addition, God gave each of these Christians special gifts—spiritual gifts. These gifts were to be used to help others in the church develop to full maturity in Christ. Instead, the Corinthians argued over whose spiritual gift was the greatest. God gave each member exactly what He wanted them to have, but they failed to use that gift while they dreamed about being someone else.

Sometimes that happens in the church today. We forget that what God gives us to do is the most important task we can do. If we do someone else's job in church and neglect our own, we fail twice.

Has God gifted you in a certain way? The only way you can be happy is to allow God to get out of you what He has put in you. He has tailor-made a gift for you. It's His choice for you, and God's choices are always right choices. Don't fail twice by salivating after someone else's gift; savor your own.

"Help me, Father, to recognize that You have given me gifts to use for others. Don't let me be jealous of others. Instead, let me be zealous in serving You with my gift."

NOT ON OUR LIST

*Psalms 137–139, **1 Corinthians 13** • **Key Verse: 1 Corinthians 13:6***

Try this with a group. Ask everyone to finish this sentence: "Love is
_____." Some of the phrases from 1 Corinthians 13 will
be suggested, but one undoubtedly will not. It is this: "Love does not
delight in evil but rejoices with the truth" (v. 6). Why is that a characteristic of love?

What we delight in we will share with those we love. A person who
enjoys fine dining will want to take others to his favorite restaurants.
The sports fan will tell others about his love of the game. A collector
may try to get her friends involved in her hobby. We want our interests to be their interests.

If we delight in evil, the same will be true. We will want those
around us to be involved in the same things, in the same way. This
is a sad but unmentioned truth.

Our desire should be to help others become more like Christ. Paul
even said that a husband should love his wife as Christ loved the
Church, giving Himself for her "to make her holy" (Eph. 5:25–26).

Do you see how delighting in evil works against that? If we delight in
evil, then we are bringing into others' lives that which pulls them
away from Christ. Love does not do that. It desires that others "rejoice with the truth."

*Are there things in your life that are wrong? Don't think about only
yourself, but also about how you influence others with what you delight
in. Determine to get the wrong out and the right in.*

THE GATEKEEPER

Psalms 140–142, 1 Corinthians 14:1–20 • *Key Verse: Psalm 141:3*

We probably get into trouble quicker by what we say than any other means. A moment of speaking before thinking can result in damage that seems beyond repair. I sometimes say that I have two goals: one is not to begin a sentence with the words, "Don't quote me on this," and the other is not to end a sentence with the words, "Just kidding."

The books of Proverbs and James have plenty to say about what we say. Both give us warnings that should help us pause before we speak. We also can learn from those books how to speak.

Still, we come back to the problem of execution—doing what we know we are supposed to do. Too often we find ourselves "hung by the tongue."

David gives us an example to follow. It is not to "count to ten" or some other technique to practice. It is what you would expect from a godly person. His approach was to pray. Notice that it was not a prayer of the moment, as in, "Help me not to say this!" but a prayer for a consistent quality of speech. He prayed, "Set a guard over my mouth, O Lord; keep watch over the door of my lips" (141:3).

We need a gatekeeper, one who watches over our mouth. If we make that our prayer, God will help us so that what goes out of our mouth is only that which the sentry allows to pass.

Pray the prayer of David, "Set a guard over my mouth, O Lord; keep watch over the door of my lips."

THIRSTY AND TEACHABLE

Psalms 143–145, 1 Corinthians 14:21–40
Key Verse: Psalm 143:10

As mentioned yesterday, sometimes the problem isn't with knowing what to do but with doing it. In Psalm 143 David prays not only to know God's will but to do it. "Show me the way I should go," he prays (v. 8), and then asks, "Teach me to do your will (v. 10)." Far too often our problem is with failing to do God's will.

Earlier in the psalm David describes his soul as longing for God like a parched land. As dry ground thirsts for moisture, David's soul thirsts for God. There is a connection with what he says in verse 6 about his thirst and his prayer to be teachable in verse 10. The thirsty soul will be teachable.

We need to keep our souls thirsty. That is done by keeping a proper attitude. When we feel satisfied spiritually, we will not be thirsty. It is tempting to stay spiritually anemic if we are satisfied with our spiritual condition. But the proper attitude is one that longs for more of God. Then when our souls are thirsty, we will be teachable.

If we are spiritually satisfied, no more is wanted—we are neither thirsty nor teachable. Stay thirsty!

Examine your heart, asking, "Do I thirst for God?" If not, ask God to make you a thirsty and teachable Christian.

POPEYE THEOLOGY

*Psalms 146–147, **1 Corinthians 15:1–28***
Key Verse: 1 Corinthians 15:10

There are words that are a part of our vocabulary today that our parents probably never heard. While we do not seem to use *codependent* as much as we used to, the word *dysfunctional* is easily attached to *family*. If you said "ACOA" a few years ago, people might have thought it was a reference to an aluminum manufacturer. Now it is an acronym for "Adult Children of Alcoholics." All these words carry the theme that people are affected by their past.

Sometimes it sounds like Popeye talking. One of his favorite lines is, "I am what I am and that's all that I am." People "excuse" themselves with words such as that. "My upbringing was dysfunctional and I am a product of my environment"—in other words, "I can't help myself."

In contrast there is Pauline theology. He said, "By the grace of God I am what I am" (v. 10). God had worked in his life and changed him. The effects of his past were overcome by the work of God.

It can be the same for us. We may have come from a dysfunctional family and bear the effects—its negativity stamped on our soul, the destructive patterns ingrained in our thoughts, words and deeds. We opt for a Popeye theology, thinking nothing can ever change it.

But by God's grace it can be changed. Our hope is that we are not inseparably bound to our past when we are children of God and have received His grace.

Do you struggle with the effects of your past? Recognize the truth of what Paul says, grasp it in your soul and do not let it go. Determine to be able to say with him, "I am what I am—by the grace of God!" Let God's grace change and heal you.

THE DONE UNDONE

Psalms 148–150, 1 Corinthians 15:29–58
Key Verses: 1 Corinthians 15:55–57

You can't unscramble an egg. That simple statement reminds us that some things, once done, can't be undone. One noticeable exception is death. In the Resurrection, all that death has done was undone by Jesus.

Death's sting is sin. As the sting of a bee injects its poison into our system, so sin injects death into mankind. We die and our bodies decay. The power of sin is the Law because it shows us our sin and condemns us. We are guilty and sentenced to death.

Yet there is complete victory over death and sin through Christ. It is not that death is destroyed so that it cannot continue to harm God's people. But its effects are reversed so that death is defeated—and we will live forever, victorious.

The hope of the Christian is expressed by the epitaph Benjamin Franklin wrote for himself: "The body of Franklin, printer, like the cover of an old book, its contents torn out and stripped of its lettering and gilding, lies here food for worms. But the work will not be lost, for it will appear once more in a new and more elegant edition, revised and corrected by the Author."

The defeat of death, the hope of the Christian, is the resurrection of Jesus.

Our hope is in Jesus, not just as a man of history but as the resurrected Lord. Thank Him now for this truth, by which you are saved, by which you know that death is defeated. Praise God!

SYSTEMATIC GIVING

Proverbs 1–2, 1 Corinthians 16 • *Key Verses: 1 Corinthians 16:1–3*

A cartoon featured the sign in front of a church. It boldly announced "Stewardship Sunday" and then meekly suggested, "Try us again next week." That may reflect our culture's thinking about giving, but it should not reflect ours.

Our giving is to be systematic, individual and consistent. On the first day of the week, each of us is to bring our offering. This is to be the pattern of our lives.

What we give is to be proportionate. God does not set a price but a standard. He does not even stipulate a percentage. Rather, we are to give as He has prospered us and as we have purposed in our heart. When we consider what is an appropriate percentage, we find that tithing (ten percent) is neither annulled nor endorsed in the New Testament, but it was the minimum for giving in the Old Testament. Setting aside ten percent is a good starting point, one that can be increased as God prospers us.

The money you put in the offering is a private matter between you and God. Paul did not want to pressure people to give, so he instructed that the collection be taken before he arrived. It should motivate you to consider that when you give, God is your witness!

Finally, our giving has a place. The Corinthians brought their offerings to the local church. That is to be the first priority of our giving. Begin there.

Stewardship is not a subject to avoid but a command to obey. Consider your giving. Do you meet the standards Paul outlined?

A GATED LIFE

Proverbs 3–5, 2 Corinthians 1 • Key Verses: Proverbs 4:23–27

The term "gated community" is used in real estate ads to describe a secure area, one that is guarded. A wall with a gate surrounds the property, and everyone who goes in and out is monitored. Often a guard stands at the gate.

Our lives should be like a gated community. In Proverbs 4 Solomon tells us to "guard your heart, for it is the wellspring of life" (v. 23).

A guarded heart will show in many ways. It will show in what we say as we put away perversity and corrupt talk (v. 24). Our conversation and speech will be affected.

It will show in what we see (v. 25). Solomon says that we will look straight ahead, not distracted by things off to the side. Television, magazines and the Internet give us things to look at that are wrong, that pull us away from God. A gated life is careful to control the eye gate.

It also will show in how we walk (v. 26). In a guarded life we choose the right paths and do not swerve.

I often say that God did not give us His Word just to increase our knowledge but to affect the way that we live. These verses point us to the truth that our lives are to be directed by His Word. As we guard our hearts, we will live gated lives.

Often we focus just on the outside, while God wants us to start on the inside. If right now you need to make changes in your heart, pray. Ask God to help you change and truly guard your heart.

WHAT GOD HATES

Proverbs 6–7, 2 Corinthians 2 • *Key Verse: Proverbs 6:16*

"God is love," says 1 John 4:8. We like that. It is comforting, like a warm blanket on a chilly night.

But like a rock dropped into the stillness of a pond are the words "God hates." The ripples that result disturb the tranquility of the water's surface. Our minds are jolted to a reality that too often we want to ignore.

God is love, but there are things He hates. This really ought to catch our attention! We should sit up and take notice when the One who loves us so much that He would give His Son to die for us says in His Word that there are things He hates. "There are six things the LORD hates, seven that are detestable to him" (6:16). This does not mean there are only six or seven things God objects to. Hebrew poetry uses a phrase like this to indicate that these are definitely on the list! It is like the flashing lights at a railroad crossing, saying, "Look out!"

Included in the list is "a man who stirs up dissension among brothers" (v. 19). Earlier in the chapter this person is described as one "who plots evil with deceit in his heart" (v. 14). His mouth, his winking, even his body language bring about alienation and conflict.

God hates this. That should be enough to keep us from causing dissension, but sadly we know that dissension can be found even among the people of God. Consider your words and what you do. Is your heart set on causing conflict?

The heart of Christianity is reconciliation—first of all to God! And we are to be people reconciled to one another. Examine you heart. Are you by words or deed sowing seeds of dissension?

OUR COMPETENCE

Proverbs 8–9, 2 Corinthians 3 • Key Verse: 2 Corinthians 3:5

Some help-wanted ads sound like only Superman should apply for the job. The job description may include the required education and the amount of experience in the field, plus the abilities that are expected of the person filling the position. We may look over the ad and wonder if anyone would be up to the job.

In 2 Corinthians 2:16, Paul asks a question that is not answered until the next chapter. It is a little like an advertisement in the help-wanted section. After describing believers as the "aroma of Christ" (v. 15) and saying how we are to the one "the smell of death; to the other, the fragrance of life," he asks, "And who is equal to such a task?" (v. 16).

We certainly aren't! It is important for us to recognize that confidence in self alone is insufficient to accomplish what God wants us to do. It is also vital that we not excuse ourselves from our God-given responsibilities by highlighting our inadequacies either. At this point we need to keep reading. "Our competence," Paul writes, "comes from God. He has made us competent as ministers of a new covenant" (3:5–6).

We may feel like the overwhelmed candidate for an overwhelming job, but we have this assurance—God can make us competent for the task. The only real question is not if He can but if we will. Will you let Him so mold and make you that He can effectively use you?

"God, help me not to be overly confident in myself but properly dependent on You. Help me see how You are molding and making me to serve as Your witness."

AUDIT PHOBIA

Proverbs 10–12, 2 Corinthians 4 • *Key Verse: Proverbs 10:9*

One of the least-welcome return addresses on mail that comes to our homes is that of the Audit Department, Internal Revenue Service. Just reading those words makes us wince. Perhaps we dread the thought of gathering up all the needed materials to answer the questions of the person assigned to examine our tax return. Honest mistakes do happen. We can copy a figure incorrectly, miscalculate or even not understand what deductions are allowable or not allowable. Still, we would rather not make the trip, returns, receipts and documentation in hand, to see the IRS agent.

The dread of an audit is worse if we know that we cheated on our return. Now the mind turns to possible explanations for the intentional error or to wondering what the penalty might be. The stomach churns, the mind races and dread hangs heavy in the air as the appointed day to meet with the auditor approaches.

Solomon said, "The man of integrity walks securely" (10:9). This person may dread an audit but only for the inconvenience. Other than a possible error in his math or a misunderstanding in the tax laws, he approaches an audit with an inward security, at peace because he knows that he has done what is right. In contrast, "he who takes crooked paths will be found out."

Integrity is not a bother but a blessing. It enables a person to walk securely, even when that walk is into the office of an auditor. Choose the secure path.

Is there an aspect of your life you live without integrity? Change that today. Choose the secure path to walk, the one of integrity.

A HOUSE, NOT A TENT

Proverbs 13–15, 2 Corinthians 5 • *Key Verse: 2 Corinthians 5:1*

It is not unusual to see a canopy tent set up in the cemetery near our house. These are temporary structures, providing some relief from the weather during a graveside service. Soon after the burial, the tent is removed.

I like those tents for two reasons. One is obvious—they do keep the sun, snow or rain off of those gathered by the grave. The other is not so obvious, but I would point it out if I were leading the service. At the committal I would reach up and grab hold of the tent. "We don't live in tents," I would say, "but in houses." Tents are fine for times such as that, but most people would not want to live in one. They would rather have a house. I like the tent because it is a reminder of the truth that we all will one day move out of current residences and into our permanent home in heaven.

Where we live now is in one sense a tent. That is what Paul calls our body, which will one day be destroyed. Until then we look forward to the building we have that is from God, "an eternal house in heaven, not built by human hands" (5:1). A tent over a grave is a vivid picture of this truth. It serves as a reminder that we will leave the earthly tent behind for the home we have in heaven.

All that is around us is temporary, even our aches and pains. Rejoice that one day you will move out of the tent and into the house, the one prepared for you by God.

COUNT TO TEN, AGAIN

Proverbs 16–18, 2 Corinthians 6 • Key Verse: Proverbs 16:32

In our fast-paced world, with lives stuck on fast forward, rage comes quicker than ever. Someone gets cut off in traffic and rage kicks in— we lay on the horn or scream out the window, if not something even more drastic. Road rage is one example; airline rage is another. I once witnessed frustrated and fearful gate agents call for the police when a passenger at the airport, frustrated by a delay, began to yell.

"Better a patient man than a warrior, . . ."

A friend caught in one of those nightmare travel scenarios, flights delayed and canceled due to weather, described what happened when he was patient with the ticket agent. After she worked out the remainder of his trip, she thanked him for his demeanor. "You made my day," she said.

". . . a man who controls his temper than one who takes a city."

The person of rage may get his way at the counter or feel better having vented his anger at other drivers. He may feel good about being a road warrior, but he is not. God's Word says that the patient person, the one who can control his temper, is better.

The impatient person may think he is in control by forcing his will on others, but he is not. He is out of control, unable to control himself. We are to be under the control of the Spirit and be people of patience.

Rage may be the rage today, but patience is honored by God forever.

Perhaps something will test your patience today. Do you think you will pass or fail? You probably already know the answer! Ask God right now to help you begin to be a patient person.

SET APART AND ACCEPTABLE

*Proverbs 19–21, **2 Corinthians 7** • **Key Verse: 2 Corinthians 7:1***

Imagine sitting down at the table for a meal. A place has been set for you. Imagine looking at the plate and seeing on it the remnants of previous meals eaten from that plate. You just might protest a bit, especially if you are in a restaurant and don't know whose food was left on your plate! Now imagine the waiter saying, "Is there a problem? We set this place for you. What more could you want?"

Your answer would be immediate. "I want a clean plate!"

Now imagine you are the one setting the table for a very special guest. You would not want him to ask you, "Would you please bring me a clean plate?" Instead, you would make certain that not only was a place set for the guest but that it was immaculate.

This illustrates holiness. To be holy means to be "set apart." In a sense the place at the table is set apart for you; it is holy. But more is needed for it to be acceptable. It must not only be set apart but also clean. So it is with holiness.

Paul tells us to be "perfecting holiness out of reverence for God" (7:1). Being set aside and available are only part of what makes a person holy. We must be acceptable to God—which will be the result of truly being set apart!

How clean is your life before God? If you know of "dirty food" on your plate, ask God to forgive you and to help you remove it from your life.

NEVER GIVE UP!

Proverbs 22–24, 2 Corinthians 8 • *Key Verse: Proverbs 24:10*

He was a paunchy, stern-looking, cigar-chewing Englishman, an unlikely candidate to stand against the tyranny of Nazism. But Winston Churchill will be forever remembered for his motivational one-liner: "Never give up!"

That's good advice for the Christian. Our verse for today counsels us, "If you falter in times of trouble, how small is your strength!" Translation: never give up.

Let's face it. Anybody can have strong faith when not being tested. It's when the storms of life come, when the report from the doctor is not good, when the voice on the other end of the line bears tragic news, that we need strong faith in God. That's not a given. In fact, it's not even likely, unless we are convinced of God's righteous character in the good times of life. It's the knowledge of who God is and how He works in our behalf that gives us strength in the day of adversity.

What has God put on your plate today? Is something too difficult to bear? Is it some unexplainable disaster? Is life getting tougher for you instead of sweeter? If so, remember the paunchy Englishman. Better still, remember the advice of King Solomon: "Don't give up when tough times come. God will help you through them. Trust Him. You'll see brighter days if you never give up."

"Lord, help me to face the difficulties of life with Your grace. Help me to hang in there when others hang it up. Give me the courage to do my best and look beyond the difficulty of today to the victory of tomorrow."

STOKING THE FIRE

Proverbs 25–26, 2 Corinthians 9 • *Key Verses: Proverbs 26:20–21*

A few years ago my wife and I decided to make the change from charcoal to liquid propane gas. We enjoy grilling and opted for convenience over taste. The flavor, in our humble palettes' opinion, is better with charcoal, but we do cook out much more with the gas grill. I have at times brushed the snow off the top to fire it up in the middle of the winter. A twist of the knob on the tank, one match and we are on our way.

There is a problem, though. With charcoal I could see how much was left in the bag, but with a propane tank, it is pretty much a guess. One time the meal was not completely cooked when we ran out of gas. No fuel, no fire. That's the way it is.

It is the same with arguments. If there is no fuel, there will be no fire and the argument will end. One of the things that can feed that fire is gossip, and when it dies down, the quarrel does also.

Some people are quarrelsome. They stir up things and keep them stirred up. That is why they are described as being like charcoal, or wood. They kindle strife.

With picturesque words, Solomon challenges us not to be the fuel for the fire. Neither our actions, as in gossip, nor our character, as in being contentious, should start disagreements and keep them burning.

Ask yourself before you say something about another person, "Am I saying this to stir up trouble?" Answer honestly. Better to be quiet than to stoke the furnace of disagreements.

COACHED TO THE END

Proverbs 27–29, 2 Corinthians 10 • **Key Verse: Proverbs 27:6**

The next time you meet a retired Major League Baseball player, ask him, "At what point in your career did you no longer have a coach?" "I always had a coach," he will answer. Even the perennial all-star, certain Hall of Famer, needs a coach.

Some coaches are great motivators, encouraging with positive statements to help the athlete maximize his potential. But all coaches are critics. They have an ability to see what is wrong, point it out and correct it. The player who wants to improve his game needs a good coach and a willingness to listen. He may prefer having his ego stroked, but knows that he needs the blows the coach can dish out.

We all need coaches who will tell us what we need to hear, not just what we want to hear. We need to be coachable, people who will listen and learn from what Solomon calls the "wounds from a friend" (27:6). The words of a friend may hurt for a while, but ultimately they will help if we will listen. The person who says what we want to hear instead of what we need to hear is more like an enemy who kisses up to us.

Later in this chapter Solomon says, "As iron sharpens iron, so one man sharpens another" (v. 17). To sharpen involves removing some from the edge being sharpened. In a sense it, too, is a wounding, but for the good.

So which do you want—ego strokes or wounds?

Has someone tried to help you but you rejected him because his words hurt? Go back to that friend and ask for his help. You can trust the wounds of a friend.

AIMING FOR THE MIDDLE

Proverbs 30–31, 2 Corinthians 11:1–15
Key Verses: Proverbs 30:8–9

The prosperity train has pulled out of the station and everyone wants to be on board. Markets have been up, "dot coms" have soared, new home starts have increased—happy days are here again. Today there are probably more advertisements for investment services than lenders, especially the lenders who bail out people financially. It seems like it used to be the opposite, more quick-fix financial ads and fewer long-term investment ones, but times have changed.

Now is a good time to review a prayer for financial balance. It is not a prayer to say before balancing your checkbook, but one to help you keep money in perspective, not allowing yourself to get out of balance. Agur writes, "Give me neither poverty nor riches, but give me only my daily bread" (30:8). These are not the words of the brokerage firm wanting your investments but of a man of God concerned about the heart. The reason for his prayer is rock solid—"Otherwise, I may have too much and disown you and say, 'Who is the LORD?' Or I may become poor and steal, and so dishonor the name of my God" (v. 9).

There is both balance and reason in that prayer. The danger is in the extremes. With poverty comes the temptation to steal, and with affluence comes the temptation to forget God. There is safety in between. More may seem better to those around you, but less may be best!

With affluence and an emphasis on prosperity, it can be difficult to keep a balanced perspective on money. Pray this prayer to God today and repeat it as often as needed!

TWISTED AND EMPTY

Ecclesiastes 1–3, 2 Corinthians 11:16–33
Key Verse: Ecclesiastes 1:15

A bundle of studs delivered to a building site will invariably have some boards that are twisted, and no amount of nails seems to be sufficient to straighten them. Then there is the frustration of running out of nails. "How many do we have?" someone will ask. When "none" is the answer, frustration sets in.

Know the feeling? When bad things cannot be undone, and the needed supplies or other people who could be of help are unavailable, realization sets in and emotions churn. Are we having fun yet? Not now.

Solomon catches our attention with this scenario. He writes, "What is twisted cannot be straightened; what is lacking cannot be counted" (1:15). It is meaningless, he says, to try to change these facts. His intent is not to leave us in despair but to counsel us to a wise perspective. There are times when we must accept things as they are.

This is not a Christian fatalism or a Christian version of karma, but it is a biblical perspective that brings peace to the heart of the believer. We need to accept what God brings into our life, be content with our situation and learn to live for His glory with our circumstances. Some things cannot be undone. Other things will be lacking. So learn to accept those facts and get on with being the person God wants you to be.

Do you have any areas of discontent right now? Accept them and ask God to help you have contentment and fulfillment in spite of, if not because of, them.

STAY WEAK

Ecclesiastes 4–6, 2 Corinthians 12 • Key Verse: 2 Corinthians 12:9

As usual, strength is "in." Join the fitness center, work out, eat right, take supplements, be strong. Then be self-reliant, capable, assured, accomplished, using your connections and abilities to get where you want to be. Overcome your weaknesses and conquer the world.

You hear this over and over again, don't you? What you don't hear is an encouragement to be weak. The closest thing to that is the current emphasis on "servant-leadership," but notice that it is still "leadership."

What Paul writes in 2 Corinthians 12:9 is truly counter-culture: "I will boast all the more gladly about my weaknesses, so that Christ's power may rest on me." When did you last hear someone say, "Let me tell you about my weak points"? We think they are to be hidden, put out of sight, covered up. But Paul said he would boast about them.

The difference is Christ. Paul knew, and we need to also, that Christ's power rests on us in our weaknesses, not in our strength. Where we say, "I can't," Christ says, "I can." And as long as we say, "I can," Christ says, "I can't." It is not that He can't but that we won't let Him. We are like a child, unwilling to let a parent help. It is only when the child in weakness admits he can't that the parent, in strength, can help.

It's the same for us. Stay strong and you are weak. Stay weak and by Christ you are strong.

"God, help me be weak, to put aside my arrogant self-sufficiency, drawing instead on the strength of Christ. I can't, but He can."

UNEXPECTED DISASTER

Ecclesiastes 7–9, 2 Corinthians 13 • *Key Verse: Ecclesiastes 9:12*

Sophisticated forecasting devices warn us when storms move into our area. Efforts are continually made to improve the equipment and techniques so we can receive even more accurate information. Long gone are the days of looking at the sky and saying, "Looks like rain." Now it is done by Doppler radar and satellite images beamed from high above the earth. We like to be forewarned, especially of impending disasters. Yet in spite of all the technological advances, we still sometimes get caught unawares. We just don't know what the future holds.

In his wisdom, Solomon says that we are we are like fish, unaware of the net that is in the water until we hit it, or like birds, not realizing that a snare has been set for our capture (9:12). Unexpectedly, we are caught by what was unpredictable. This happens, he says, so be prepared.

God does not give us a pass to avoid all difficulties. Nor does He give us advance warning of every challenge that lies ahead. He does let us know that in this life we will have problems. That does not sound like much encouragement until you remember that whatever comes, He will be with us. God does not keep us from all difficulties, but He does stay with us and sees us through them.

Face the future with realistic confidence. Whatever comes, God will be with you. Ask Him to help you brace yourself for the days ahead and for Him to help you get through the unexpected things that lie ahead.

THE KISS OF LIFE

Ecclesiastes 10–12, Galatians 1 • *Key Verse: Ecclesiastes 12:13*

Sometimes we need to be reminded of the importance of KISS. That word can be an acronym reminding us to "Keep It Short" or "Keep It Simple." I know that is only "KIS," but I prefer to leave off the last "S" because typically that stands for "Stupid." Why call someone a name when you can get across the point without demeaning him!

There is another version of KISS. It is "Keep It Strictly Scriptural." A great admonition, especially for those of us who teach the Word, but it's not just for teachers. All of us should want to live a strictly scriptural life, doing and saying and thinking only what is strictly based on God's Word.

Maybe Solomon heard of KISS when he summarized all of what is important in just six words. He wrote, "Fear God and keep his commandments" (12:13). It is the "KISS of Life," short, simple and strictly scriptural. In those six words are contained the foundation for our life—loving reverence of God. The content is there as well—keep His commandments. There is a completeness in this command, as Solomon notes that it is the "whole duty of man." Far from the meaninglessness of things pointed out in Ecclesiastes is the fulfillment of life found in these words.

This, then, is how we are to live, in the fear of God, keeping His commandments. Remember this "KISS."

Put this verse into your memory, say it daily and live it always. It is the KISS of Life.

REPETITION AIDS LEARNING

Song of Solomon 1–3, **Galatians 2** • *Key Verse: Galatians 2:16*

Those who are taught how to teach will sooner or later hear that "repetition aids learning." Repeat your point, in a different way, restating it so your hearers will have more than one opportunity to learn the lesson.

Sometimes we find repetition in the Bible, and when we read a passage with repetition it should really catch our attention. If God thought it necessary to repeat a point, it is extremely significant.

In Galatians 2:16, we are told the same thing three times. As is pointed out in the *New International Study Bible*, "Three times it tells us that no one is justified by observing the law, and three times it underscores the indispensable requirement of placing one's faith in Christ." Read the verse again, looking for the repetition. It says that man is "not justified by observing the law . . . . not by observing the law, because by observing the law no one will be justified." The point is made, remade and made again!

God repeats it because we struggle to learn this lesson. People try to earn salvation, work their way to heaven, keep the Ten Commandments, even though God clearly says it doesn't work that way. Salvation is by faith alone, never by works or faith and works.

Have you learned this lesson? The final exam is when you die. See if you pass this one-question mid-term exam: Why should God let you into heaven? The wrong answer is "works."

God gives salvation to those who believe, who by faith receive Jesus as their Savior. You cannot trust in anything or anyone else and be saved. Make sure your hope is based on Jesus and Him alone.

SWEET WORDS

Song of Solomon 4–5, Galatians 3
Key Verse: Song of Solomon 4:11

Try to go a day without any sugar. That might be close to impossible! There is sugar or a sweetener of some form in many of the things we eat. Read the labels and you may be amazed. Since that first suggestion is probably impossible, spend one day noticing the sweets you eat. Perhaps at some point in the day you'll get one of those "cravings," maybe even while just reading about sweets.

Let's face it—we enjoy the sweet treats, pieces of chocolate, mints, candies, as well as the spoonfuls of sugar we ladle into coffee or tea. Sweet is nice.

With that in mind read again these words: "Your lips drop sweetness as the honeycomb, my bride; milk and honey are under your tongue" (4:11). Here the "Lover" of Song of Solomon compares the words of his bride with the sweetness of the honeycomb. She must have been an expert at sweet talk!

Too often we are better at sounding sour than sweet. Sour words come more naturally. Yet we all like to hear the sweet words, the words that encourage, build up, motivate, calm and lift up our souls. Like the taste of a special piece of candy, the words of others can be sweetness to our hearts.

Now, knowing how much you appreciate the kind words of others, consider your own words. Are they sweet or sour?

Would you be described as one whose lips "drop sweetness as the honeycomb"? Think as you speak today.

JOY ROBBERS

Song of Solomon 6–8, Galatians 4 • *Key Verse: Galatians 4:15*

Paul asked the Galatians an agonizing and penetrating question, "What has happened to all your joy?" Biblical Christianity allows us to live life to the fullest extent intended by God, a life of blessing, one that is to be characterized by the joy of the Lord. We should be concerned when God's people are robbed of their joy.

The joy robber in Galatia was the restraints of legalistic Judaism. Later Paul would describe these people as ones who "cut in on" them as they were running a good race (5:7). They sought to enforce rules that were not of God but of man.

The problem is not with rules or with having "standards" in our lives. The problem is with the reason we keep them. If we observe special days or rules, especially those legislated for us by others, in hope of gaining some spiritual merit, then we are sinning. We regress from liberty to bondage and in the process can lose our joy.

In Christ we have liberty, which includes liberty from legalism. We can express our liberty in Christ and enjoy the blessing of it by keeping rules or having standards. Those are not wrong in themselves. The wrong comes from our motives if we do so to gain favor.

Joy will be found when we live a life of liberty, doing what we do to express our love for Jesus. Don't lose your joy.

Christian liberty is often misunderstood. Do what pleases God not to gain merit, but to show your love for Him. Ask yourself if your Christian life is one of joy.

NOT GOOD ENOUGH

Isaiah 1–2, Galatians 5 • *Key Verse: Isaiah 1:15*

It seems inconceivable to think that God would not listen to our prayers, yet there are times when that is exactly the case. Our concept of God is that He always hears, always listens, but that is an incomplete concept. It may be the one that we like, but it is not what the Bible teaches.

What makes the difference between God hearing or not hearing our prayers is a matter of our heart. Some think, *If I have the right "form," if I pray with the right words, in the right place, at the right time, then it is a done deal. I prayed. God will answer. That is the way it is supposed to be.*

That attitude toward prayer is very man-centered, one that views God as the cosmic servant rather than the holy, sovereign Creator. His view differs drastically. Isaiah 1 makes that apparent. God looks at the heart of the one praying. Even His view of the raised hands is penetrating as He sometimes sees the uncleanness of the supplicant's life (1:15). In this chapter Isaiah also condemns strongly the sacrifices and festivals of the people, making the point that it is not a matter of art but of heart that makes what we do acceptable to God.

Flowing out of these rebukes are the gentle words, "'Come now, let us reason together'" (v. 18). Notice, though, that between rebuke and reconciliation is repentance (vv. 16–17). When there is wrong in our life it must be made right, a process that starts in the heart.

Perhaps you go through all the right motions, but is there wrong in your life? Don't just trust your routines to indicate all is right in your relationship with God. Look at your heart.

FARMERS' MARKET

Isaiah 3–4, Galatians 6 • *Key Verse: Galatians 6:9*

Two words that will get a person to wake up early on a Saturday morning are "garage sales." Two other words are "farmers' market." Both have their own appeal, but there is something extra special about fresh fruits and vegetables, picked just a few hours before, trucked in from the country in the back of a pickup. These are not the processed, hauled long-distance, waxed, sprayed, treated versions, but the real deal.

We enjoy wandering through the stalls, picking and choosing, feasting on the fruit of someone else's labor. But ours is a different view of those items from the person selling them. The fruit of the harvest is the fruit of their labor. They may remember tilling, planting, cultivating, fertilizing, pruning, staking, watering—then finally came harvesting. Giving up is not in the process, unless the person wanted a bed of weeds.

Life is like that. Paul uses farming as an illustration to teach us both the importance of sowing and of not giving up. We will reap a harvest if we do not lose heart (6:9), and what we reap will depend on what we sow (vv. 7–8).

At the farmers' market, we reap the benefit of what others have sown, of their hard work. That is the way it can be with fruits and vegetables but not with the blessing of God in our life. We cannot buy His blessings from a vendor. We must sow and reap, not giving up. The blessings do come!

Look at what you are sowing in your life. Remember that you will reap what you sow. When it is difficult to keep doing right, remember that the good harvest will come for those who do not give up.

PURPOSE-DRIVEN

*Isaiah 5–6, **Ephesians 1** • **Key Verses: Ephesians 1:6a, 12b, 14b***

It is not unusual to see posted in a business or printed in an organization's literature things like a vision statement, a mission statement or objectives. Being purpose-driven has become one of the trends of business that has been adopted and adapted by some churches. Even some families and individuals have decided to write vision/mission statements.

Long before any writer or consultant suggested having a clear sense of vision, God communicated to His Church that what He was doing was purpose-driven. Three times in Ephesians 1 we find the same basic expression that says, "to the praise of his glory." Each time the phrase is attached to another aspect of God's plan for our salvation, and each time it is in regard to another Person of the Trinity.

God purposed and planned our salvation to the praise of His glory. The provision for our salvation is in the finished work of Christ, in whom we hope that we might be "for the praise of his glory." The Holy Spirit is given us as a pledge of our inheritance—again, "to the praise of his glory."

Purpose-driven? Definitely. What God did in eternity past, what Jesus did on Calvary's cross, what the Spirit does in our life, is all with purpose. It is all intended to bring glory to God.

So let's not mess it up! Let's live in a way that brings glory to God and in no way cause Him shame.

It is easy for us to see salvation as just for our benefit. Ask God to help you focus your heart and life on bringing glory to Him. Do not think only about how what He has done is for your good. It is also for His glory.

SERIOUS ABOUT THE WORD

Isaiah 7–8, Ephesians 2 • *Key Verse: Isaiah 7:9*

The phrase, "Is that your final answer?" has recently become part of our lexicon. The hope of winning a million dollars seems to be the key to a highly watched television program. Repeatedly there is the tension and anticipation of a contestant saying, "Yes, that is my final answer." After a dramatic pause he is then told if his answer was correct.

Isaiah gave King Ahaz the final answer. It was the word of the Lord, a prophecy, one that the Lord would confirm with a sign. What more could a person ask for than that? God's word, confirmed!

Still, man being what man is, with a hesitancy to declare that something is his "final answer," can waver. So Isaiah, in a very straightforward way, said to Ahaz, "If you do not stand firm in your faith, you will not stand at all" (7:9).

This is an either/or statement, not a both/and. It is a one-way street. Our faith is to be our final answer.

We need to study the Bible, learning what it says so we can live what it teaches. That will bring blessing and confidence. And as we correctly understand and apply the Word of God to our lives, we will be able to stand. It is a stand we take in faith, but not in a blind faith. It is a faith based on the revealed Word of God.

Isaiah will not come knocking on our door, giving us new revelation. Isaiah is in our home, though! He brings us God's message in written form. Continue to read, learn and live the Word. Make it your "final answer."

MR. WONDERFUL

Isaiah 9–10, Ephesians 3 • *Key Verse: Isaiah 9:6*

Many people do wonderful things for us. The doctor performs a wonderful operation and removes a cancerous tumor. The newspaper editor runs a wonderful article on our church. The guy at the garage gives us the wonderful advice just to ignore the check engine light on our car. But there is only one person who can be our wonderful Savior. That person is Jesus.

In one of the most thrilling and inclusive prophecies of the Bible, Isaiah predicts some of the qualities we should expect in the Savior. "For to us a child is born, to us a son is given, and the government will be on his shoulders. And he will be called Wonderful Counselor, Mighty God, Everlasting Father, Prince of Peace" (9:6).

Jesus Christ is "Mr. Wonderful," in every sense of the word. He has given us a wonderful salvation because of His wonderful sacrifice at Calvary (2 Cor. 5:21). He calls us to a wonderfully abundant life now because of His wonderful resurrection (John 10:10; 14:19). And He is preparing a wonderful home for us in heaven because of His wonderful promise (John 14:1–3).

It is true that Jesus Christ is the Prince of Peace. He is the Mighty God. He is the great Counselor. But in this world where the quality of almost everything is suspect, it's good to know we have a wonderful Savior. He is Mr. Wonderful.

"Thank You, Lord, for being a wonderful Savior to me. May I today be a wonderful witness to You."

BITTER, NOT BETTER

Isaiah 11–13, Ephesians 4 • *Key Verse: Ephesians 4:31*

Do you remember the medicines your mother tried to give you as a child? There was aspirin, cough syrup, cod liver oil and more. And for some reason mothers were always trying to get kids to take castor oil. All I remember is that they all tasted terrible.

Sometimes bitter tastes make us healthy; sometimes they don't. Bitterness is a bit like that. It tastes terrible, but it doesn't do us any good. That's why Paul said, "Get rid of all bitterness, rage and anger, brawling and slander, along with every form of malice" (4:31). Did you notice what topped the list of bad medicine? Bitterness.

Bitterness is the only substance that does more damage to its container than it does to those it is applied to. It destroys people, but not those who are its recipients. Bitterness destroys those who are bitter towards others.

If you are bitter toward your spouse, your boss, your pastor, your sibling, your parents, your neighbor or anyone else in your life, they are untouched and unharmed by your bitterness.

Identify your bitterness. Admit it. Confess it. Discard it. It's the only way to have a relationship with others that benefits both of you. Replace bitterness with forgiveness and you will replace acid with honey.

"Lord, don't allow me to retain bitterness. Help me to confess it as sin and forsake it. Help me to realize the personal harm bitterness causes, not to those toward whom I am bitter, but to me."

LIFE IS SHORT

Isaiah 14–16, Ephesians 5:1–16 • *Key Verses: Ephesians 5:15–16*

Perhaps you have seen this slogan: "Life is short. Play hard." Perhaps you also have seen the rewritten version: "Life is short. Pray hard." One letter makes all the difference. It is the difference between a temporal mind-set and an eternal one.

A temporal mind-set thinks primarily about the things of now. It focuses on this world as if it is all there is. The time is now because there is no other time. It embraces an "eat, drink and be merry for tomorrow we die" philosophy of life.

The Christ follower, however, knows that this life is only temporary; the world to come is permanent. So, we have only this much time and we better make good use of it—good use not in the sense of getting maximum pleasure as we play hard, but as we make it count for all eternity.

It is foolish to waste time. Paul both warns and encourages us: the time we have is limited and the days are evil, so we need to make the best use of our time to impact this world for Jesus while we have opportunity.

Opportunity is originally a Latin word that means "toward the port." When the winds and tides were favorable, the sailing ship would take advantage of the "opportunity." The days are evil, Paul says, which sounds like unfavorable winds, not favorable. Still, this is our time, our opportunity. Life is short. Pray hard.

Think about how you spent your day yesterday. Did you make it count for eternity? Now think about today. In what ways will you make it count?

IDOL WORSHIPERS

Isaiah 17–19, Ephesians 5:17–33 • Key Verses: Isaiah 17:7–8

Man has the innate ability to look more to what can be seen and made than to the unseen God, who is the Maker of all things. That is the lure of idolatry. A person can see an idol or make or designate something to be an idol. The problem with idolatry has always been that whatever the idol is, it is worthless. It may have some monetary value, depending on the materials in it, but it has no spiritual worth.

Even Christians, while perhaps not actually putting an idol on a shelf in their home, can have eyes that wander from the true God to other things. It may be the skill of their hands that becomes the object of their trust. A person's investment portfolio can be viewed as the source of security. Someone might rest in his accomplishments, as if having done this much will enable him to get through whatever might come his way.

To the people in Damascus, the prophet said that a day would come when "men will look to their Maker and turn their eyes to the Holy One of Israel" (17:7–8). When people forget God, living as if He doesn't exist, they become like the people of Damascus, who had turned their eyes from God to idols.

We might chafe at being compared to an idol worshiper, but when our eyes are off God and on other things, we are really the same.

Is your trust in God or other things? Think hard about this. If your trust is first in yourself, then get your eyes right. Look to God.

ALL!

Isaiah 20–22, Ephesians 6 • *Key Verse: Ephesians 6:18*

Some words are so simple and clear that they should not need definition. *All* is one of those words. It means . . . well, you know, it means all! While we may understand the word, there are times when we need to be reminded of just how much *all* includes. Nothing is left out when all is included. To see what I mean, look at the *all's* of this verse:

"And pray in the Spirit on *all* occasions with *all* kinds of prayers and requests. With this in mind, be alert and always keep on praying for *all* the saints."

Paul uses the word *all* repeatedly to stress the "all-ness" of prayer. We are to pray on *all* occasions, which leaves none out. *All* kinds of prayers and requests are to be brought to God. Praying is something we should *always* be doing. Finally, notice that we are to pray for *all* the saints. No one is to be left out of our praying.

One of the things going on in your life all the time is your heartbeat. It beats all the time. What does that *all* mean? It means all the time; no time is excluded.

You are to pray "all the time." What does that *all* mean?

Now, pray as if your heart beats with that kind of all, and let your heart beat like you pray with that kind of all. Would you live?

Praying always does not mean that you must always have your head bowed and your eyes closed. It does mean you are in constant communication with God. Consciously think today about keeping communication going with God.

WORSHIP IN JUDGMENT

Isaiah 23–25, Philippians 1 • *Key Verse: Isaiah 24:14*

A typical view of worship is much more narrow than what is found in the Bible. It may be that you conceive of worship as a Sunday morning service, something to attend once a week at most. Perhaps your view is a bit wider, recognizing not only corporate but also personal times of worship, such as daily devotions. Some people consider worship as being a response to something good: God does something good so we praise Him.

When we look for worship in the Bible, our understanding is stretched. In chapter 24, Isaiah records a worship scene far different from the one in chapter 6. Now the prompting to worship is not a vision of God in heaven but the carrying out of His wrath on earth. We typically do not think of God's judgment as a call to praise, but it is.

In His judgment, God declares His majesty and righteousness. He is the rightful Ruler of all creation. One day He will declare His majesty, putting down all rebellion, displacing all rulers. Also, the wickedness of the world will be brought to an end as God establishes His reign of righteousness.

Can God's judgment prompt you to worship? It should. But it won't unless you see this world as God sees it, a place of sin deserving His judgment. It will when you see judgment as God setting all things right, demonstrating Himself to be the Sovereign of the universe.

"God, help me worship You in Your majesty and righteousness. May I truly see You as the King who rules in holiness and praise You for the day in which You will establish Your righteous reign on this earth."

TRANQUILITY

Isaiah 26–27, Philippians 2 • *Key Verse: Isaiah 26:3*

There is something peaceful about the sound of the word *tranquility*. Life typically is lived on the edge—the ragged edge. Peace, an over-used word, is reduced to a slogan, something known but not experienced. But since we have not overused the word *tranquility*, it sounds so appealing, so peaceful.

God makes tranquility available to us. When He promises us "perfect peace," that is tranquility. It is important to note that perfect peace is not a product that He offers but a result. It is the result of a steadfast mind, one that trusts God.

The better we focus our minds on God, the better we trust, the more we will experience the perfect peace that comes from God alone. This peace, or tranquility, passes all understanding.

Sounds nice, doesn't it? It is such a contrast to the noise and congestion of traffic, the interrupting ring of the phone, the beep of the answering machine letting you know that you have messages, or the sound of children's voices clamoring for attention.

Perfect peace is not the result of God removing all of these, along with the other sights, sounds and smells of a stress-filled life. Instead, it is the result of a mind that is focused solely on Him.

Upon what is your mind focused? Determine today to keep God at the front of your thoughts, viewing everything through a God-conscious grid. Ask Him to help you know His perfect peace.

PAINT-BY-NUMBERS

Isaiah 28–29, Philippians 3 • ***Key Verse: Isaiah 29:13***

Remember paint-by-number sets? The pictures were divided into numbered sections, each number indicating the color to go into that portion. People could paint just by putting the right-numbered paint into the corresponding areas of the picture. When done, the person had a painting. Usually you could tell that it was a paint-by-numbers. It looked too much "by the numbers"!

Some people try to do worship "by the numbers." It's as if the worship of God could be printed out with spaces to fill in, the end result being a picture entitled, "Worship," but looking more like a painting done by filling in numbered spaces.

The difference between worship that is acceptable to God and that which He despises is the heart. Isaiah delivered God's rebuke when he said that the people's words may have sounded right but their hearts were wrong. God will always reject right words from wrong hearts. Worship by the numbers, or rules, is not what God desires.

So when we gather with others for worship, or spend time alone with God, we must not let ourselves be like these people, whom God strongly rebuked. Worship is not a matter of art but of the heart. We must look inward, determined that the words we offer in worship are ones that come from the heart. Keep your heart close to God and your worship will be pleasing to Him.

This week ask God to help you worship in a way that pleases Him. If you find that your worship is a paint-by-numbers approach, ask for forgiveness and for help to change.

DON'T WORRY!

*Isaiah 30–31, **Philippians 4** • **Key Verse: Philippians 4:6***

Unlike the popular song a few years back, God never tells us, "Don't worry, be happy." Mindlessness is never the answer to anxiety. Avoidance may be a chosen path, but going that direction typically contributes nothing to the solution and may only aggravate the problem.

Instead, God tells us that we are not to be anxious about anything. That could be shortened to, "Don't worry—period." What follows is choosing the path that will take us in the direction of resolving our worries. Paul tells us that we are to take our anxieties, package them up as requests, then by prayer and petition, with thanksgiving, present them to God. Included in this instruction is the word *everything* because God wants us to understand how all-encompassing this command is. Give everything to God in prayer.

To the worrier, this is unnatural. Give away your worries and you have nothing left to worry about! But if you give them to God and take care of what you are supposed to do, you can leave the rest to Him. There's no need to worry over them any longer because you have given them to God. He never fumbles.

God does not want you to be a worrier. Do what He wants. Make a list right now and give your worries to Him. Pray, asking God to take those things out of your mind and put them into His hand.

ONLY ONE CAN HAVE IT

Isaiah 32–33, Colossians 1 • *Key Verse: Colossians 1:18*

Supremacy is a rather limited word. We may try to use it broadly, but when something or someone has supremacy, it really is singular. Only one can be supreme. Anyone else may be close, but not quite. The same is true of preeminence.

Paul says that preeminence and supremacy belong to Jesus because of the Resurrection. We need know that and remember that preeminence is His by right, not ours to grasp. In Colossians 1, the emphasis of verses 15–19 is on Jesus.

Contrast this with Diotrephes, the church leader characterized in 3 John as a man "who loves to have the preeminence" (v. 9, NKJV). The root word in Colossians 1 and 3 John is the same in the Greek. The only difference is that in 3 John it is a compound word, the other part meaning "he loves to be." Diotrephes loved to be first, to have the preeminence.

It is striking that this word appears only twice in the New Testament. When Paul used it, he was stating what rightfully belongs to Jesus. When John used it, he was condemning a man who wanted what belongs to Jesus. The desire to control, to be the center of attention, to have the power to exclude others, came from a heart that wanted what belongs to Jesus.

The preeminence is His to have, not ours to take. Watch your pride, lest you become like Diotrephes.

Do you have the heart of a servant or a usurper? Read carefully the description of Diotrophes and then again the one of Jesus. Ask God to help you be humble, not seeking in any way what belongs only to Him.

GOD WILL COME

Isaiah 34–36, Colossians 2 • *Key Verses: Isaiah 35:3–4*

A writer was describing his experience of hiking in the Grand Canyon. I was surprised when he said that coming back up the trail at the end of the day was easier than his earlier descent into the canyon. It seems like uphill would always be harder, especially when it is the last part of the hike.

But knowing that the hike would soon be over, that he could return to his air-conditioned room, that dinner was waiting at the end, made the climb up easier than the climb down. Basically, hope made the last part less difficult. What he knew was ahead kept him going. His knees felt better and his thoughts were not on cardiac arrest, either! The rim was just ahead, and with it would come rest, refreshment and relief.

Far greater than a motel room with an air conditioner is the word of hope given to the redeemed by the prophet Isaiah. His message was, "'Be strong, do not fear; your God will come'" (35:4). Those words would "strengthen the feeble hands," "steady the knees that give way" and encourage those with "fearful hearts." Better than a room on the rim of the Grand Canyon is the truth that God will come!

The way our life takes us can be hard. The world in which we live can be difficult. Our souls may weary, weakening our hands, our knees, our hearts—but to the weary pilgrim God gives words of hope. He will come.

"God, fill my heart, mind and soul with hope. Help me climb, renewed and reinvigorated by the reminder that You will one day come."

HABIT TRAILS OF THE SOUL

Isaiah 37–38, Colossians 3 • *Key Verses: Colossians 3:1–2*

Show me three things and I can probably tell what is important to you: your checkbook, your calendar and your home. The first will show me what you do with your money, the things that you value enough to spend your earnings attaining. The second will show me what you do with your time, that in spite of how busy you might be, these are things for which you still find time. The third will show me your interests. Items accumulated or displayed, even the books and magazine on a coffee table, can reveal your interests.

The things that we devote time and money to have captured our minds and our hearts. Thinking about and being involved in those things results in habit trails developing in our souls. We just seem to keep returning to those thoughts, those things.

First and foremost in our habit trails needs to be the things of God, the things of above. Paul tells us to set both our hearts and minds on things above. It is easier, more natural, to think about and love earthly things. After all, we can see them, hold them, collect them—love and think about them. Yet that is exactly what we are to do with the things of God—love and think about them, not totally to the exclusion of other things, but with a priority.

As we discipline our hearts and minds to fall in love with and think about what God teaches us from His Word, this will happen. Consider your habit trails. Are they of things above or below?

A good first step is Bible memory. Memorize Colossians 3:1–2. Then ask God to help you develop heavenly habit trails.

AN AWESOME GOD

Isaiah 39–40, Colossians 4 • **Key Verse: Isaiah 40:12**

A popular praise song says, "Our God is an awesome God." Verses such as Isaiah 40:12 reinforce that truth. Allow yourself a moment to meditate on this description of God.

He has measured the waters in the hollow of His hand. See how much water your hand can hold. Maybe an ounce, maybe two, but probably not much more. Then go look at a body of water, add to it all water you have seen, and toss in all the oceans. God is described as being able to measure all of the water in His hand.

He has marked off the heavens with His hand. I sometimes use my hand, from the tip of my thumb to the tip of my little finger, as a basic measuring device. It is about nine inches from tip to tip. That is my span. Compare that to God's. Isaiah said that God could mark off the breadth of the heavens.

We all know what dust is and how much of it there can be. God can put it all in a basket. He can even take the mountains and the hills and put them in a scale or a balance, much like we might weigh fruit at the grocery store.

Granted, this is only a representation of God. He does not have a body like ours but is spirit. Sometimes the Bible describes God in physical terms to help us understand Him. This description leaves us with only one thought: "Our God is an awesome God."

Take a moment to meditate on the awesomeness of God and then pray, praising Him for His majesty.

NO FEAR

Isaiah 41–42, 1 Thessalonians 1 • *Key Verse: Isaiah 41:10*

Have you seen this on a T-shirt, cap or car window—"No Fear"? It's a strong sentiment, but I sometimes wonder if the words match the reality of life. When life is going well and we are moving along in familiar circumstances with things seemingly under control, it is possible to have no fear. The problem is that what can look like smooth sailing may at any time change to treacherous waters without warning. A person might be tempted to change out of their "No Fear" T-shirt at the same time!

Yet God wants us to be "no fear" people, not in apparel but in the calmness of our hearts. He tells us not only in Isaiah 41:10 but elsewhere that we should neither fear nor be dismayed.

As is the case with God, He does not just tell us what to do but also enables us to do it. He says, "For I am your God." Remember this! Realize this! Be strengthened by this truth!

What this means is that He will strengthen and help us. He will also uphold us with His righteous right hand. Help is not on the way; help is here!

Knowing this truth is one thing. Making it real is another. To help calm your fears, memorize this verse. Then when you are starting to feel uncertain, remind yourself of this truth. And one other thing—pray this verse. Ask God to keep you from fear and to help you feel His strengthening so that you will know that He is upholding you.

Begin right now to memorize this verse. Learn it well and say it often, especially when fear begins to show itself in your heart.

FORGET IT

Isaiah 43–44, 1 Thessalonians 2 • *Key Verse: Isaiah 43:18*

One of the most difficult things we can attempt to do is to forget. But sometimes forgetting is easy. Usually that is when we are trying to remember someone's name or what we were supposed to pick up at the grocery store. Other things get so firmly embedded into our minds that nothing could ever dislodge them. Our past can "haunt" us, actually affecting our present.

It is a challenge for us to forget the past, with its pains and failures. Yet God does not want us to be controlled by such things. Instead, He wants us to live with a clear sense of forgiveness.

To His people, Israel, God said, "Forget the former things; do not dwell on the past" (43:18). To give added emphasis to this instruction, God also said, "I, even I, am he who blots out your transgressions, for my own sake, and remembers your sins no more" (v. 25).

This is a tremendous picture of forgiveness. Our minds, which can't remember names or that we were supposed to pick up milk on the way home, hang on to hurts and wrongs for decades! Yet God, who knows even the number of hairs on your head, says, "I will not remember your sins." Forgiveness is fantastic!

If only we would let forgiveness accomplish all that it can. It can free us from the pain of our past. Forget it. Don't dwell on it. These are not trendy phrases but biblical truth.

Is anything in your past affecting your present? Right now make sure it is forgiven and then ask God to help you not bring it up again. Remember it no more.

NO OTHER GOD

Isaiah 45–46, 1 Thessalonians 3 • *Key Verse: Isaiah 45:22*

The God of the Bible is not reticent to say that He alone is God. In the Book of Isaiah, Jehovah often claims divine exclusivity: "I am the first and I am the last; apart from me there is no God" (44:6, see also 44:8, 24; and 45:5).

We could dismiss these claims and believe that there are many gods, one for each of us to discover in our own way. But the Bible doesn't give us that option. Jehovah says, "All who make idols are nothing . . . . He bows down to it and worships. He prays to it and says, 'Save me; you are my god.' . . . A deluded heart misleads him; he cannot save himself" (44:9, 17, 20).

God will not make room for pretenders to His throne. And nowhere is this more critically important than when it comes to our salvation. Jehovah says, "Turn to me and be saved, all you ends of the earth; for I am God, and there is no other" (45:22).

Make sure you have trusted the right God, the only God who can save you from your sins. You'll know who He is when you meet Him in a personal way. Read John 14:1–6 to know Him personally.

"God, I believe there is but one God, that You have revealed Yourself through Your Son, the Lord Jesus Christ. Help me to be bold in my witness to those who are still searching for a relationship with You."

HOPE MAKES THE DIFFERENCE

Isaiah 47–49, 1 Thessalonians 4 • *Key Verse: 1 Thessalonians 4:13*

We all have times of grief, times of mourning the loss of a family member, neighbor or close friend. There is a sadness that comes with death, a sadness intensified by the finality of it. For some, their mourning is intensified by both finality and uncertainty. They do not know for certain what happens after death and find themselves facing an unsure future, one that looks hopeless.

When Paul wrote to the church at Thessalonica, he wanted, among other things, to clear up any misunderstandings they might have regarding death. His intent was to do more than just give them information. He wanted them to realize the certain hope of the Christian and to have that hope affect their mourning. Knowing that in Jesus we have eternal life and that those who die in Christ are forever with Him should keep us from grieving like those who have no hope. We will still miss those who have died, but we should not grieve like others might.

We have hope in Christ. When a Christian dies, he is with Jesus, eternally. The day will come when we will join those who have died before us, either through our own death or through Jesus coming to take us out of this world. Our time together here on earth is temporary, as is the separation when our loved ones join Jesus. When we are all with Jesus, that will be permanent. There will be no more separation.

Perhaps you are grieving a loss. The truth of these verses can help you through your grief. You have a certain hope in Jesus!

HUGS AND HELPS

Isaiah 50–52, 1 Thessalonians 5 • *Key Verse: 1 Thessalonians 5:11*

Much can be said in just a few words. One example is the following: "Life is hard." Our knees may buckle at times, our shoulders droop under the load, and a weariness can settle even into our breathing. We sigh, and sigh again. That's life! Good times are interspersed with difficult times.

The good news for the Christian is that we do not go through the tough times alone. When we are involved in a local church, a body of believers that practices fellowship, others will come alongside to give hugs and to help. They are following Paul's command to "encourage one another and build each other up" (5:11).

Paul is not reminding us of a blessing but of a responsibility. It is easy for us to say, "Someone should do this for me!" And they should. But don't just sit back and remind yourself of what others should be doing. Paul wrote these words to you, about what you should be doing.

God wants the Body of Christ to be a place of encouragement and help. That will happen as we all get involved in giving out the hugs and helps to those who need them. The more we sit back, waiting for others to do it, the less likely it will happen. Yes, you may be in need, but so are others. So, get up, go out, and give of yourself to encourage and build each other up.

Is there someone you can encourage or help? If so, do it—today.

BOTTLED WATER

*Isaiah 53–55, 2 Thessalonians 1 • **Key Verse: Isaiah 55:1***

It's a bit ironic that while drinkable water is free, bottled water, which costs, has become very popular. When ordering a sandwich at a fast-food restaurant, your request for water to drink has to be very specific. If you just say "water," a bottle might be put on your tray—and on your bill! Some people do have good reasons for drinking bottled water, but it still seems odd to buy it when water is free.

Isaiah contains very beautiful invitations, ones God gave to His people that also have meaning for us. The call of God, "Come, all you who are thirsty, come to the waters," is a touching one. God cries out to us. He has water that will quench our thirst, and it is free. Jesus used the water imagery to describe salvation, a free gift that satisfies the deepest thirst of our souls (John 4:14).

Just as people will pay for water, which is free, some will try to pay for salvation, which also is free. There is a major difference though. You can pay and get water. You cannot pay and get salvation. It is free and only free. God offers it, and we receive it.

There is a sense in which salvation is not free. It did cost a high price, which Jesus paid when He died on the cross. But it is always free to us. We can never pay for what God gives.

Have you received the free gift of salvation? If so, thank God for the Living Water. If not, pray today, asking to receive this gift. It is yours, already paid for, available for the asking.

TRANSCENDENT AND IMMINENT

Isaiah 56–58, 2 Thessalonians 2 • *Key Verse: Isaiah 57:15*

A friend one day contrasted the music she prefers with the music style her teenage sons like. She used two words in particular to describe the difference. She prefers the music in which God is transcendent, while her sons like music in which God is imminent.

Her comment stuck in my mind. It was very insightful. Some do prefer music that describes God as high and lifted up, the One who reigns from above in heaven. Others gravitate to the songs that help them "feel the power." God is described as working in them and through them. He is right there with them. That is the basic difference between transcendent and imminent—high and exalted compared to right here with us.

In reality God is both. Through Isaiah, God said, "I live in a high and holy place" (57:15). His next statement adds the fact that God is "with him who is contrite and lowly in spirit." God is both transcendent and imminent.

This affects our worship when we, as Isaiah describes in chapter 6, see the Lord high and exalted. This affects our daily living as we realize that God is right here with us and in us, working through us. Our view of God needs to be as large as all the universes He created and as specific as our street address. It is not a contradiction but a completion. He is transcendent and imminent.

How do you view God—as off in the distant, or right here right now? Thank God for His immensity and for His immediacy.

NEVER GIVE IN

Isaiah 59–61, 2 Thessalonians 3 • *Key Verse: 2 Thessalonians 3:13*

Among the familiar quotes of Sir Winston Churchill is the line from a speech he gave at the Harrow School on October 29, 1941. They were not darker days, according to Churchill, but sterner ones. England was engaged in the war against Germany. It was there that he uttered the famous line, "Never give in, never, never, never, never." Some think that is all he said, but there was more. It is this sentence, though, that stands most firmly in our memory.

Among the sayings of Paul, this one is not as well remembered but should be. He said, "And as for you, brothers, never tire of doing what is right" (3:13). Had Churchill said it, it might have been, "Never tire, never, never, never, never, never." But we do. We grow weary in well doing, which is exactly the opposite of what God wants.

What causes us to tire?

Other activities. We get involved in more than we can handle and as a result sometimes tire of things that are good for us to do.

Opposition. Satan opposes our efforts to do right. That can be wearing, causing a spiritual battle fatigue.

Distractions. Maybe instead of distractions I should say *attractions.* Other things catch our attention and may appear to be more appealing. Then we tire of what we are doing; the luster is gone because something else is more attractive.

These are just a few reasons. Remember Paul's words: "Never tire of doing what is right." Don't give in or give up.

Are you weary in your soul? Examine the source or cause. If it is something that is pulling you away from doing right, don't let it. Ask God to renew your strength.

DID I TELL YOU ABOUT . . . ?

Isaiah 62–64, 1 Timothy 1 • **Key Verse: Isaiah 62:1**

Our family plays a game as we drive. Certain places along the road remind us of a past trip, so someone says, "That's where . . . ," and the rest of us remember. Part of the game is guessing what someone in the car will say in advance. It is our *Ground Hog Day* game—like the characters in that movie, we say the same thing over and over again every time we come to that point in the road.

We are good about telling some things over and over to anyone who will listen. We like to share what we have experienced and enjoyed. If only we were as persistent in telling people about God!

Isaiah had that kind of heart about God. He said, "For Zion's sake I will not keep silent" (62:1). Only one thing could get him to be quiet. He said that he would keep doing this "till her righteousness shines out like the dawn, her salvation like a blazing torch."

A day will come when righteousness and salvation will not only pierce the darkness but drive it away forever. Until then, Isaiah would keep on talking, telling about the things of God.

What will you tell about today? Perhaps a bend in the road will spark the sharing of a remembrance. A phone call will get you talking about what you are doing today or what your plans are for tomorrow.

Isaiah wouldn't stop talking about God. Will you?

Decide that today you will share with someone else a blessing or a lesson you've learned from God.

CHARACTER COUNTS

Isaiah 65–66, 1 Timothy 2 • *Key Verse: Isaiah 66:3*

The world has its heroes. We find them in action figures, on trading cards, posters, Web sites and newsletters. From athletes to entertainers, from politicians to authors, people have their heroes, those whom they admire. They may like the sound of their voice, the emotions they invoke, the skills they possess or perhaps something as superficial as how the person looks.

If you could meet one person who is alive today, or get his autograph, or spend some time with that person, who would it be? And why?

Now contrast that with the kind of person whom God esteems. It may surprise you that anyone would have God's respect, but there is such a person. "'This is the one I esteem: he who is humble and contrite in spirit, and trembles at my word'" (66:2). Earning God's esteem is not a matter of looks, abilities or talent but of character.

Since character counts, being esteemed by God is within reach of all of us. If it were based on ability, talent or attractiveness, we could not all attain it. Remember that man looks on the outside, but God on the inside. While many are driven to earn the esteem and respect of others, our priority should be to gain that from God. So, work on humility, being contrite and responsive to the Word of God.

Is your character like the person's who is esteemed by God? Write out this verse and meditate on it today, asking God to help you be one whom He esteems.

ACCEPTABLE CONDUCT

Jeremiah 1–2, 1 Timothy 3 • *Key Verses: 1 Timothy 3:14–15*

Sometimes we read signs that begin with the words, "Rules for Use of . . . ." They might be posted on the wall at a swimming pool or an exercise room. The purpose is to inform or remind you of how you are to conduct yourself there.

Paul did that for the church. He made a list that could be posted by the door as a reminder of what is acceptable and unacceptable conduct. Typically this list is applied only to the leaders of the church. Yet Paul said, "I write so that you may know how you ought to conduct yourself in the house of God, which is the church of the living God." Yes, these rules apply to leaders but they are the standard of conduct for all believers.

Now read again 1 Timothy 3:1–13, marking the specific "rules." Imagine writing them out and posting them on the wall of the church. "Be blameless" would be rule number one, followed by statements on marital fidelity, temper, self-discipline, hospitality and gossip. Hopefully, this list would make quite an impression on Christians.

Far more significant than pool regulations against running and obeying the lifeguard is this list for conduct in the church. Those pool rules are for your safety, to keep you from getting hurt, and for your enjoyment so that your time at the pool will be pleasant. Following the list in 1 Timothy 3 will do the same: it will keep people from getting hurt at church and help make their time there a blessing.

It is easier to apply rules to others. But don't miss how your life should measure up to this standard. If you are a leader in your church, this passage is especially applicable.

IN TRAINING

Jeremiah 3–5, 1 Timothy 4 • *Key Verses: 1 Timothy 4:7–8*

Sports dominates our society. We read about it in the newspaper and watch it on TV. Our cities spend enormous sums of money on facilities, and shopping malls include stores that specialize in helping you become an athlete—or at least look like one. Unfortunately, putting on running shoes will not make you a runner. You must train to be a runner, work at it and discipline yourself.

Paul never said, "Don't exercise." He did say that the effort we put into physical conditioning is of some value, but more valuable is training ourselves to be godly. Athletic training is good for now, but godliness is good for now and forever!

The athlete knows the need for training as well as the discipline needed to train. But it is one thing to know and another to do. Somewhere between knowing and doing is discipline. The athlete must discipline himself to do what will ultimately benefit him.

It's the same for the Christian. We can know that we should be godly and that godliness doesn't just happen—it's something we need to work on. It's also true that we can know what to do but not do it because we lack the discipline.

Isn't it ironic that people will watch what they eat, follow an exercise routine and avoid the things that will hurt them physically, but fail to apply the same discipline to their spiritual lives? Just as physical conditioning doesn't simply happen, neither does spiritual fitness.

Are you spiritually fit? Or are you more of a Christian coach potato, willing to watch but not do? Paul says, "Train yourself to be godly" (4:7). This is a command. Are you obeying it?

GET DIRECTIONS

Jeremiah 6–8, 1 Timothy 5 • *Key Verse: Jeremiah 6:16*

"Should you call for directions?" my wife asked.

"No," I replied, "I have a map." Actually, I was printing a map off the Internet as she asked. I knew of a Web site where I could enter the address and get a map. So, off we went, map in hand, into a part of town that was new to us. We found the house on our first try. It sure was better than wandering around lost—or worse yet, having to stop and ask for directions!

I really like the maps I get off the Web. They can be very specific, showing me the exact location of the place I am going, and I don't have to fold them up again! A person needs to be a cross between a professional accordion player and an origami expert to refold maps.

Jeremiah gave a warning to Judah. The people had wandered off the road, the path of God's righteousness. So the prophet said, "Ask for directions. Get back on the right road." He also promised that they would find rest for their souls if they did this.

We all know the tension of getting lost trying to find someone's house. However, there is a greater tension—a spiritual one—when we get off the path of God's choosing. That is why Jeremiah's instruction is critical for us today. We need to keep the map in hand, the Word of God, because in it we will find "where the good way is" (6:16).

Consider your path today. If you are off course, decide to get back on the right path and find the rest that God promises.

SOMETHING TO BRAG ABOUT

Jeremiah 9–11, 1 Timothy 6 • *Key Verses: Jeremiah 9:23–24*

Sports can bring out boasting in a person—both before and especially after the game. On any given weekend, players and teams let anyone who will listen know that they are number one. Some players wear their achievements literally on their shoulders with letterman jackets. Championship rings are flaunted, trophy rooms built and museums are opened to display their accomplishments.

Others brag about what they have without saying a word. They drive flashy cars or have a haughty walk and look. A wad of bills pulled from the pocket is meant to impress.

A common challenge is to keep our pride under control, whether it's pride about our intelligence, athletic ability or financial position. Pride happens, and so does boasting.

But God says, "Don't!" These are not the things to brag about.

Instead, He says, "Let him who boasts boast about this: that he understands and knows me" (9:24). Knowing God is the only thing in which we should take pride.

The athlete will grow older, his skills diminished by age. The wealthy person will one day realize that the abundance of life is not found in possessions. Even the intellectual may see others pass him by and ultimately realize that his mental abilities are less than they once were.

Knowing God, though, just gets better and lasts for all eternity. Now that is worth boasting about!

Can you say, "I know God"? If you can, think about how great and permanent that is. It is a blessing worth telling to others.

MOUTH AND MIND

Jeremiah 12–14, 2 Timothy 1 • *Key Verse: Jeremiah 12:2*

When a person does or says something that causes hurt, saying "sorry" can help—but only if it is said from the heart. Sometimes when you hear the way an apology is made, it makes you want to ask, "Do you mean it?"

There are other ways that people can be insincere in their words. As Jeremiah complained to God about the people to whom he was ministering, he described how God was "always on their lips but far from their hearts" (12:2). They would say the right words about God but not mean them. Isaiah said the same thing, as did Jesus (Isa. 29:13; Matt. 15:8–9). It was not a new problem in their day, and it is still a problem today.

People can say one thing and mean another, or they can say something and mean nothing. What Isaiah, Jeremiah and Jesus all join in condemning is the religious-sounding person whose words seem right but whose heart is wrong. God does not just listen to our words; He also looks at our hearts and knows what is going on in our minds. We need to say, and mean, David's prayer: "May the words of my mouth and the meditation of my heart be pleasing in your sight, O LORD, my Rock and my Redeemer" (Ps. 19:14).

Examine your heart. Is your Christianity of the lips only, or does it come from the heart?

TARNISHED MEDALS

Jeremiah 15–17, 2 Timothy 2 • Key Verse: 2 Timothy 2:5

Every two years, the interest of the world is drawn to the Olympics, alternating between the winter and the summer games. Sporting venues around the world are used, allowing opportunity for a particular country to showcase itself. As much as the host cities would like to be the focus of attention, the real center of attention is the athletes. Stories abound of dedication, determination and years of discipline as these individuals "go for the gold."

Yet every year the news that comes from the games includes stories of tarnished medals, as individuals are disqualified for one reason or another. Performance-enhancing drugs, unapproved or altered equipment and various rule infractions are some of the reasons that athletes are disqualified. The bottom line is that they broke the rules.

Athletic competition, rules and disqualifications are not new. When Paul wrote 2 Timothy, he used that familiar scenario to encourage Timothy to compete according to the rules. Realize, though, that Paul was not writing as a coach to his young competitor but more as a mentor to his disciple. Using the examples of a soldier, an athlete and a farmer, Paul was setting before Timothy valuable instruction. Included in that was the statement that "if anyone competes as an athlete, he does not receive the victor's crown unless he competes according to the rules" (2:5).

God has given us the Bible to teach us how to live and how to serve Him. To receive the reward that He has for us, our service must be "by the rules."

Ask yourself if you are following God's rules in your life. Just as an athlete can lose a medal, so you can miss out on the reward God has for His faithful servants.

SPIRITUALITY WITHOUT RELIGION

Jeremiah 18–19, 2 Timothy 3 • *Key Verse: 2 Timothy 3:5*

One of the sad trends today is spirituality without religion. In a general and widespread way, the interest in being spiritual has grown. People want spirituality, to be known as a spiritual person, to have the benefits of a spiritual life. They just don't want to be religious.

To be religious is to be perceived as enslaved to a system of rules, regulations, rights and wrongs. In 2 Timothy 2:1–5, Paul describes the antithesis to a "religious" person. Man is at the center of what he describes. He is narcissistic, greedy, proud, looking out for number one. There are no restraints for the non-religious person.

The list of characteristics of this type of person ends with an intriguing phrase: "having a form of godliness but denying its power." This is the spiritual, but not religious, person. He has an outward appearance that looks spiritual, but the reality of a spiritual life is missing. He has never experienced the power of God in his life.

The warning Paul gives is very direct—"Have nothing to do with them" (v. 5). Don't get pulled into the trap. That lifestyle may look appealing, but it is to be avoided. What God wants is godliness that comes from lives changed by His power.

Do you seek a spiritual life? Make sure, in prayer to God, that you have Christ in your life.

RESCUE

Jeremiah 20–21, 2 Timothy 4 • *Key Verse: 2 Timothy 4:18*

"I couldn't help myself" might be one of the most correct and incorrect statements ever spoken when someone is trying to explain why he did something wrong. You might be thinking that those words can't be both correct and incorrect at the same time, but they are.

It is a correct statement when spoken by someone who realizes that he cannot in and of himself resist temptation. It is incorrect when it is said to justify doing wrong, as if a person has no hope at all of resisting.

The truth is that we alone cannot resist but must draw upon what God has promised. He has stated clearly that by His help we can resist temptation. Paul understood this clearly when he wrote, "The Lord will rescue me from every evil attack and will bring me safely to his heavenly kingdom" (4:18). He knew that God would not allow him to face temptation greater than he could handle and that God would help him withstand it as well.

Does this sound familiar? Perhaps that last sentence brings to mind 1 Corinthians 10:13. Read that verse again. It will help reinforce the truth that we cannot help ourselves, and yet we can—because God will deliver us.

The only question that remains is, will you allow God to work in your life, in every situation to help you overcome temptation? It is not a matter of "I can't" but of "I won't." It is not that you can't resist; it is that you won't let God deliver you.

You have a choice to make: either allow God to help you or not. Pray right now, asking God to help you resist temptation today.

NO SKELETONS

Jeremiah 22–23, Titus 1 • *Key Verses: Titus 1:6–7*

Do you know what it means to be blameless? It's not something we think much about today.

The Bible teaches that leaders in the local church must be blameless (1:6–7; see also 1 Timothy 3:2). To be blameless does not mean to be sinless. If that were the case, none of us would qualify.

The word translated "blameless" in the original language is *anegkletos*. It is made up of two words: a negative suffix and *egkaleo*, meaning "to accuse" or "to call into question." Thus, the word literally means one who cannot be called into question, one who is irreproachable. It means church leaders must have no skeletons in their closets. They must always live blameless lives before the Lord. That's what God said to His servant Abram: "I am God Almighty; walk before me and be blameless" (Gen. 17:1).

Often today church leaders are selected because of their money or influence or availability, with little regard to whether they have walked blamelessly before the Lord. Better to select a blameless leader than a popular one.

Pray for your pastor and the other leaders of your church. They have tough jobs, and the qualifications are stringent. And ask God to enable you to walk blamelessly before Him and allow Him to lead you as He wills.

"Lord, I cannot be sinless, but I can be blameless. Help my life to be an open book before You. May there be no skeletons in my closet that would cause You to be embarrassed and me to be disqualified from service to You."

A HEART FOR GOD

Jeremiah 24–26, Titus 2 • *Key Verse: Jeremiah 24:7*

The heart is a very fickle thing. One day your teenager is in love with the guy of her dreams. The next day he's history. Often our hearts are like that toward the Lord.

Israel was God's chosen nation, the object of His special love (Deut. 7:7–8). But the Jewish people had fickle hearts. Time and again they promised their love to Jehovah alone, and time and again they snubbed the Lord and lusted after the false gods around them. Divine punishment was inevitable. It finally came when Israel was carried into Babylonian captivity.

Still, God loved them. He promised, "My eyes will watch over them for their good, and I will bring them back to this land. . . . I will give them a heart to know me, that I am the LORD. They will be my people, and I will be their God, for they will return to me with all their heart" (Jer. 24:6–7).

Think for a minute of how patient God is with us when we sin (Ps. 86:15), how faithful He is to forgive us when we confess our sin (1 John 1:9), and how He gives us a heart to thirst for Him (Ps. 42:1–2). Let that thought deepen your desire to have a heart for God. Let Him give you that kind of heart today.

"Father, let my heart beat with Your heart, let it be consumed with the things that consume You, and let it be set against the things that You condemn. Give me a yearning heart, a longing heart, a loving heart."

CASTING YOUR BALLOT

Jeremiah 27–29, Titus 3 • *Key Verse: Titus 3:1*

In the United States, the month of November includes the day we vote. Campaigns are concluded as votes are cast for office holders on the national, state and local levels. Some will be reelected, while others will be elected to their first term. Some of those for whom you vote will be elected; others will not. No matter who wins, the day comes when those chosen by the voters will assume office; they will form our government.

It may not be our typical way of thinking about these elected people, but they are our "rulers and authorities." From the local collector of taxes to the president of the United States, this is the phrase the Bible uses to describe them.

The Christian is given straightforward instruction regarding the authorities in our cities, states and nation. We are to be subject to these authorities, obeying the government without compromise but with a ready submission. While others around us might be disrespectful of those in authority or even purposefully disobedient, it is our responsibility to be good citizens.

We are "to be subject to rulers and authorities" (3:1). Not just to those for whom we voted. Not just the ones of the same political party. Not just in regard to the laws with which we agree or that we like. Paul gives no exceptions, just a blanket reminder: "be subject to rulers and authorities."

You need to be that good citizen, one who models biblical truth in your attitudes and actions regarding our government.

What are your attitudes and actions about government? Take time right now to pray for those who are in government. Pray by name for our president and other leaders.

IT'S JUST NOT FAIR!

Jeremiah 30–31, Philemon • *Key Verse: Jeremiah 30:11*

Breathes a child who has not at some time said, "It's just not fair"? And that is only the beginning of what he says. "How come I . . . ?" is the follow-up question, drawing attention to the perceived injustice. Actually, if "justice" were left up to children, it would probably be closer to "all of grace" rather than "fitting the crime."

There probably were times when the Israelites wanted to cry out, "It's just not fair!" After all, they were the people of God who had received His blessings and promises. It just didn't make sense that God would then punish them—especially when other people were far more wicked, far more deserving of judgment.

Through His prophet Jeremiah, God told the people of Israel that they would not "go entirely unpunished," but that He would correct them "with justice." This was a "good news/bad news" scenario. The bad news was punishment but the good news was justice.

Sometimes when people adjust God to their preference, they leave out the idea that He would punish anyone for anything. They emphasize His forgiveness and mercy to the extent that they eliminate punishment and justice. That may be the God of man's idea, but it is not the God of the Bible. If this were true, there would be no need for Jesus to have died.

God is the God of justice—and of mercy and grace. So Jesus died, that we might live.

"I thank You, God, that You are the God of justice and grace. Thank You for Jesus, who died that I might live."

ENDLESS LOOP

Jeremiah 32–33, Hebrews 1 • *Key Verse: Jeremiah 32:40*

Sunrise, sunset. The two words go together, like tick and tock. Sometimes when we hear pairs of words like these, we repeat them. They roll off the tongue naturally, easily repeated, communicating endlessness: sunrise is followed by sunset, which is followed by sunrise . . . and so on.

There is a loop of sorts that God promises will one day come, just as sure as sunrise will follow sunset. It is a loop of two parts, one His and one His people's.

For God's part, He will "'never stop doing good to them'" (32:40). That is His promise, contained in this prophecy uttered by Jeremiah. A day will come when God's everlasting covenant will be established, and without fail He will do good for His people.

The other part of the loop will be the faithfulness of God's people. Jeremiah said that "they will never turn away from" God. As He does good to them, they will not forsake Him.

In between the two parts of the loop is another thing that God will do to insure the everlasting nature of this loop. He will "'inspire them to fear'" Him. This fear is not a terror of God but a reverential respect of Him. As His people have that fear in their hearts, they will stay faithful.

The day is coming when this endless loop of doing good and faithfulness will be in effect. But we should live that way today. In our hearts we should have a proper fear of God, one that affects the way that we live, that keeps us close to Him.

Do you fear God? The Bible speaks repeatedly of how fear is the beginning of wisdom and of knowledge. The fear of God should affect the way we live. Do you truly have this reverential respect of Him?

PRONE TO DRIFT

Jeremiah 34–36, Hebrews 2 • *Key Verse: Hebrews 2:1*

If I were choosing a material to make a model of the human heart, something that would show the nature of our hearts, I would use driftwood. You have probably seen those pieces of wood floating by on a river or along the shore of a lake, wood that is rootless, just drifting wherever the current carries it. Our hearts are like that, prone to drift.

Throughout the Book of Hebrews we are warned about our propensity to wander away from God. Chapter two begins with the warning that "we must pay more careful attention, therefore, to what we have heard, so that we do not drift away" (2:1). As you read through Hebrews, watch for this theme and hear the repeated warnings. The warnings often come with instructions, things to do to keep this from happening.

In chapter 2 the instruction is very basic: "pay more careful attention . . . to what we have heard, so that we do not drift away." To hear is one thing; to heed is another. We can hear, even read, the Word of God and its instruction, but this is not enough. We need to pay careful attention because the help we need to stay close to God comes not from just hearing but from heeding.

If I were choosing the material that I wish would make a good model of a Christian's heart, my choice would be an anchor. Now I know that an anchor is not a material per se, but I want it to be the image that best represents my heart—one that is anchored close to God.

The hymn writer's words were, "Prone to wander, Lord I feel it" ("Come, Thou Fount"). Do you feel prone to wander? Ask God to help you anchor your heart close to Him. Do it by both hearing and heeding His Word.

A WORD FOR "TODAY"

*Jeremiah 37–39, **Hebrews 3*** • ***Key Verses: Hebrews 3:12–13***

Many a long-distance runner has come around that final turn wondering if he has enough energy left to finish the race, only to be energized by the cheering of the crowd. He may feel like he's running the remainder of the race in slow motion, but his exertion is fortified by the voices of onlookers.

Words can have a powerful effect. They can build up or tear down. Our words can, and should be, encouraging ones, words that help others—especially those who are running the race of faith alongside us. The race is hard, the challenge real, and the temptation to sin constant.

Hebrews warns us of the possibility of drifting, of allowing our hearts to harden, of being deceived by sin. That is a very real danger that each Christian faces. Our natural tendency is away from God, not toward Him.

An antidote for this is encouraging words. The community of believers should daily give exhortations to help keep one another from developing a hardened heart. As each of us has a responsibility to keep our hearts anchored close to God, so each has a responsibility to help others do so as well. Notice that we are to encourage one another "Today" (3:13). Any day that you can call "today" is a day that you are to be an encourager.

Your assignment is to encourage someone in his faith today. Who will it be and what will you do? Now do it.

EXPOSED

Jeremiah 40–42, Hebrews 4 • *Key Verse: Hebrews 4:13*

We keep many things in our lives private. Some people are very private about their finances. They do not want others to know how much they earn, what they have in the bank or any other details about their money. Physical health is another very private subject. Some people will undergo a surgical procedure and not tell even their closest friends about it.

Any list of things that people try to keep private includes sin. We may have—should have, in fact—a sense of shame when we do wrong. Along with feeling shame, though, we might hope we get away with our sin. Things can be hidden in computer files, underneath clothes in a drawer or tucked behind a loose brick. Perhaps the hidden sin is an activity. A person traveling away from home might think he can get away with sin in a town where he's unknown.

But God knows. The Bible says, "Everything is uncovered and laid bare before the eyes of him to whom we must give account" (4:13). That verse says two things to us. One is that God knows. Nothing we think or do is hidden from His sight. We are naked. The other is that we will give an account to Him, and it will be an account that covers everything!

God tells us this for a reason. He wants us to live right and not try to get away with wrong. He knows everything we do, say and think—and one day we will have to tell Him about all of it.

Are you trying to hide anything from God? If so, then you need to stop doing wrong, get rid of the hidden things, ask for forgiveness and live right. Take those steps today.

HARD OF HEARING

Jeremiah 43–45, Hebrews 5 • ***Key Verses: Jeremiah 44:4–5***

The sign said, "Stop." That much I read, and that is what I did. As I pulled away from the stop sign, my wife asked, "Did you see what that sign said?"

"'Stop,'" I replied.

"It also said, 'Look again,'" she told me. I hadn't noticed that second line.

I wonder how many warnings we miss because we aren't looking or listening. The answer is probably more than we could imagine. The saddest of these are the warnings from God we ignore.

God sent His prophets to the people of Israel to especially warn them against the sin of idolatry. Again and again they were sent, but the people did not listen or pay attention. In Jeremiah 44:6 God says that the result of the failure to listen was judgment. No more messengers were sent. Instead, God sent His fury and wrath.

While Jeremiah spoke to a specific time in the history of Israel, his message is one we need to hear. We, too, can hear the Word of God again and again. We can read the Bible, hear it taught and ignore what it says.

God did not give us the Bible just to increase our knowledge but to also affect the way we live. For it to have that affect on us means that we must not only hear but also heed. When it says "stop," we must stop. Those things that it says "do," we must do. What we must not do is what the people of Jeremiah's day did—neither hear nor heed.

Is there anything in particular that you know God wants you to change in your life today? If so, make that change now.

AN ANCHOR

Jeremiah 46–47, Hebrews 6 • *Key Verse: Hebrews 6:19*

Among the symbols that Christians have held dear are the fish and the anchor. Over 60 such pictures have been found in the catacombs of ancient Rome. The outline of a fish on the back of a car can be a testimony. The picture of an anchor also is a strong statement of what Jesus means to the Christian. People put their trust in anchors, and we have put our trust in Christ.

During a storm at sea, hope is placed in an anchor. It can keep the boat from drifting and help it weather the storm. The better the anchor, the more firm the hope.

For us, Jesus is the Anchor, the One who not only can keep us from drifting but help us through every storm. To emphasize the security we have in Christ, the author of Hebrews describes this anchor as "firm and secure" (6:19). It is "firm" in that it cannot break and "secure" in that it cannot slip. That cannot be said of any other anchor, only of the Anchor of our soul—Jesus.

The next time you see an anchored ship, watch how the waters move but the ship does not. Storms may come that are greater than an anchor, but there are no storms greater than the Anchor of our soul. In this Anchor we have hope and confidence, whatever the storms we face.

"Thank You, God, for giving me an Anchor that is sure and steadfast. Help me today and every day to rest secure in this knowledge."

HE PLEADS OUR CASE

Jeremiah 48–49, Hebrews 7 • *Key Verse: Hebrews 7:25*

When needed, an effective lawyer is very appreciated, especially one who can plead our case for us. A good attorney knows what to say and how to say it as he represents us before a judge or magistrate. With him pleading our case, we have high hopes for a favorable ruling or verdict.

Everyone has a case that we cannot win without the help of Jesus. If we were to stand before the Judge of the universe and plead our case, we would lose. There is nothing we can do or say that can change the fact that we are guilty sinners before Him. Still we have hope—because of Jesus.

When Jesus pleads our case, He does it not on our merit but on His own. It is His sacrifice that satisfies the requirement of God, and it is our receiving of what He did on our behalf that saves us. The writer of Hebrews says that it saves us completely (7:25). There is no appeals process or partial settlement. We are saved completely, and unlike a human attorney who may move on to other cases once ours is settled, Jesus continues to intercede for us.

Notice the simplicity of this statement: "He is able to save completely those who come to God through him, because he always lives to intercede for them." Jesus saves—no doubt. He saves completely—nothing is left undone. And He keeps us saved as He ever lives to intercede for us.

Thank God today for the salvation you have in Christ. Even now He is interceding for you!

MISGUIDED

Jeremiah 50, Hebrews 8 • *Key Verse: Jeremiah 50:6*

When traveling by car, my wife and I usually have a road atlas in the front seat with us. Sometimes we have just the basic map that comes when you rent a car at an airport. At other times we use maps from the Internet. Then there are times we stop the car and ask for directions—a last resort for any guy!

It would be extremely rare today to get lost following a map. Technology and publishing advances provide us with accurate and highly detailed maps. Sometimes, though, a person you ask directions from can err and send you on the wrong path. Or, shunning the help of a map, we can get lost on our own.

God uses the images of being lost and misguided to challenge us. He said through His prophet Jeremiah that His people were like lost sheep that had been misguided, led astray, taken away from the places of rest. The image is not of physical but of spiritual wandering. It is a sad picture that God's people could be like wandering, misled animals.

You probably don't like it when you get lost while traveling or trying to find a certain place in town. Even a wrong turn can be annoying. And if someone gives you wrong directions, you know the irritability that you can feel.

So if that is how you react to getting lost on the road, how do you feel about wandering spiritually? The Bible is like your map. You need to read it and know it to keep from wandering. Also, watch out for those who give poor directions. Compare their teaching with the Word. Don't be like lost sheep, led astray.

You need to read and know the Word to keep from wandering spiritually. Commit yourself anew today to reading, studying and learning the Bible.

NOTHING BUT

*Jeremiah 51–52, **Hebrews 9*** • ***Key Verse: Hebrews 9:12***

The glass doors, front windows, display cases or even cash registers of stores tell us the variety of ways we can pay for our purchases— VISA, MasterCard, American Express, Discover, debit cards, checks and cash. Some retailers also have a coupon program or voucher system, maybe a card filled with stamps. Options abound.

That is the way it is at gas stations, department stores, restaurants and other places of business, but not the way it is in regard to salvation. In the words of the old hymn, it is "nothing but the blood of Jesus" that can make the payment for our debt of sin.

This chapter of Hebrews draws our attention to what Jesus has done for us. It especially reminds us that we are not saved by His life or by His example but by His shed blood. We also must remember that salvation is nothing in or of ourselves but is totally of Him. Again, as a songwriter put it, "Nothing in my hands I bring, simply to Thy cross I cling." As this chapter says, "He entered the Most Holy Place once for all by his own blood, having obtained eternal redemption" (6:12).

While some people might want to turn away from this imagery, preferring instead to focus on Jesus' life and example, we must remember that it is by His death, burial and resurrection that we are saved. Again, quoting from a modern writer, "We had a debt we could not pay; He paid a debt that He did not owe."

"Thank You, God, for my salvation. It is a gift given freely to me but one that was purchased at great price. I thank You for the shed blood of Jesus."

ANY OTHER WAY?

Lamentations 1–2, Hebrews 10:1–18 • *Key Verse: Hebrews 10:4*

In many situations we understand that only certain things are acceptable. Show up for a football game with a ticket to a baseball game. Think you will get in? Go to a concert with an admission pass for an amusement park. Won't work. Try to get backstage without a pass hanging around your neck. You'll be turned away. It's easy to come up with example after example where there is only one way in; no others work.

So why do people understand this principle at the auditorium, stadium or amusement park but think it will be different with heaven? Salvation is through Jesus, nothing else, not even through sacrifice.

God had given His people rituals that symbolized the covering of their sins. These pointed to Christ's atoning death for sinners, looking forward to the ultimate sacrifice, Jesus Christ, who died for the sins of all people. His sacrifice eliminated all need for other sacrifices and eliminated those sacrifices totally. We read that "it is impossible for the blood of bulls and goats to take away sins" (10:4). Nothing else can accomplish what Christ alone did on Calvary's cross.

We need to know this so that we do not wrongly think that there is some other way into heaven. There is only one way, and it is Jesus. No sacrifice we offer, no deeds we do, no gifts we bring, will work. Just Jesus.

Friend, be sure you are saved. If you are hoping in some other way, you will be disappointed. Salvation is found in Jesus alone.

I HAVE HOPE

Lamentations 3–5, Hebrews 10:19–39
Key Verses: Lamentations 3:19–20

When the weather is nice, temperatures are pleasant, and a gentle breeze blows, people will sing, "This is the day that the Lord has made, I will rejoice and be glad in it." But when the weather is horrible, temperatures are at the extremes, and perhaps the wind is a gale force, people aren't as likely to sing. Yet God makes both kinds of days.

We need to remember that God is good all the time. His goodness is not dependent on how much we like our current situation. That must have been Jeremiah's perspective. At a time when his soul was "downcast" within him (3:20), he could look beyond the immediate to the eternal. Rather than allowing his circumstances to drag him down, he focused his attention on God's faithfulness and said, "I have hope" (v. 21).

You probably know the next verse: "Because of the LORD's great love we are not consumed, for his compassions never fail. They are new every morning; great is your faithfulness" (v. 22).

It's easy to sing the hymn "Great Is Thy Faithfulness" when things are going well. Yet the verses from which that theme is taken did not come from a time of smooth sailing for the prophet. Instead, it was a time of extreme difficulty. Jeremiah knew that God is good all the time and that even in the worst of times He is faithful.

Even when life looks hopeless, remember that looks can be deceiving. Hope in the ever-faithful God.

Ask God today to help you be a person of hope. Don't let the immediate cloud your view of the eternal. Hope in the ever-faithful God.

HOW TO PLEASE GOD

Ezekiel 1–2, Hebrews 11:1–19 • *Key Verse: Hebrews 11:6*

Someone once said, "Faith is getting yourself in so deep only God can get you out." Be careful—that could define stupidity too.

I like this definition much better. Faith is confidence in the righteous character of God that fosters trust and hope, even when the evidence fosters doubt and despair.

Hebrews 11 is a cast of characters, all of whom had great faith. From the first verse all the way to the middle of verse 35 are recorded the success stories of the heroes of faith. But there's a dramatic change beginning in verse 35. "Others were tortured . . . . still others were chained and put in prison. They were stoned; they were sawed in two . . . . They went about in sheepskins and goatskins" (vv. 35b–37).

These were heroes of faith, too, but their circumstances were very different. Still, they had faith in God. Why? Because faith is unrelated to our circumstances. If you have faith in the righteous character of God before tough times come, that faith will see you through the tough times. If you aren't already convinced of God's righteous character, the moment disaster strikes is no time to wrestle with that issue.

Do you want to please God today? Then don't allow your circumstances to determine your faith. Have faith in God. He can change your circumstances, but He Himself cannot change.

"Lord, help me to live above my circumstances today. Help me to have faith in who You are and recognize that no matter what happens to me, You are faithful and trustworthy."

ON YOUR FACE

Ezekiel 3–4, Hebrews 11:20–40 • *Key Verse: Ezekiel 3:23*

Have you ever sat in church and wished the song leader would give you an opportunity to stand and stretch your legs for a minute? Probably. Have you ever grumbled that the song leader had you stand up and sit down too much? Probably. While we are on the subject, are your pews too hard or too close together—or just plain uncomfortable? Probably.

Having comfortable seats during worship is important to most people. They want adequate but not too-bright lighting, along with cool—not cold—temperatures. And they don't want to feel crowded.

Yet as you read your Bible, one of the things you will not find is people sitting during worship. The only One who sits is God. Others stand, kneel, walk and get on their faces. Now what would it take to get you to put yourself flat on the ground with your face on the floor? When Ezekiel saw "the glory of the LORD," he says, "I fell facedown" (3:23). Worship put him on his face.

True worship is not about us. It is about God. Too often we focus on ourselves, making ourselves comfortable, designing worship to fit our tastes, whims and wishes. Put our face on the floor? Unheard of— until we catch a glimpse of the glory of the Lord.

It is not the physical act that makes something an act of worship. It is the heart from which that act originates. Ezekiel's heart responded to the glory of the Lord with this act of worship. His focus was clearly on God, not himself.

Which is more important to you: your comfort in church or your worship of God? Would you ever put your face on the floor, or even bend your knee? Ask yourself if your worship focus is on yourself or on God.

ACCEPTABLE WORSHIP

Ezekiel 5–7, Hebrews 12 • *Key Verses: Hebrews 12:28–29*

Imagine you've ordered your favorite pepperoni pizza. The delivery person arrives at your house and greets you with the words, "Here's your anchovy pizza!"

"But I didn't order anchovy. I ordered pepperoni," you would protest.

"Yes, but anchovy is my favorite kind," he replies.

Would this be acceptable? Of course not. While this situation may never happen in the world of pizza, it happens too often in our church pews. We may want God to accept any and all forms of worship, expecting Him to let us approach Him as we want, but He does not. Some of our ideas about God, how we perceive Him to be, and our approaches to worship—based on our wishes, not His will—are not acceptable. Just as we would not accept any and all pizza when we ordered pepperoni, so God does not accept any and all worship. Some is acceptable and some is not.

In an anything goes world that has given some people the idea that anything goes in worship as well, it is important for us to understand that when it comes to worship, anything doesn't go. Understanding what is and is not acceptable to God will bring us to a decision point. Either we seek in our worship to please Him, or we seek to please ourselves. And when it comes down to doing what we want because it is what we want, we are no longer worshiping God but serving self, satisfying self, putting what we desire above what God requires.

"God, help me know Your will in worship, that my worship will be acceptable to You."

GOING, GOING . . .

Ezekiel 8–10, Hebrews 13 • *Key Verse: Ezekiel 9:3*

I have a collection of mental images filed under the heading of "Used to be churches." There is a certain sadness in my heart when I see restaurants, bookstores and antique and furniture stores that obviously used to be churches. People of God had sacrificially given to build that structure and had gathered there, joined together in ministry. Sometimes a cornerstone remains, inscribed with words such as, "Dedicated to the glory of God."

Reasons for the change vary, for sure. Some churches relocate to new facilities, but sometimes the building is empty because the church no longer exists. The ministry there is over. Among the saddest images in my mind is that of a sign in the front yard of a church. It simply said, "For Sale by Owner." The ministry there was going, going, gone.

Ezekiel describes over a series of three chapters a vision of the glory of God departing from the temple in Jerusalem. The glory moved from above the cherubim (9:3) to the threshold of the temple (10:4), to the east gate (10:19) and finally out of the city (11:23). It was a slow, sad departure of the glory, unseen except by the prophet.

Our heart's desire should be that the Lord's glory remain in our churches! That will take more than just wishing. It requires staying true and faithful to God and to His Word. When we move away from correct interpretation, clear teaching and correct application of His Word, then we move closer to a time in which the glory may leave.

Be people of the Book. Read the Word, learn the Word and live the Word.

"God, help my local church to stay true to Your Word. May Your glory continue to be proclaimed through my church."

AND A CHILD
SHALL LEAD THEM—MAYBE

Ezekiel 11–13, James 1 • *Key Verse: James 1:21*

I started using computers before my daughter was born, and therein lies the difference. While I have learned, she has always lived with computers. There has never been a time in her life when a computer wasn't in the house. Using electronic gadgets seems to come easier for her than learning to ride a bike! When she has my cell phone, I wince, wondering how it might be reprogrammed before she returns it. I keep my PDA out of her sight, just in case.

Then comes the time when, looking over my shoulder, she says, "Dad, you need to . . . ." You know, it can be hard to take instruction from a preteen, especially about something that you have been doing before she came on the scene—and especially when she is right. There is something challenging about saying, "You're right, child of mine." You can't do it without either being humiliated or without being humble enough to listen.

The same is true about the Word of God. We sometimes fail to learn from what it says because we are not humble enough to listen. That is why James says, "Receive with meekness the implanted word," which means that a person must have the right kind of attitude to accept the Word. The proud person does not receive any instruction well.

Pride can keep a father from listening to his daughter. It also can keep you and me from listening to the Word. The result from the first refusal might be having to learn the lesson the hard way—and that may well be the result of refusing to listen to God's Word too.

"God, help me today to have a teachable spirit, humbly receptive to Your Word. Guide me and I will follow."

TRIPPING OURSELVES

Ezekiel 14–15, James 2 • *Key Verse: Ezekiel 14:3*

Is there something in your house that you consistently trip over? Or perhaps it is a low-hanging light fixture that you often encounter with your head. You know it is there, but at the moment you are walking by—well, it's like you didn't know it was there! Once again you trip or bang your head.

Wouldn't it make sense to move whatever it is on the floor or raise that fixture hanging from the ceiling? Of course it would. Then again, we don't always do the sensible thing, do we?

Of far greater significance are the things in our lives that can cause us to stumble spiritually. A group of men, leaders of Israel, came to Ezekiel. God told the prophet that these elders had "set up idols in their hearts and put wicked stumbling blocks before their faces" (14:3). It was as if they had deliberately put things in their own path to trip over! The specific obstacle God mentioned was idols, objects of worship valued above the true God.

On the one hand this verse reminds us of the wrong of idolatry. On the other, it points to an ongoing problem: setting up in our lives things that cause us to stumble spiritually. In the same way a footstool should be moved, these stumbling blocks need to be taken out of our lives. God even questioned whether He should let them inquire of Him at all. The things we keep in our lives that cause us to stumble spiritually hinder our prayers as well.

Do you have a favorite "stumbling block"? Look for something you keep around or have in your heart that causes you to sin. God wants you to remove it. Do that right now.

TONGUE IN CHECK

Ezekiel 16–17, James 3 • Key Verse: James 3:2

Among the most difficult sins to remove from our lives are those we commit with our words. James makes this so clear when he writes, "If anyone is never at fault in what he says, he is a perfect man, able to keep his whole body in check" (3:2).

The word translated "perfect" does not mean "totally without fault or sin." As it is used here, it speaks of the Christian's maturity. The mature believer will control what he says. The implication plainly is that if one does not control his tongue, he is not mature.

A second important truth in this verse relates to the rest of our character. Since the tongue is so hard to reign in, the believer who can control the tongue gains control of himself in all other areas of life also. It's like in a war: when major cities are captured, the rest of the country is as well. So when we are able to keep our tongue in check, we have developed the discipline and maturity to keep other aspects of our life in line as well.

God wants us to be mature believers, not spiritual infants in our thinking and actions. Control of the tongue is a crucial component of spiritual maturity. It is not impossible, just supernatural. You cannot do it on your own, but you can do it with God's help.

The question is not if you can learn to control your tongue but whether you will. Study James 3. Get the Word into your heart. Ask God to help you mature by keeping your tongue in check.

SOUR GRAPES

Ezekiel 18–19, James 4 • *Key Verse: Ezekiel 18:2*

In chapter 16 Ezekiel quoted the proverb "like mother, like daughter" (v. 44) to tell Israel that the nation had become like the people of Canaan, giving into that heathen environment. Now he uses a proverb to drive home another point as he writes, "'The fathers eat sour grapes, and the children's teeth are set on edge'" (18:2).

Unless you have eaten sour grapes, you can't relate. Expecting a sweet taste, you instead encounter sour. It may literally set your teeth on edge as you react to the sourness. The next time you have some sour grapes, eat one while sitting next to another person. Ask the person if the sour grape you ate left a bad taste in his mouth. The person may wonder about your mental state! "Why would something you ate leave a bad taste in my mouth?" he might reply.

Ezekiel is not writing about grapes but about how a father's actions affect his children. We might say "the apple does not fall far from the tree." The people, though, had misapplied this principle. They were fatalistic in regard to judgment, thinking that they were being judged because of the past wickedness of their fathers.

God then said directly that judgment will come to the one who sins (v. 4). A righteous father can have a wicked son. That wicked son may have a righteous son. Each will be judged on his own merit.

You will stand before God as an individual, not as someone else's child, and be judged yourself. Be sure that you have trusted Christ for salvation and do not rely on the righteousness of your ancestors.

It is so important that we individually receive Christ! Having a godly heritage is a wonderful blessing, but our heritage will not get us into heaven.

WAITING FOR THE HARVEST

Ezekiel 20–21, James 5 • *Key Verses: James 5:7–8*

The fields are about empty now, and so are the gardens. Last spring, with hope, the farmers planted their fields, as did the gardeners. Dirt was turned over, seeds sown and young plants set. Then with water, fertilizer, care and good weather, a day came when the corn was harvested or the tomato picked from the vine. Between planting and harvesting was watering, cultivating, fertilizing, protecting and patience. "A watched pot doesn't boil," nor does a watched plant sprout.

In a world that wants instant gratification, the farmer and gardener go against the flow. That is why they are such a good picture of patience. Notice, though, that James is speaking of a particular kind of patience, the one that gets us through the long summers of our life. It is a patience that is based on a certain hope—that one day Jesus will come again.

This spring, plant a small garden with a child. Watch her enthusiasm as you show her the pictures on the seed packets. Let her pick her favorite foods to grow. Then watch as her enthusiasm wanes, especially when the heat of summer arrives. Take her out to the garden to weed. She'll probably wilt! The pictures of fresh fruits and vegetables are no longer in her mind. Her patience is exhausted. She'll be content with store-bought food.

Look beyond the challenges of today. Jesus is coming. Just be patient.

James gives us a good word picture here. Ask God to help you be patient, always looking forward to the return of Jesus.

SCRATCHED AND DENTED

Ezekiel 22–23, 1 Peter 1 • *Key Verses: 1 Peter 1:3–4*

Perhaps someday you will receive an inheritance. As hard as you may try, that inheritance will not stay as you get it. Money will be spent. A car will wear out. Furniture will become scratched and dented. Dishes will chip and break. Clothing may become moth-eaten. And the list goes on. Getting an inheritance is one thing. Keeping it is another.

This is what makes these words of Peter so amazing. He tells us that we have an inheritance that "can never perish, spoil or fade" (1:4). No scratches. No dents. No depreciation. It is unlike any other inheritance.

One other great aspect about this inheritance is that it is "kept in heaven for you." You have heard of contested wills. A person may have made his wishes known regarding the dispersal of his worldly goods, but sadly, those wishes are not always followed. A person may have the experience of looking forward to a promised inheritance only to not receive it. But that will not happen with this inheritance. God has reserved it. No one can contest His will in this matter. It is reserved not by a legal document that can be challenged in a court, but by His divine decreed will.

So the next time you look at something you or someone else has inherited, notice the scratches and dents. And the next time you hear of a contested will, remember that you have an inheritance that is incorruptible, undefiled, unfading and reserved.

Even Christians can get distracted by the things of this world. Look beyond this temporary life to that which is eternal. There your inheritance waits for you.

AGAINST THE ODDS

Ezekiel 24–26, 1 Peter 2 • Key Verse: Ezekiel 26:3

Lottery tickets are sold in grocery stores, convenience food marts and gas stations. People buy the tickets even though the chances of them winning are infinitesimally small. The odds are against them, just as with all forms of organized gambling. If the odds were not in favor of the "house," the casinos and lotteries would all go out of business. Still, with just a slight possibility of winning, people will gamble away their money.

Consider these odds: 1 in 400 million. Doesn't sound very favorable, does it? Yet in Ezekiel 26 there is a situation that would occur against similar odds. In verses 3–6 there are seven prophecies: many nations will come against the city of Tyre; its walls will be destroyed, and its towers pulled down; the rubble will be scraped away, leaving a bare rock; the place will be used to spread fishnets; it will become plunder for the nations; and the settlements on the mainland will be ravaged by the sword. Someone has calculated that the possibility of all of that happening as prophesied was 1 in 400 million.

The betting person would not like those odds, but this is not about gambling. Instead, this prophecy draws our attention to the certainty of the Word of God. God's prophets could say something that looked impossible but in reality was more than possible. It was a sure thing because God said it.

Ezekiel 26 is just one of many examples of fulfilled prophecy. The complete accuracy of the Bible in regard to the prophecies it contains as well as its accuracy regarding events of the ancient world are added evidence to the truthfulness of God's Word.

Actually, the odds were not 1 in 400 million. Since God said it, the odds were 1 in 1. What God says is a sure thing. Never doubt the Word of God.

THE PERIL OF PROSPERITY

Ezekiel 27–29, 1 Peter 3 • *Key Verse: Ezekiel 28:5*

We live in prosperous times. Not everyone shares in the prosperity, but it is still a time of abundance. Increasingly, there is a desire to be wealthy. Advertisements are intended to create a dissatisfaction that can be assuaged only by getting more. Investment firms then add their enticements to help people gain more to have more. The mailbox contains offers of credit so that we can have instant gratification.

Some will get caught in the trap; the lure of easy credit will put them in financial bondage. Others will prosper. Their investments will do well; their portfolios will flourish.

But with prosperity comes the peril of pride. The words Ezekiel spoke to the prince of Tyre apply to us as well: "'By your great skill in trading you have increased your wealth, and because of your wealth your heart has grown proud'" (28:5). He warned the ruler who had done well financially that his prosperity had damaged his heart. The damage was not physical but spiritual.

It's easy for our hearts to grow proud when we are prosperous. It's especially easy for this to happen when our prosperity is the apparent result of our own wisdom. When we have worked hard, invested well and made our first million, so to speak, pride grows. We are tempted to rest in our own accomplishments.

One antidote to pride is giving. Giving our money to support the Lord's work reminds us that money is temporary. Only the things of God are eternal.

READY FOR HIS RETURN

Ezekiel 30–32, 1 Peter 4 • *Key Verse: 1 Peter 4:7*

What will you be doing on the evening of April 15? Millions of Americans will feverishly be finishing their income-tax returns. Postal workers will be stationed at the post office waiting to collect the forms of those last-minute filers. If you wait until the literal eleventh hour to do your taxes, then the evening of April 15 is a night of singular focus. You are intent on one thing, refusing to be distracted until the envelope is in the mail, postmarked before midnight.

God wants us to have a singleness of mind, living, thinking and using our time as one approaching a deadline—because in reality we are facing a deadline. "The end of all things is near. Therefore be clear minded and self-controlled so that you can pray" (4:7).

The Bible does not tell us when the end of all things will come, but we are to live with the expectancy that it could be soon. None of us knows how long we will live nor when Jesus will come again. Our time on this earth will conclude with either our death or with the Rapture, both of which could happen at any time. Either way, we will instantly be in God's presence.

Peter wants us to realize and remember this in such a way that it affects the way we live and pray. More important than being ready for a tax deadline is being ready for Jesus' return.

It seems easier to focus on tax returns than on Jesus' return. Ask God to help you live with a sense of immediacy. Jesus could come today.

EASIER SAID THAN DONE

Ezekiel 33–34, 1 Peter 5 • *Key Verse: 1 Peter 5:7*

Some things are easier said than done. One of those things is casting "all [our] anxiety on him," even though we are told that "he cares for [us]" (5:7).

We do have anxieties. Our concerns range from physical needs to financial needs, from family needs to the needs of our friends. These are things of which prayer lists are made—or at least should be made.

But we have a God who cares for us! We are not a burden, an afterthought or something of which He is not aware. He cares for us more intensely than we can ever imagine. The omniscient God knows our needs, all of them, and is concerned about every one of them.

Peter tells us what we are to do with our cares. We are to "cast" them onto Jesus. As a coat is tossed to someone else with the request, "Would you carry this for me?" we are to take the cares of this world and toss them to Him.

The problem is, we tend to do that but then take back the cares. We are willing to say that we will give our anxieties to Jesus but then continue to mull over and carry them ourselves.

Do not confuse continuing to pray with failing to cast the burden on Him. God doesn't tell us to stop praying but to let Him carry our anxieties.

Do you have a prayer list? If you do, that is good. Don't stop praying. But do you worry about these things on your list? That is bad. Ask God to help you give Him the worries. Keep praying, but stop worrying.

EVERYTHING WE NEED

Ezekiel 35–36, 2 Peter 1 • **Key Verse: 2 Peter 1:3**

Complete is a wonderful word, especially when putting together something like a computer system. It's encouraging when the advertisement promises, "Everything you need is included." All the necessary parts are there, with no additional cables to buy. You open the boxes, follow the instructions and ultimately the system is up and running.

God gives us a complete offer. Peter puts it this way: "His divine power has given us everything we need for life and godliness through our knowledge of him who called us by his own glory and goodness" (1:3). Everything we need for life and godliness has been given to us. Nothing has to be added!

Sometimes we look for the fine print of a too-good-to-be-true offer. But Peter doesn't put anything in fine print. This offer is made possible "through the knowledge of him who called us." When we truly know God we are given all that is needed for life and godliness. Eternal life is a gift to those who know Jesus as Savior. This is not just knowing about Jesus but knowing Him personally.

When we know Jesus, we are changed. God changes us so that we are no longer under the penalty or the power of sin. Freed from sin's power, we can live a life of godliness. Then the better we know God, the better we will know how He wants us to live.

Knowing God begins with salvation. Knowing God better ought to be the desire of our life, one fulfilled by learning His Word. God's offer is a complete one, found in Him.

"God, I thank You for what You have given me—everything I need for life and godliness. Help me know You better so that my life may please You more."

DRY BONES

Ezekiel 37–39, 2 Peter 2 • *Key Verses: Ezekiel 37:3–7*

Someone has said that an archaeologist is a person who makes his living digging up dead people. If you lived in Israel today, you might believe that is true.

Israel is bustling with archaeological activity. Professionals and volunteers are digging up mounds of past civilizations, finding pottery, coins and, occasionally, human bones. They gather the artifacts carefully, but they do not anticipate that the pottery will ever again be used for cooking or the coins for trading. And they certainly do not anticipate that those dry bones will ever live again.

No so with the Lord God. He called the prophet Ezekiel to a valley full of dry bones and asked, "Can these bones live?" Ezekiel was cautious in his response: "O Sovereign LORD, you alone know" (37:3). God was promising that the nation Israel, which was all but obliterated due to enemy invasion, would one day live again.

For almost 20 centuries Israel did not exist as a nation. There was no Jewish homeland. The Hebrew language all but died out. And then God performed a miracle. He gathered Jews from all over the world and brought them to Palestine, and in 1948 the modern state of Israel was born. It was proof that, just as He had predicted to Ezekiel, God would not abandon His people forever. God keeps His promises, even in a valley full of dry bones.

"Thank You, Heavenly Father, for being a God of integrity. Thank You for bringing Your people back to their land and for giving us one more example that You are a God of Your word."

THE DAILY DOUBLE

Ezekiel 40–41, 2 Peter 3 • Key Verse: 2 Peter 3:18

Have you noticed how some things just naturally go together? Like bacon and eggs. Batman and Robin. Peanut butter and jelly. That's true in the Bible too. Adam and Eve. David and Goliath. Priscilla and Aquila.

The last verse of 2 Peter highlights one of these biblical dynamic duos—grace and knowledge. Peter says, "But grow in the grace and knowledge of our Lord and Savior Jesus Christ" (v. 18).

Growing in knowledge requires the discipline to find a time and a place, and then to focus on a plan to get to know God better through His Word. Growing in a knowledge of God means both understanding what He did for us and what He wants us to do. It means applying the Word to our lives daily.

Growing in grace also requires time in the Word. It means growing in the graces that become a Christian, like brotherly kindness and love. You can read about some of these graces in the first chapter of 2 Peter.

Grace and knowledge. We need to grow in them every day. We get both from God's Word. It's a daily double that will make a difference in your day.

"Lord, help me to find the time and place and discipline myself to read Your Word each day and thus grow both in Your grace and in Your knowledge. And may others around me sense that I've been with You and my life is different as a result."

EVIDENCE TO THE CHANGE

Ezekiel 42–44, 1 John 1 • *Key Verse: 1 John 1:6*

There is a simple phrase that goes like this: "Do you walk the walk or just talk the talk?" The alliteration and rhyming make it catchy, easy to remember. But don't lose sight of the insightfulness of the question just because it rolls off the tongue so easily.

The apostle John never pulled his punches. He called for a commitment to Christ that included "walking the walk." To the person who said that he had fellowship with God but lived as if he did not, John's message was blunt: "You lie." Read again verse 6: "If we claim to have fellowship with Him yet walk in the darkness, we lie and do not live by the truth."

There are two opposite lifestyles from which we can choose. The one is characterized by wickedness and error. John calls it walking in the dark. The other is characterized by holiness and truth. It is walking in the light. For John there was only one choice, and it was to walk in the light as Jesus is in the light. To walk in darkness was not an option.

A Christian's life should show that commitment. Christianity is not just forgiveness of sins with no change in lifestyle. We are saved not just from sin but to live a life of godliness. Do you walk the walk?

Consider your words. Do they match your life? You can lie to others and even yourself but never to God. To say you have fellowship is meaningless unless your life gives evidence to the change.

THREE ENEMIES

Ezekiel 45–46, 1 John 2 • *Key Verses: 1 John 2:15–16*

First John 2 contains a much-needed reminder about the three enemies who are constantly trying to defeat the Christian. The more
conscious we are of their existence and activities, the more likely we
will be to have victory over them. John clearly identifies them and in
his direct way warns us that affection for these enemies is an indication that a person does not have the love of God in him.

The world is the present system that is under Satan's control. Sadly,
it seems that many churches have quit warning against worldliness.
Loving this world is contrary to loving God.

The flesh is an enemy, not in the sense that the human body is evil
but that it can be used for evil and it contains the desires that enable
Satan to entice us to sin. We are not to hate our bodies but to recognize how they can be used for wrong.

The devil is the personal enemy of the believer. He is not just an
influence but an individual who opposes God and the people of
God. He is a fallen angel who should be respected for the damage
that he can do but not feared because he was defeated at Calvary.

We need to be reminded of these enemies so we will be vigilant,
keeping up our guard at all times. None of the three can be escaped,
since our bodies are in this world. Escape is not the answer anyway.
Victory is, and there is victory in Jesus!

*Ask God to help you remember these enemies and to give you victory. Do
not live a defeated life. Satan was defeated, not you. Remember that
your strength is found in Jesus.*

TOGETHER FOREVER

Ezekiel 47–48, 1 John 3 • *Key Verse: Ezekiel 48:35*

Weddings are special events filled with hope, commitment and happiness. The day finally has come when the bride and groom are no longer separated; from now on the two are one. Being together is one of the great blessings of marriage. No more saying good-bye at the end of the day because husband and wife are home together. Times of separation due to travel may come—but they also go.

The Book of Ezekiel concludes with a great and decisive declaration. This final prophecy is about the reuniting of the scattered people of Israel with their God. A day will come when God's people will never again be separated from Him through judgment. Forever they will live as God's people and He will be their God.

To drive home this joyous truth, Ezekiel announces that the name of the city will be "THE LORD IS THERE." Some see in the Hebrew phrase a wordplay on the name "Jerusalem." There is a similar sound. Either way it is a name of great encouragement, to be where God is—forever.

It is good for us to remember that the blessings of salvation include eternity with God. We live in a sin-sick, sin-cursed world. One day this world will be past and eternity will be our neverending present. Then the promise will be fulfilled that we will always be with God, He will be our God, and we will be His people.

"I praise You, God, for the promise of eternity with You. Help me keep my eyes fixed on what is to come!"

RESOLVE

Daniel 1–2, 1 John 4 • *Key Verse: Daniel 1:8*

In any newspaper of any size you will find a sports section. The larger ones devote an entire section to the subject and at times even have more than one. With the focus on performance and results, sometimes it's lost on the reader what it took for athletes to reach their level of competitiveness. Saying it took diet and exercise is a very simplistic summary that leaves out an intangible, without which no athlete can excel. That intangible is resolve.

Resolve essentially is determination. It means that a person has a fixed purpose. The successful athlete has a determination that will enable him to endure the rigors of training in order to achieve at the desired level of performance.

If we are to excel in our spiritual lives, we need resolve as well. Many Christians are content with a low level of "performance" in the spiritual life. Their discipline is poor, inconsistent at best, and they fail to develop the maturity that God desires.

Daniel was a man of resolve. As a young man, promoted to the king's palace, tapped for success, he "resolved not to defile himself with the royal food and wine" (1:8). He had a fixed purpose and the determination to accomplish that goal. Without resolve, the enticement of the delicacies would have entrapped him. He would have been defiled. But he was not, because he was determined.

Are you determined to be all that God wants you to be? It will mean refusing those things that defile you spiritually. Satan will test your resolve, as he did Daniel's.

The spiritual resolve we need is not temporary like most New Year's resolutions. It must be the consistent character of our lives. Watch for times today that your resolve is tested, and then ask God to help you be like Daniel.

THE FIRST MARTYRS

Daniel 3–4, 1 John 5 • *Key Verses: Daniel 3:17–18*

The following is a "trick" question, not intended merely to fool a person but to provoke thought. The question is, who were the first martyrs? In one sense the correct answer is Stephen in Acts 7. He died for refusing to renounce his faith. The thought-provoking answer is Shadrach, Meshach and Abednego. Now the argument begins. How could they be martyrs since they did not die in the fiery furnace?

A martyr is one who sacrifices his life rather than renounce his belief. That is exactly what these three men did. They should have died. The temperature of the furnace into which they were thrown had been increased to seven times hotter than normal. The flames were so fierce that the soldiers who took them to the blazing furnace died. But Shadrach, Meshach and Abednego did not. God protected them.

Martyrs or not? There's no argument that they were willing to die for their faith. To the king they said, "We will not serve your gods or worship the image of gold you have set up" (3:18). Still, they are not remembered as martyrs but as men who stood for God even when threatened with death.

Few of us will ever be in the same situation, yet the sad truth is that thousands of people around the world die every year because of their faith. We should pray regularly for those who are confronted with the choice to renounce Christ or die.

And we should pray that if we ever face that choice, our resolve will make us stand for the One who died for us.

Ask God to help you resolve to never deny your faith.

HAND IN HAND

Daniel 5–7, 2 John • Key Verse: 2 John 6

If we were to define love the way it is portrayed in the media today, the result would be a definition of something not found in the Bible. Love is not the unexpected emotion that justifies a deserting of commitments and the abandonment of morals. Yet that is the "stuff" of love stories today. Emotions run hot and heavy. Spouses are deserted as well as other obligations. Morals typically do not enter the picture.

Yes, we are told to "love one another" (v. 5), but read on. The very next verse states, "And this is love: that we walk in obedience to his commands" (v. 6). Love and obedience go hand in hand.

First, notice that love can be commanded. The first part of loving one another is an act of obedience, not a rush of emotion. Certainly emotion is involved, but essentially the love commanded is an act of the will.

Then notice that love and obedience must go together. We cannot separate our relationship with God from our relationship with others. When we seek to live according to God's Word, how we act toward others will be affected positively. It may sound like an oversimplification, but the truth is this: live the Word and those around you will be loved.

To love without obedience is to conform to the world and its view of love. But to love one another and obey God is to conform to the Word. Love and obedience are to go hand in hand, always.

Have you tried to love and not obey? It can't be done. Decide today to obey God's Word and look for ways that this will help you "love one another."

CONFESSION IS GOOD FOR ...

Daniel 8–10, 3 John • *Key Verses: Daniel 9:4–5*

Remember this phrase—"Confession is good for the soul"? It seems like we readily agree with that statement, especially when we are trying to get someone else to confess! At the same time, it's quite possible that the least frequently offered prayer is one of confession. We do best with requests, remember to at least say thanks, are possibly passable with the amount of worship in our praying, but fail miserably in regard to confession.

So if you agree that confession is good for the soul, when was the last time you practiced it?

One of the great prayers of the Bible is in Daniel 9. Daniel offered it in response to reading Scripture. He understood what the Word said, and it affected him tremendously. He prayed, fasted and confessed.

Read again carefully this prayer of Daniel. Note the request portion. It is very short, toward the end and really no more than one phrase —"turn away your anger and your wrath from Jerusalem, your city, your holy hill" (9:16). Then immediately Daniel returns to confession.

Our prayers should be balanced. They should include worship, thanksgiving, requests and confession. It is not necessary that each prayer have all four, but as we examine our prayer life, all should be evident, including confession.

Think now about your prayer life. Perhaps it isn't much. (That is a subject all its own to consider!) Whatever the current condition is of your prayer life, do you confess?

"Father, right now I need to confess that . . ."

UNDER CONSTRUCTION

Daniel 11–12, **Jude** • *Key Verse: Jude 20*

What is the biggest room in your house? The room for improvement, of course! There is always room for improvement in our lives. No matter how much we may think we have arrived, there are still rough edges and missing pieces that need work. The typical homeowner knows that there is always something that needs to be fixed, replaced, removed or added. That means he has two choices—either get to work on those things or forget about them. Obviously, the former is preferred over the latter.

The same is true with our spiritual lives. There is always room for improvement, and we can either work on it or forget about it. God's will is that we "build [ourselves] up in [our] most holy faith" (v. 20).

You started out your Christian life as a baby believer, one needing to be fed the milk of the Word. As you grew and developed, you moved from milk to meat. The parallels between physical growth and spiritual growth make it easy for us to understand. As the child is fed, he grows and develops. As the believer is fed the Word, he also grows and develops.

Sometimes, though, a Christian may be content to stay a child in the faith. That is not the same as childlike faith. Also, there is no excuse for stunted spiritual growth. God wants, expects and commands us to mature. It is a building process that should occur in the life of every believer.

Are you growing in your faith, or are you stagnant? Reading the Bible is part of the growth process, as is praying, which is also mentioned in this key verse today. Be sure to do both every day.

LOVED

Hosea 1–4, Revelation 1 • *Key Verse: Revelation 1:5*

The apostle John knew Jesus. He walked with Him, heard Him teach and joined with Him in ministry. When Jesus died on the cross, John was there and was given a special responsibility, that of caring for Mary, the mother of Jesus. He is remembered as the Apostle of Love—but he was not always known by that name.

In the list of disciples in Mark 3, John and his brother James are called the "Sons of Thunder" (v. 17). When the Samaritans would not receive Jesus, John and James were ready to command fire from heaven to destroy the place (Luke 9:54)! John not only was with Jesus, but he also was changed by Jesus. He went from one who would react with a call for judgment to being characterized as a man of love. John knew the reality of being loved and became one who loved.

In the opening chapter of the Revelation of Jesus Christ, John gave greetings and a doxology. Doxologies are words of praise. His praise of Jesus includes this phrase: "to him who loves us and has freed us from our sins by his blood" (v. 5). John had experienced both the love of Jesus and the cleansing that can be received from Him.

John may not have been the most lovable of individuals. Typically, someone described as a "son of thunder" does not invoke images of relational warmth! Yet there is no more tender picture of closeness and purity in relationship as that of John at the table during the Last Supper, leaning on Jesus. He knew love and was changed by the love of Jesus.

We are loved and it should show. How do others see you? If you are more like a son of thunder than an apostle of love, ask Jesus to help change you like He changed John.

REPENT, PART 1

Hosea 5–8, Revelation 2 • *Key Verse: Hosea 6:1*

Perhaps we should make a list of the "lost words of Christianity." It seems like some things are not talked about as much today. *Worldliness*, for instance, is a forgotten word, erased from usage by an overemphasis and sometimes misapplication of Christian liberty. *Sin* and some of the classic words for it have been dropped from the vocabulary. Adultery is an "affair" or a "fling," for example. Seldom do we hear the word *repent*.

Repent implies the need for change. Something is not right; actually, something is wrong. The tendency today is to teach how God can meet man's need and not so much about how man needs to change. The concept that God would judge is foreign to the minds of some people yet is essential to His nature as a God of justice and righteousness.

To the people of Israel, God sent Hosea, a man who became a living parable of repentance and return. His story is shocking: he was married to a prostitute whom the Lord commanded he love as the Lord loved the Israelites (3:1). The reality of Hosea's marriage teaches us the reality of God's love for His wayward people, for us. We are told, "'Come, and let us return to the LORD. He has torn us to pieces but he will heal us; he has injured us but he will bind up our wounds'" (6:1).

That is not what people may want to hear, but it is what we need to hear. God will work in our lives, sometimes in forceful and unpleasant ways. His goal is not to destroy but to bring us back to Him.

Examine your life and think about areas in which God wants you to change. Repentance is not just something of the past. It needs to be a part of our present.

REPENT, PART 2

*Hosea 9–11, **Revelation 3*** • ***Key Verse: Revelation 3:19***

About the time we start to think that repentance is only an Old Testament idea, along come verses like this one from the New Testament: "'Those whom I love I rebuke and discipline. So be earnest, and repent'" (v. 19). There is an interesting blend of two contrasting actions—love and rebuke.

We may not understand how love and rebuke go together, but they do. It is vital to our understanding of God and the development of our spiritual lives to understand that both are a part of our relationship with Him.

God loves us. That is a comforting thought. We do not typically draw as much comfort from the thought that God rebukes us—until we realize that His rebuke is an act of love. He cares for us enough to correct us, and His desire is to help us change.

Several times in these letters to the churches the message of Jesus includes a call to repentance. It is a message that we must not miss nor misunderstand. Do not misunderstand it as being anything but an expression of God's love for us. And do not miss the need for change, removing from your life those things that God says are wrong. We are saved from the penalty and power of sin. God desires that we turn from those sins and determine to do that which is right in His sight. *Repent* truly is a word for us today.

Do you need to change something in your life? Repent *is still a word for today!*

GOOD CHOICE

Hosea 12–14, Revelation 4 • *Key Verse: Hosea 14:9*

We make choices every day about a multitude of things, some of which are of little or no consequence. But some of our choices are of great significance. How well we choose can set us apart from the crowd. The person who makes good choices will be known for his wisdom and discernment.

Hosea concludes with a statement that describes the wise person. This truth summarizes well the choice every one of us should make. He says that the wise, prudent person should understand that "the ways of the LORD are right; the righteous walk in them, but the rebellious stumble in them" (14:9).

Choose to accept the truth that the ways of the Lord are right. That is the crucial decision that needs to precede all others. The Bible teaches us the ways of the Lord. We need to read it and learn it with an attitude of acceptance. God's ways are right.

Then choose to act on the truth that the ways of the Lord are right. Accepting is one thing, acting is another. Someone may agree but not practice. The wise person does more than just agree with truth— he lives it. That is the crucial next step. Transgressors, on the other hand, do not walk in the ways of the Lord and they stumble.

Choose wisely and prudently. Choose the ways of the Lord.

We must read, learn and live the Word. Today renew your commitment before God that you will choose His ways.

STRIKING IMAGERY

Joel 1–3, Revelation 5 • **Key Verse: Revelation 5:6**

John's vision of the heavenly throne room is one of the most moving worship scenes in the Bible, one filled with rich and striking imagery that joins Old and New Testament truth in a single person, Jesus Christ. He is the Lion of the tribe of Judah, the Root of David and the Lamb of God, the only One worthy to open the scroll and to loose its seven seals.

Allow for a moment your mind to dwell on this scene. John "wept and wept because no one was found who was worthy to open the scroll" (v. 4). Then he heard that the Lion of the tribe of Judah had "triumphed" and was able to open the scroll (v. 5). He turned to see the Lion and saw the Lamb. Old and New Testament converge and contain a striking imagery not seen in our English translations.

The Lamb is described as looking "as if it had been slain" (v. 6). That phrase is a translation of a Greek word that means "with its throat cut." Our English versions emphasize that the marks of death are visible, but the original language communicates the picture of a sacrifice. How else would a lamb have been sacrificed? Its throat would have been cut.

Yet notice that the Lamb is standing. He is not dead, even though slain.

Jesus is the Lamb of God. He died for our sins, yet He lives! And He alone is worthy "'to receive power and wealth and wisdom and strength and honor and glory and praise!'" (v. 12).

We prefer a nicer image of the death of Christ to this bloody one. Yet the truth is that Jesus died a cruel death for us. Meditate on this truth today. Thank God for the Lamb, the One who was slain.

GOD'S NOBODY

Amos 1–3, Revelation 6 • Key Verse: Amos 1:1

My hometown had only one building, which contained the train station, general store, gas station and post office. I used to say that it was "just five miles south of resume speed." There's something about coming from a small town that makes you feel insignificant.

I'm sure Amos was like that. He came from the tiny village of Tekoa. If you rode your donkey south out of Jerusalem you soon came to Bethlehem. If you rode six miles further, you came to Tekoa. And if you rode even further you came to nothing. Tekoa was a frontier town, on the edge of the harsh Judean wilderness.

There, Amos was a shepherd. He was not the mayor of the town; he was a sheep breeder. He was a nobody.

Still, God came to this nobody and called him to become His servant and spokesman (read Amos 7:14–15). Amos wasn't eloquent nor was he educated. But he was available and he wholly obeyed the Lord. Eleven times in his tiny book Amos says, "Thus says the LORD . . ."

Maybe God has something special for you to do too. It doesn't matter what you are now; it only matters what He intends to make of you. Be available. Be clean. Be ready. You may be His next Amos.

"God, make me the kind of person who is clean and pure before You, so that if You have some special task for me to do, I will be ready, willing and able to do it."

TOO AT EASE IN ZION

Amos 4–6, Revelation 7 • *Key Verse: Amos 6:1*

You've probably heard about the meeting that was called to deal with the problem of apathy—no one cared enough about the problem to show up! The better things appear to be, the easier it is to grow complacent. Yet there are dangers inherent in complacency. Ruin can set in when diligence is set aside. For example, don't worry about changing the oil in your car because it seems to be running fine. One day the warning light will come on, and it may be too late for your engine. Or as an ad for a dentist advised, "Ignore your teeth and eventually they will go away."

Complacency in the spiritual life is a great danger too. Just as a car or our physical health can suffer from benign neglect, so can our spiritual health. We may fail to see the damage that is occurring when we do not maintain our spiritual life. We may one day wake up to realize that just like ignored teeth, our spiritual life is in shambles due to our complacency.

The prophet Amos cried out to the people of Israel, "Woe to you who are complacent [at ease] in Zion, and to you who feel secure on Mount Samaria" (6:1). At the heart of the complacency was pride. "We have Zion, the city of God," they might have said. The people of Samaria viewed themselves as economically and militarily secure. Their vision did not match the reality of their situation. They faced judgment. God declared, "I abhor the pride of Jacob and detest his fortresses; I will deliver up the city and everything in it" (v. 8). We can be too at ease in Zion.

"God, help me to rest in You but not grow complacent about Your Word and my spiritual life. May I rest in You but keep my walk with You vibrant."

THE SOUND OF SILENCE

*Amos 7–9, **Revelation 8*** • ***Key Verse: Revelation 8:1***

During the premier of Handel's *Messiah*, King George II was so moved by the "Hallelujah Chorus" that he spontaneously rose to his feet and stood for the remainder of the performance, his eyes glistening with emotion. The rest of the audience, when they saw the king reverently standing as the music swelled, also stood—a tradition that remains to this day.

Remember that chorus? Wave after wave of hallelujahs sweeps over you. And then—the orchestra and the choir suddenly stop! There is silence, a thundering silence, full of awe and intense anticipation. There is a sense of drama, of suspense, of mystery. We know it is not over. The last hallelujah is yet to sound. Suddenly the silence shatters under the triumphant blow of the final majestic, "Hallelujah!"

Handel used a dramatic pause to get the attention of the audience, just like God used a dramatic pause to get our attention in Revelation 8:1. The rapidly moving drama of the seven-seal judgment stops. The breaking of the final seal brings an unexpected result: silence. The captured attention is then drawn to the seven angels who are given seven trumpets—but still no sound. Finally in verse 5 the silence is broken with "peals of thunder, rumblings, flashes of lightning and an earthquake."

God used silence to catch our attention to show us His judgment. He does not do this for mere dramatic effect but that we might repent. Sadly, the Bible tells us, men will ignore God's acts of judgment and will instead curse Him. When God catches our attention, we better listen!

Do you really listen to what God says to you through His Word? The real evidence is the changes you make in your life. What evidence do you have to show that God has your attention?

THE SERIOUSNESS OF SIN

*Obadiah, **Revelation 9** • Key Verse: **Revelation 9:20***

This chapter of Revelation does two things. First, it tells of events that will occur. It is a prophecy detailing part of the judgment God will pour out on this earth. It also serves as a warning of the seriousness of sin.

The seriousness of sin is seen in the increasing severity of judgment. As you read through Revelation you will notice this. The warning at the end of chapter 8 is given in a way that none will fail to see or hear. The movement through the seal and trumpet judgments, on to the bowl judgments, is one of increasing severity.

The seriousness of sin is also seen in the severity of the judgments themselves. Torment and death are the results of the fifth and sixth trumpets. We sometimes focus more on the description of these judgments rather than reflect on their severity. These will make all other disasters pale in comparison.

And how does mankind react? Incredibly, with great stubbornness. In verses 20 and 21 we're told that people refuse to turn to God. Their hearts are set in their hostility toward Him. Not even torment and death lead them to repentance. They "still did not repent of the work of their hands; they did not stop worshiping demons, and idols of gold, silver, bronze, stone and wood . . . . Nor did they repent of their murders, their magic arts, their sexual immorality or their thefts."

Sin can so grip the heart that even the judgment of God does not break its grasp. Don't just learn about the future from these verses but see the warning for the present. See the seriousness of sin.

We sometimes are too casual about sin and its effects. Consider your life today, looking to see if sin is gripping some part of it. By God's grace and power you can break its grasp.

SWEET TO TASTE,
BUT HARD TO SWALLOW

Jonah 1–4, Revelation 11 • *Key Verse: Revelation 10:11*

Have you ever put off going to the doctor because you did not want to hear what might be said? Or delayed taking your car to a mechanic for the same reason? Or avoided your accountant for fear your financial picture was rather bleak? There are times when we need to hear from the doctor, mechanic and accountant. We know that what they have to say may be for our good, but it is hard to hear. It may be good for us, but it is hard to swallow.

Sometimes the Word of God is sweet to taste but hard to swallow. That was John's experience as he was given a little scroll and told to eat it. In his mouth it was sweet, but in his stomach it turned sour.

The Word should be as sweet as honey in our mouths. In it we read of God's promises, of hope and of heaven. God's Word teaches us about salvation and gives us the instruction we need to live godly lives. It is sweet to align ourselves with God and His truth.

Yet God's Word also contains judgment. That is the part that can be hard to swallow, yet it also is God's truth. We do not find pleasure in the prospect of the wrath of God.

John would rather have stayed with the sweet things of the Word, but God recommissioned him to carry the prophecy of judgment, to tell the hard truth to people. Sometimes we also have to tell others what they do not want to hear.

It can be hard to tell of God's judgments, but we must be faithful to the Word and its message.

SATAN RULES, BUT GOD OVERRULES

Micah 1–3, Revelation 11 • *Key Verses: Revelation 11:1–2*

A time is coming in which it will seem like Satan is on the throne. His kind of government, church and economic world system will be in place as well as his kind of control. In those days it will look like Satan rules, but consistently God will show that He overrules. In what is considered to be one of the most perplexing chapters of Revelation, God demonstrates this.

That God is in charge is seen in an act of protection found in verses 1 and 2. He instructed John to mark off the boundaries of the temple and to count the worshipers there. That place and those people are then set aside, Satan notwithstanding. God can draw the line on Satan anytime, anyplace because He is in charge. What He protects is protected.

That God is in charge is also seen in an act of proclaiming. The next portion of this chapter tells of the two witnesses. In the midst of darkness, they are light. They also are protected until they finish their testimony. This may seem to be Satan's time, but God's message will still be going out and His messengers will be triumphant.

The scene of the people celebrating the death of the two witnesses should scare us in the sense that again we see the deceitfulness of sin. It should also embolden us because at that precise time God again demonstrates Resurrection power!

It should also amaze us. God has been rejected but still reaches out. Even in that day of abomination, God will have a witness.

"Some days, God, it seems like Satan is in control. Help me remember that You alone are the Sovereign of the universe, that you overrule Satan."

THE DARK SIDE OF CHRISTMAS

Micah 4–5, Revelation 12 • Key Verses: Revelation 12:1–2

Once upon a time there was a kingdom. The person who ruled the kingdom was not the rightful ruler but a usurper. One day he learned that a baby would be born, one who would be the rightful heir to the throne. He knew that if the baby were allowed to live, it would be able to claim the throne and take it from him. So he decided to kill the baby. He tried but failed because the baby was safely taken to another kingdom.

Do you recognize this story? It's not a fairy tale. It is the Christmas story, told without the usual emphasis on angels and shepherds and magi, or bright lights and joyful songs. It is "the dark side of Christmas." The usurper is Satan. The rightful ruler is Christ. This is the version of the Christmas story found in Revelation 12.

Too often we forget this aspect of Christ's birth. Satan desired that the Child die. Thankfully, the truth of the Christmas story includes not only Satan's enmity toward Jesus, but also Christ's ultimate victory over him. Revelation 12 pictures the cosmic struggle and the celebration song. The kingdom comes! The accuser is thrown out! Rejoice!

The chapter concludes somewhat ominously. Satan has failed but does not accept defeat without a bitter struggle. The victory has been won, but the battle grows fiercer and darker for the Church. Still, we are assured that satanic evil on earth is really a defeated power.

Rejoice in the truth that Satan is a defeated power, but don't let down your guard. He will ultimately go down, but not without a fight.

THE PARDONING GOD

Micah 6–7, Revelation 13 • ***Key Verse: Micah 7:18***

Someone has said that humor is only the truth thinly disguised. The phrase "I don't get mad, I get even" is intended to be humorous, but the truth is evident. For some people, this phrase is like a mantra for relationship management. Its corollary statement is, "Do unto others before they do unto you." Sadly, some people live with anger and revenge in their hearts—and at times that shows in their lives.

Consider this description of God: He "pardons sin and forgives the transgression . . . . [He does] not stay angry forever" and it is His "delight to show mercy" (v. 18). If that isn't contrast enough, add the next verse: "You will again have compassion on us; you will tread our sins underfoot and hurl all our iniquities into the depths of the sea" (v. 19). With God, the only thing that gets walked over is our sins!

This is an amazing picture of God. He pardons, forgives, shows mercy and has compassion. Don't miss the application of all of this. What He does is done for you and me. We are the ones who have sinned and need forgiveness. He is the One who through Jesus offers salvation to us. When we receive Jesus, we receive all the benefits of the God who pardons, forgives, shows mercy and has compassion.

And as you think of what this means for you, remember the responsibility that comes with the blessing. Paul put it this way: "Forgive as the Lord forgave you" (Col. 3:13).

"Lord, I thank You that You are the pardoning God and ask that You will help me to be a forgiving person."

THE DIFFERENCE A DAY CAN MAKE

Nahum 1–3, Revelation 14 • *Key Verse: Revelation 14:1*

God does not give us just a hope for a tomorrow. He gives us a hope-filled tomorrow. The opening scene of Revelation 14, the Lamb standing on Mount Zion with the 144,000, comes on the heels of one of the darkest chapters in the Bible. In chapter 13 there is only darkness and apparent defeat for the people of God. But what a difference a chapter can make! The text moves from hopeless to hope-filled and helps us focus on a future of victory and vindication.

The hope-filled future is one of victory as described in verses 1–5. The Lamb stands on Mount Zion, not on the shifting sands of the seashore like the dragon in Revelation 13:1. His followers stand not in defeat but victory. They stand on Zion, not in exile but in Israel, the place where Messiah will gather the redeemed. They stand and sing, not in sorrow but with a new song, one of redemption and victory. And they stand before God.

The hope-filled future is also one of vindication. The climactic announcements in the remainder of the chapter are of the everlasting Gospel, the fall of Babylon and the torment of the beast worshipers. There is promised rest and more angels of judgment.

If Revelation ended with chapter 13, we would be left with a picture of defeat. But chapter 14 encourages us to patient endurance and to remain faithful to Jesus. There will be victory and vindication.

After reading both Revelation 13 and 14, we should be convinced that God is ultimately in control and nothing should shake us—ever. Since that is true, do not let the events of this day shake you.

GOD IS GOOD, ALL THE TIME

Habakkuk 1–3, Revelation15 • **Key Verse: Habakkuk 3:19**

We need to remind ourselves that God is good all the time, with special emphasis on "all the time." When things are going well, it's easy to say, "God is good." But in difficult times those words can be hard to say. At any time we should be able to join Habakkuk in saying, "The Sovereign LORD is my strength; he makes my feet like the feet of a deer, he enables me to go on the heights" (3:19).

Notice the verses immediately before that one. Habakkuk is writing about difficult times. In particular he points to crop failure and the absence of livestock. Those are indications of economic ruin, financial disaster and food shortage. It is not a pleasant picture—no buds on the fig trees or grapes on the vines. The olive crop has failed and there is no food in the fields. Even the sheep pens and cattle stalls are empty. "Yet," he writes, "I will rejoice in the LORD, I will be joyful in God my Savior" (v. 18). Habakkuk understood both that God is good and that He is good all the time.

How clearly do you understand that? If things are going well for you today, it is easy to say, "God is good." But what will happen when your situation changes? It is then you should read Habakkuk 3 again to be reminded that God is good—all the time.

Pause right now to thank God for His goodness. Make this a daily prayer.

IMMANUEL

Zephaniah 1–3, Revelation 16 • *Key Verse: Zephaniah 3:17*

If there is one direction our thoughts should head today, it is to the birth of Jesus Christ. This is the great moment in which God physically entered into our world. He "became flesh and made his dwelling among us" (John 1:14). If we were to put all this into one word we would say, "Immanuel," which means, "God with us" (Matt. 1:23).

We also must remember that He did this "to save His people from their sins" (Matt. 1:21). Jesus did not just come for a visit, nor was His birth just the birth of another man. Rather, His birth was the intentional, preplanned act of God whereby He entered our world to become our Savior. He was born to die. That is a simple statement, but do not let the simplicity of it belie the significance of what it says.

Zephaniah the prophet wrote of these two things—God with us and His work of redemption—when he said, "The LORD your God is with you, he is mighty to save. He will take great delight in you, he will quiet you with his love, he will rejoice over you with singing" (3:17).

On Christmas Day our focus can become blurred by all the cultural trappings of the holiday. Passages such as this call our attention back to what is central to the celebration. It is Jesus, Immanuel, God with us, who came to save.

The greatest gift is not found under a tree but in Jesus.

"Thank you, God, for the greatest gift, one not of tinsel and glitter but of eternal value. Thank you for Jesus and for the gift of salvation we receive from You."

BE STRONG, BE STRONG, BE STRONG

Haggai 1–2, Revelation 17 • *Key Verse: Haggai 2:4*

In spite of so many blessings and so many benefits, people still struggle with depression. When we are "down" emotionally or mentally, it can even pull us down physically.

In the days of Haggai the people were discouraged. Why? Among other things, the new temple they had built was inferior to the old one. One of the common effects of depression was evident—their initiative was stifled. Depressed people often slow down, even stop altogether. Having lost their motivation, they sit. And the longer they sit, the more depressed they get.

God gave very specific instruction to His people, instruction that can help us. He said first, "Be strong." Then He said, "Be strong." After that He said, "Be strong." Mark it in Haggai 2:4. Three times God says, "Be strong." That is spiritually based emotional resolve! It's not psychological self-help talk but divine instruction. It is also something that we must determine to do, to be strong.

God instructed one other thing—"work." This was not a "don't just sit there, do something" kind of instruction. It is amazing how much healing can take place when we start being constructive again.

Don't miss the bottom line. God said, "For I am with you." His presence indeed makes all the difference.

Is something depressing you? Then decide what you can do about it! Work on it, remembering that God is with you.

LIVE UP TO YOUR NAME

Zechariah 1–4, Revelation 18 • Key Verse: Revelation 18:4

"If God doesn't judge America, He will have to apologize to Sodom and Gomorrah." Those words caught my attention the first time I heard them and every time I've heard them since. It is a striking statement. Rest assured, God will not have to apologize to Sodom and Gomorrah. Recognize also that God is not going to judge just America. The day is coming when God will judge in its entirety the great satanic system of evil that has corrupted earth and mankind.

Revelation 18 opens with a scene of desolation. Babylon is fallen and ruined. There is a reason for the judgment—"'her sins are piled up to heaven, and God has remembered her crimes'" (v. 5). God is not a cosmic bully but a righteous Judge. His wrath is related to the out-working of sin. The world sought luxury, elevated itself in pride and was smug in its avoidance of suffering, saying, "I will never mourn" (v. 7). Instead she will experience all that she has avoided.

The scene in the chapter is one of ruin, but notice that it is a scene Christians can avoid. "'Come out of her, my people, so that you will not share in her sins'" (v. 4). We are called to come out, to be separate, to shun the charms and entrapments of this world. Like the warnings to the seven churches, this is addressed to those of us who claim to be Christ followers. Satan attempts to seduce us so we will abandon our loyalty to Jesus, but we must not.

The most common New Testament designation for a believer is "saint." It means "to be set apart to God for a holy purpose." Are you living up to that name?

THE BATTLE BELONGS TO THE LORD

Zechariah 5–8, Revelation 19 • *Key Verse: Revelation 19:11*

In 47 B.C., the Roman army under Julius Caesar soundly defeated the forces of King Pharnaces, who fought the Romans for control of the kingdom of Pontus in Asia Minor. After his victory Caesar returned to Rome and made the famous announcement, "Veni, vidi, vici," or, "I came, I saw, I conquered."

Some 1,700 years later a Polish military strategist, King John III Sobieski, led a brilliant campaign to drive the Ottoman invaders out of central Europe. Leading a force of 25,000 men, he came to the aid of the German emperor Leopold I and beat the invaders back from the walls of Vienna, saving the city and the emperor. The Polish king was given an audience before Pope Innocent XI, who congratulated him on his victory.

King John's reply was: "I came, I saw, God conquered."

In Revelation 19 John describes for us the last battle, one fought between the rebellious forces of this world and the Warrior-Messiah, the One who is rightly described as the King of kings and Lord of lords. Those two titles indicate His universal sovereignty and anticipate His ultimate triumph. A day is coming when Jesus will return and conquer the evil systems of this world.

That is the way it will be. The Lord will come, the world will see, and God will conquer. As John MacArthur so aptly summarizes what is recorded in this chapter, it is "not so much a battle as an execution." It is a quick account as God brings to a close the Tribulation.

Notice that the first part of the chapter is a scene of worship. The "hallelujahs" ring out! Worship God for the truth that Jesus is the King of kings and Lord of lords.

REBELLION RUNS DEEP

*Zechariah 9–12, **Revelation 20** • **Key Verse: Revelation 20:7***

The signboard in front of a Littleton, Colorado, church near Columbine High School announced the sermon title for the Sunday after the tragic shootings at the school in April 1999. It asked the question, "Where Was God on Tuesday Afternoon?"

That was a question many people wanted answered. However, it was not an expression of sincere inquiry but of shifting blame. The world wants to shift the blame. Man has been doing that since Genesis 3 when Adam said, "It was the woman you gave me." The sad irony is that people also ask, "How can a loving God send anyone to hell?" Yet that Tuesday they wished that God would have stopped the killers, even by death if necessary.

Where was God? He was—as He always has been—continuing to offer His grace and forgiveness to sinful, inherently evil man. Not willing that any should perish, God was continuing to demonstrate loving patience.

Not all agree that man is evil, yet he is. Revelation 20 is often thought of as teaching about the Millennium. It does say a little about that subject, but the chapter really is about the sinfulness of man and how God takes a thousand years to prove that point.

For a thousand years God will restrain Satan while Jesus reigns on this earth. Without Satan and his deception, an ideal environment will be in place. Yet when Satan is released, man will still rise up in rebellion against God. Therefore, the problem with man is not our environment (culture) but our heart. The reality is that man's rebellion against God runs deep.

The answer to man's deepest need is not more metal detectors but Jesus. He alone can change the sinner's heart. Have you received Him as your Savior?

THE REFINER'S FIRE

Zechariah 13–14, Revelation 21 • *Key Verse: Zechariah 13:9*

The process of refining metals is used in the Bible as a metaphor of spiritual purification. In a sense, if you have something made of pure gold or pure silver, it is made of the leftovers. Refining is a process by which everything else is removed and only the pure metal remains. It is accomplished through firing, putting the metal over the fire until it is a liquid from which can be drawn all the dross.

Our lives are not pure gold by any means. God's desire is that we be holy as He is holy. That means there are things that need to be removed from our lives. It also means that He will assist in that process!

God's intent is not to destroy us but to purify us. Sometimes His method is akin to the intense heat of the refiner's fire. Our response to the process is crucial. We can either allow Him to work in our lives, cooperating in removing that which is impure, or we can resist or rebel.

To His people, God sent the message through the prophet Zechariah that He would "refine them like silver and test them like gold" (13:9). That is painful, but look at the promise: "They will call on my name and I will answer them; I will say, 'They are my people,' and they will say, 'The LORD is our God.'" The blessing will be ours.

Don't resist or rebel against God's refining fire. Learn from the tough times. Look for the ways in which God is using your difficulties to refine you.

GOOD TO GO

Malachi 1–4, Revelation 22 • *Key Verse: Revelation 22:20*

Jesus often told His disciples that He would one day leave them. But He also told them He would return for them: "I am going away and coming back to you" (John 14:28).

One day, as promised, He left. He ascended into the clouds from the midst of His gathered followers. But even then two angels promised, "Men of Galilee, why do you stand here looking into the sky? This same Jesus, who has been taken from you into heaven, will come back in the same way you have seen him go into heaven" (Acts 1:11).

In the last chapter of the Bible, Jesus again makes the promise, "I am coming soon! . . . I am the Alpha and the Omega, the First and the Last, the Beginning and the End" (22:12–13). The final recorded words of Jesus are, "Yes, I am coming soon" (v. 20).

If you know Jesus as your Savior, you are awaiting that day when Jesus will come quickly. It will happen soon. Don't be caught unprepared. Jesus is "good to go"; He is ready to return. Are you ready for Him?

"Lord, help me to live in such a way that I won't be caught off guard when You return. Help me to keep short accounts with You. Help me to be good to go too."

Back to the Bible is a nonprofit ministry dedicated to Bible teaching, evangelism and edification of Christians worldwide. If we can assist you in knowing more about Christ and the Christian life, please contact us without obligation.

Back to the Bible
P.O. Box 82808
Lincoln, NE 68501
1-800-759-2425
www.backtothebible.org